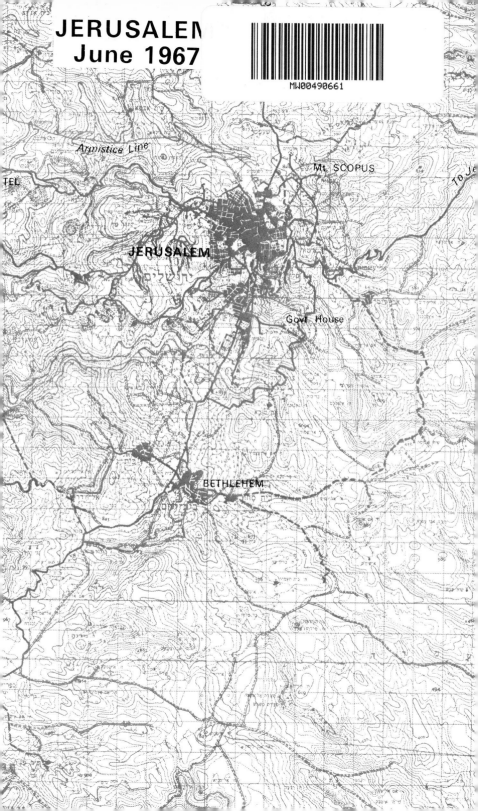

JERUSALEM
June 1967

Armistice Line

TEL

Mt. SCOPUS

TO J

JERUSALEM

חירושלים

Govt. House

BETHLEHEM

THE LIBERATION OF JERUSALEM

THE LIBERATION OF JERUSALEM

The Battle of 1967

GENERAL UZI NARKISS

With an Introduction by
ELIE WIESEL

VALLENTINE, MITCHELL

First published 1983 in Great Britain by
VALLENTINE, MITCHELL AND COMPANY LIMITED
Gainsborough House, 11 Gainsborough Road,
London, E11 1RS, England

and in the United States of America by
VALLENTINE, MITCHELL AND COMPANY LIMITED
c/o Biblio Distribution Centre
81 Adams Drive, P.O. Box 327, Totowa, N.J.07511

British Library Cataloguing in Publication Data

Narkiss, Uzi
 The Liberation of Jerusalem.
 1. Israel—Arab War, 1967—Jerusalem
 I. Title
956'.046   DS127.9.J/

ISBN 0 85303 209 2

Printed by Adlard & Son Ltd, Dorking, Surrey

This book is
dedicated to the memory of all those
whose gave their lives fighting for Jerusalem,
and the roads leading to it.

CONTENTS

LIST OF ILLUSTRATIONS

1*

LIST OF PLANS

The plans were drawn by Mrs Odeda Sagy-Ben Yehuda

INTRODUCTION

I envy the author of this book, I admit this without reticence or embarrassment. I envy him the experiences he describes. I would have liked to be there with him, to see what he saw and to feel what he felt.

He was one of the first Jewish officers to break into the old city of Jerusalem, which Colonel Motta Gur's parachutists had just liberated at General Narkiss' command. He does not say so, but he wept, just as everyone did. And yes, I envy him his tears on that day.

That day, Wednesday, June 7th, 1967, was a turning point in the history of Israel. The whole nation was aware of it. Everybody knew it, sensed it. The battle of Jerusalem – the battle *for* Jerusalem – was like no other. It had developed almost outside of politics. Its quasi-mystical dimension outweighed all others. That mad rush up to the Temple Mount, those palpitations, those cries of grief and joy, those songs to the sound of the Shofar, those non-religious soldiers who, heedless of the continuing gunfire, caressed the Wall, crying like children. What can we call that moment if not mystical? It is as if that moment bestowed meaning on the war.

Yet Uzi Narkiss is anything but mystical. Intellectual, a soldier since adolescence, he was commander in 1967 of the central front, whose line of defence included the country's chief cities. Like the majority of the High Command, he initially thought that King Hussein did not want to make the first move and should not be provoked. The tranquillity of the Jordanian frontier seemed more important than the liberation of the old city. Yet this attitude was a source of conflict in him. He had been dreaming of the old city ever since he left it nineteen years before, routed by an enemy superior in manpower and weaponry. So near, yet inaccessible, it was both a reminder and a challenge. Israelis seemed to think and speak of Jerusalem with guilt. Secretly – and unjustly – they blamed themselves for having lost it. Should they now attempt to recapture it, to liberate it? General Narkiss tells of the hesitations, the fears, and the preparations before the decisive battle. Day by day, hour by hour, he retraces the events: indecision in the political sector, diplomatic pressure both from the West and from Russia, the atmosphere among military men. Narkiss shows them as they were, the famous as well as the unknown, before, during, and after the fighting.

Fighting, moreover, which was developing in places other than Jerusalem. Bethlehem, Nablus, Jenin and Ramallah: each name evokes memories of exploits. Each struggle is a story in itself. Certain passages in Narkiss' account have a familiar ring, while others tell of what has been neglected: a remark by Dayan, another by Rabin. Yet above all else we are reminded of the losses. Can anyone reckon what they were? Can anyone measure the price in human life which the Israeli army and people had to pay for their devotion to Jerusalem?

You will read this narrative with pride, but also with sadness. You will not be able to free yourself from either emotion as you enter Jerusalem with the author as guide. As for myself, I have already confessed to yet another feeling: yes, I envy my friend Uzi Narkiss.

I envy him his memories.

ELIE WIESEL

(Translated from the French
by Martha Hauptman)

FOREWORD

I thought it best to preface the story of the battle for Jerusalem with the one of a Jerusalem whose heart, the Old City, had been gouged out in the 1948 War of Independence; to describe how Jews existed in a city once, as the psalm says, "builded as a compact together," but now, after '48, were penned in a blind alley, dismembered, divided between Israelis and Arabs; to chronicle the courage of a people who, despite loss and hardship, refused to be reconciled to their situation and prayed ceaselessly for the Old City to be returned; to discuss the action taken by those responsible for the safety of this hard-to-defend city when suggested remedies failed to meet the exigencies of the problems that arose; and, finally, to record that, once begun, the battle of Jerusalem was essentially a network of improvization.

The Jerusalem infantry battalion, for instance, charged with capturing Abu-Tor, had to march from the radar position to the battlefront for lack of other transport; the parachute units, prepared to capture El-Arish on the Mediterranean coast of the Sinai Peninsula, were diverted instead to the Jerusalem front with neither ammunition nor equipment; the armored units were abruptly diverted from the defense of the command boundaries to terrain unknown to them and totally unsuited to tank warfare.

I have drawn the typical picture of war, of confusion during battle, of death and weariness and chaos, of soldiers overburdened with the tragic evidence of it all. I have written of scattered ammunition, empty cartridge cases, indicator-arrows and signboards, packs and haversacks, smashed and damaged weapons and vehicles, jumbled together beside the pitiful bodies of the dead and wounded.

I have tried also to illuminate the shadowy recesses of war, the difficulties of making and executing changes in original planning, the impromptu improvization that replaces pre-planned strategy, the bulldog adherence to objectives and the toll in dead and wounded.

I want to thank those who, during its years of gestation, helped complete this book: Abraham Rad, for his generous assistance; Jacob Sharett, who meticulously kept the War Diary; Aviezer Golan, a great journalist who with talent and devotion assisted my literary efforts; Stanley Broza, who made the translation; and last but not least Mr Leon Tamman; without whom the English edition could not have been realized.

A DIVIDED CITY

My Jerusalem

Dawn in Jerusalem: The sun rises and climbs above the Church spires on Mount Zion, casting its pallid lustre on the stone buildings of the city. The walls redden and the roofs turn purple.

A Jerusalem dusk: The sun slowly disappears behind the Abu-Gosh Monastery.

The metal sheets which protect the western walls of Jerusalem buildings from the rain and all the windows of the City facing the setting sun become a blaze of lights, flashing and glinting until it vanishes completely.

That is how I always recall a Jerusalem day. Between the sun bursting forth and rising above the Church in Mount Zion to the east, and the sun sinking behind the Monastery to the west.

I was born in Jerusalem in 1925. Memories of my youth take me back to the Bezalel Art School where my late father worked and where we lived. Earlier memories, from my childhood days, are of a two-storey house in the Nachlat-Ahim Quarter; it was during the 1929 Riots, and several families from among the inhabitants of the Quarter came to our house to stand united against the Arab marauders. That is one of my earliest recollections. Indelibly imprinted in the mind of a four-year-old are the large verandah at the front of the house and stairs leading out of it on to an unpaved street. Men walking up and down the verandah armed with thick wooden staves, of the sort Jerusalem women used to stir the steaming laundry in the boiler. Near the wall a pile of stones for throwing: the "armoury". These, and an atmosphere of worry and tension which even a four-year-old boy could sense.

Later memories:

We lived in the Nachlat-Ahim Quarter in a road inhabited by Yemenite Jews. We had a grandma called Hama'ama, who used to bake Yemenite pitta-bread in a "Tabun".

In 1930 I started school. The school was a simple one-storey structure, which everyone called "the small schoolhouse", for indeed there were only two grades in it, "A" and "B". The instructor, the teacher and the Headmaster, were one and the same, Joseph Cohen-Zedek: wearing a Russian shirt-blouse, a small beard on his chin, smoking a pipe and arousing our admiration and amazement with his matches, which he used to light by striking them on a polished stone which had its place of honour in the yard. We were also impressed by the fact that he spoke Esperanto even though we had no idea what that language was.

When I graduated from grades "A" and "B" of the "small school-house", I went to the Rehavia Gymnasium, where I spent the next ten years. There I learnt Hebrew properly, but what is more, there I learnt to know and love this land. English I studied with reluctance because of the Englishman who then ruled the country, and my poor marks in this subject sullied my school certificates.

The 1936 Arab uprising aroused my dormant awareness that Jerusalem was inhabited by two races. Until then I had looked upon the Arab children as neighbours. I learnt their language from them, I competed against them in throwing stones, and together we sprained our ankles playing football on the local pitch next to "Sha'arei Hessed". Certainly there were occasions when the game turned into a free-for-all, resulting in torn trousers and broken heads, but these were nonetheless still neighbourly fracas. Then suddenly the riots started and it was not possible to go down to the bottom of Jaffa Road and dangerous to walk in Mamilla Road; and the Nablus Gate, well, don't even mention it, there it was worst of all.

At our house we were taught to be satisfied with what we had. My father was an employee, and never well-to-do, yet I never felt deprived of anything. Those things Jerusalem's youth aimed at and longed for could not, in any case, be bought for money. On the contrary, I felt I was rich and lucky compared to many of my friends, for my parents never hit me and never prevented me from joining youth movements or, at a later stage, the Haganah. They never stopped me going on a hike or a march, for training or on a mission.

I joined the Machanot Haolim (Youth Movement) at a young age and was at once enraptured with it. To me it was wonderful and through it I was gripped with a love for my country and people; I was intoxicated by its keen enjoyment of life, by its rousing community singing, its Sabbath and Holiday eves when we did our "thing" in the shed which was our clubhouse. With the Machanot Haolim I learnt to know Jerusalem, its districts and byways, its highways and alleys. In its ranks I went on hikes and marches in Judea and Samaria, from the sea to the Jordan, from the Gilboa Heights to the mountains of Hebron.

I was received into the ranks of the Haganah at a ceremony in the middle of the night in the "Mizrahi" Talmud Torah building whose red roof still juts out in the centre of Jerusalem. My heart pounded with emotion and pride when on the Holy Book and a pistol, I swore eternal loyalty.

And once again treks and marches, now with the Haganah. Drilling on the "Hapoel" football ground in the Boucharian Quarter, training in Kiryat Anavim; dismantling a pistol and putting it together again with bandaged eyes at the "Tachkimony" school.

We were already carrying out missions; we carried messages from one commander to another, and sometimes from an officer to his wife. We pasted anti-Government posters on walls; guarded the Jewish Agency Building; took part in demonstrations against the British Government's White Paper on Palestine, and even broke windows of shops whose owners kept them open during the strike.

The end of my schooldays and my enrollment in the Palmach took me away from my city. I returned to Jerusalem after four years of living in Palmach tents all over the country, and there I was appointed commander of a Palmach Company at Ramat Rachel.

Those were the days of the Resistance Movement: blowing up railway lines at the Jerusalem Railway Station; "Wingate Night" in Tel-Aviv; and non-stop reconnaissance in every Quarter of the city and its environs. There was not a single Police station in the area or the house of an Arab Mukhtar (Headman) which had not been scouted out and prepared and planned as "objectives" for blowing up when the time came. And along with these we traversed the desert, to Ein Gedi and Massada, to develop our imagination and kindle our love for our country.

The "Night of the Bridges" was the last operation in which I took part – we blew up Allenby Bridge. The Resistance Movement ceased operations. Thus, after several weeks of regrets and vacillation, I found myself a student of History, Philosophy and Arabic at the Hebrew University.

Every morning a No. 9 bus bore me from its station near Histadruth House across Mea Shearim, turned towards Sheikh Jarrah, ran the gauntlet at the British War Cemetery on Mount Scopus and on to the

University, to the scenery on the Mount, so breathtakingly beautiful.
From there on 2nd November 1947, between one lecture and another,
I saw the Jerusalem Commercial Centre near the King David Hotel
engulfed in flames. My studying had come to an end.

I was given command of the Northern part of the Dead Sea. Later
of Gush Halav. From there I was transferred to Kiriyat Anavim, to the
Harel Brigade. And with this battle-scarred high-casualty unit I
fought in the Jerusalem Hills – the "Butcher's Theatre" was the
nickname given it by the men of that Brigade, who would ask themselves, "When will it be my turn?" At Kastel, Katamon, Nabi
Samuel, and on Radar Hill, at Beit Mahsir and Mount Zion, at Ramat
Rahel and Sheikh Jarrah – at all these places the men of Harel had
spilled their blood.

Throughout this time, Jerusalem was our hinterland and we its
frontline. Jerusalem, which was cut off from its water sources at the
Rosh-Ha'ayin wells, with only a dribble of rainwater collected in the
town's wells to save her from dying of thirst; Jerusalem, whose life-
line was the road to the coastal plains, beleaguered for weeks with her
food supplies dwindling rapidly; Jerusalem surrounded by enemies,
and shelled without restraint; festering from hunger and thirst, her
entrails torn asunder by the exploding shells – Jerusalem did not
surrender.

One day, during the blockade, I happened to be in town and went to
visit my parents. They were not home. I found my father, may his soul
rest in peace, who was then the acting Mukhtar of the Newe Bazalel
and Nachlat Zadok Quarters, standing near the Quarters' well, drawing water from it in a tin attached to a rope, and rationing it amongst
the women and children standing in a queue. One quarter of a tin for
each person per day, and that for drinking, cooking, washing and
laundering. All the time Arab Legion shells were bursting all around;
but those in the queue did not budge. Nobody ran for their life. I
stood watching and my heart went out to them – to my father and all
who stood there. Their courage was not a whit less than that of my
comrades, fighting in the hills.

The War of Independence ended. I brought my wife to Jerusalem,
and we set up home in the Katamon Quarter together with the
evacuees from the Old City. The war was over – but not the shortages.
Fresh water was delivered once a week, and our food – one egg a week,
a frozen fish fillet, and now and again a slice of lean meat and
vegetables.

And the town was in the throes of constant crises: business was at a complete standstill; government institutions had moved to the plains, and with them the clerks. There was nothing to do and no way of making a living in town.

And there was fear too: the town was divided, and barbed wire entanglements and minefields separated the two parts. Now and then sporadic shooting broke out from across the border, the victims' blood spilling out onto the white paving stones ... Jerusalem, a city well-versed in war. And like the city, so were its inhabitants. There was no panic. Quiet, stubborn, determined. They could stand up to the shortages, the lack of work, of money and the hardships of defense duties; for years they had been living next to barbed wire fences and in the shadow of Arab Legion positions, and had stayed put. The basement was always ready to be turned into a shelter. In the larder were a can of oil, a small quantity of rice and flour, candles and a tin of Kerosene. In many homes the well was still given an annual spring-cleaning, so it would fill up with rainwater in winter, in spite of the fact that meanwhile a new water pipeline had been laid, and water in the town was no longer in short supply.

In 1965 the Chief of the General Staff, Zvi Zur, appointed me Commander of the Central Region. For the next two years my thoughts were centred on the tortuous boundary-line that cut through my city and my heart was to cry out for its disappearance.

A dawn in the Jerusalem of today. The sun bursts out above A-Tur Tower on the Mount of Olives. Jerusalem is built of stone and in the light of the rising sun the houses in the Beth Israel and Rehaviah Quarters are bathed in crimson red, as are the former High Commissioner's Palace, Ramat Eshkol and Givat Hamivtar.

As the sun sinks nowadays it casts a noble light upon the Abu-Gosh Monastery, and turns into sparkling mirrors the tinsheets with which Jerusalemites cover the western side of their houses; it gleams from myriads of windows, from Har Gila in the South to the Ramot Quarter in the North.

The "War" of the Military Parade

At 10 o'clock on Monday, May 15, 1967, the Independence Day Military Parade began in Jerusalem. Past the reviewing stand at the University stadium fluttered the Zahal standards from brightly polished and gleaming jeeps, infantry companies, artillery, police and border-police jeeps, trucks and a variety of other equipment, included to swell the ranks of the parade without violating the armistice agreement between Israel and Jordan.

In the reviewing stand the President of the State of Israel, Zalman Shazar, greeted the parade, his hand raised in salute as each unit passed by. Next to him were Prime Minister Levi Eshkol, the Chief of the General Staff, Major-General Itzhak Rabin and I, the G.O.C. Central Command.

Every passing unit increased our recognition of how sadly diminished was this parade, meant to display Zahal's might to the Arab states and world governments. It had been emasculated of just the strength it was supposed to demonstrate – armor and air force units – without which it was a "mini" parade.

But this was Jerusalem, where our hands were tied by the inconsistencies of the 1949 Armistice Agreement. I wondered if we would be dogged forever by the problems of a Jerusalem whose '48 wounds remained and whose status as capital of Israel was purely nominal.

The Israel-Jordan armistice agreement, which cut Jerusalem in half and ran a boundary-line through its heart, was signed in April, 1949, a few months after the fighting ended. The agreement was to have given place shortly afterwards to a peace treaty and had been worded with that in mind. As a temporary document it had many restrictive clauses, difficult to live with over time. But the drafters and signatories surely thought it would soon be invalid; why, then, struggle over such temporary inconveniences? This particular agreement, however, only confirms the popular wisdom that nothing is so permanent as the temporary: surely, in any case, between Israelis and Arabs. For nineteen years Jerusalem was bound and fettered to those "temporary" clauses, one of whose conditions restricted the size of the military force each side could maintain in Jerusalem. Israel was allowed one infantry battalion of no more than 800 officers and men, whose armaments must not exceed 48 machine-guns, 16 2″ mortars, four 6-pound anti-tank guns; one headquarters company; medium fieldguns from 25 pounds; medium anti-tank guns from 40 mm. And that was all. No armor, not even half-tracks, and no air force, not even light reconnaissance planes. With such a feeble force, how could there be a military parade worth the name?

There had been two previous Independence Day military parades in Jerusalem, the last in 1961, when the Government decided upon a full-scale operation, since nothing in the armistice agreement restricted such parades in Jerusalem, despite Jordan's contrary interpretation. Attempts at logical discussion were made: the Jordanians were assured that this was a celebration, that the units brought into Jerusalem would have no ammunition, the tanks and artillery pieces no secreted shells; it was even suggested that the Jordanians check to see that everything was as promised. Beyond all this we guaranteed that the forces would leave Jerusalem immediately after the parade.

The attempt at discussion failed, the Jordanians obstinately demanding meticulous adherence to the terms of the agreement. Israel having ignored the objections and the parade having taken place, Jordan brought up the subject at the Security Council, which charged serious violation of the agreement and severely reprimanded Israel.

Israel was so sensitive to such reprimands that for years arguments, pretexts and excuses were given for not holding the parade in Jerusalem. But in 1967, on the 19th anniversary of Independence, when it was again Jerusalem's turn, the Central Command was ordered to parade in the Holy City. Strict adherence to armistice agreement restrictions – no tanks and no planes – was a *sine qua non*. Prime Minister Levi Eshkol said in a *Davar* newspaper interview, "We do not want to quarrel with the United Nations, nor do we want a reprimand from the Security Council."

1967 was the year of the "battle for the water sources." The Syrian effort to divert the tributaries of the River Jordan to cut off water from Israel resulted in exchanges of fire across the northern border. These incidents increased in frequency and belligerency and often involved tanks and artillery. On April 7th, 1967, about six weeks before Independence Day, large-scale shelling of settlements in Upper Galilee broke out. The air force finally came in and in several dog-fights shot down six Syrian fighter-planes. Tension ran high, with the government and the general staff concentrating upon the northern border, so that there seemed little point in opening a diplomatic "second front" over so marginal a matter as the annual military parade.

It was nonetheless opened.

Months prior to Independence Day, the Jordanians had begun to put pressure on U.N. Observer H.Q. concerning the parade, which thereafter began to question its nature and proportions. At the end of March, Norwegian General Od Bull, Chief of U.N. Observer H.Q., was told about the units scheduled to take part, whose numbers would not exceed those permitted by the armistice agreement. We, therefore, imagined the matter resolved.

We were, however, grievously mistaken. Jordan used the parade to make repeated diplomatic attacks on Israel. Today as I leaf through the papers that deal with it, I find it incredible that so much trouble and travail ensued.

On May 6th, the Jordanian representative at the U.N., Mohammed el-Farah, complained to the U.N. Secretariat that "it is known that the Government of Israel is determined in its decision to hold a military parade in Jerusalem on May 15th. Israel's obstinate determination to manifest her offensive strength is a serious provocation against my government and a demonstration of non-compliance with U.N. and Security Council rulings, which condemned the holding of just such a demonstration in 1961. In order to prevent a deterioration in the situation, the Secretary of the U.N. is urgently requested to bring the contents of this letter to the attention of Israel and request her not to hold the parade."

The next day, May 7th, Jordanian outposts espied a military column going up to Jerusalem, carrying, according to them, twenty 25-pound guns. They complained to the Israel-Jordan Mixed Armistice Commission (which was deputed to see that the Israel-Jordan armistice agreement was observed), whose deputy chairman hurriedly demanded that we take him to the column. We told him that the artillery column in question also included anti-aircraft guns, which, however, did not exceed the permitted number. We nevertheless agreed to let him inspect the column, but he said it would be unnecessary. The Jordanians refused to drop the matter, informing the Armistice Commission that, from their observation post at Beit Iksa, they had seen another column making for Jerusalem, with armor and heavy artillery. U.N. observers who visited the post recorded seeing tents and soft vehicles only, but Colonel Stanaway, the New Zealand Chairman of the M.A.C., demanded inspection of the encampment. Since the U.N. observer had not turned up on the previous day, our representative on the committee refused the request, whereupon the Jordanians called for an emergency meeting to discuss the "blatant violation" of the armistice agreement. We objected, not to the discussion but to the urgency, but the chairman voted in favor of meeting immediately to placate the excited Jordanians.

We soon realized that the Jordanians had no intention of being placated, for while the M.A.C. was in Jerusalem examining the situation, the Algerian representative at the U.N. protested to Secretary-General U Thant about the "Israel provocation," and the Arab ambassadors to western countries launched a diplomatic fusillade against the parade. As expected, Britain pressured Israel to cancel the parade, and U.N. Ambassador to Israel Walworth Barbour was instructed to boycott it, as were other ambassadors.

In any case, the argument over the parade was in the hands of the Mixed Armistice Commission.

The hearing on Jordan's complaint took place on the evening of May 10th, and the chairman suggested postponement until May 13th. The Jordanians did not object. When discussion was resumed, the Israel delegation appeared in its full strength of three representatives, at which the chief Jordanian delegate, Colonel Mohammed Daoud, immediately demanded that Israeli attendance be limited, like Jordan's, to two delegates.

The meeting was postponed until the following day, when a discussion of an hour-and-a-half ensued over Israel's insistence that the chairman strike the statement that he had been refused permission to inspect the Zahal camp at Givat Shaul. Afterwards we demanded that the Jordanians present a written complaint that specified the clause in the armistice agreement which we had violated. The Jordanians refused, on the grounds that any concentration of military forces in Jerusalem, even for parade purposes, was prohibited; the committee must therefore forbid us to parade. We denied violating any agreement terms and demanded to be shown the sentence forbidding a parade in Jerusalem.

Since it transpired that the U.N. observers were not properly prepared for a discussion, they summoned their councillors later that evening, changing the time of the meeting from 6 p.m. to midnight. After the councillors had presented their opinion, the meeting was further postponed until 8.30 a.m. on May 15th, at which time, the parade having already started, the chairman suggested a solution.

"Both delegations," said Colonel Stanaway, "give opposing interpretations to the armistice agreement in connection with the right to hold military parades in Jerusalem. Because of the political implications possibly attaching to such parades, I do not find that the armistice agreement is authorized to rule upon the matter. Hence we shall take no stand and shall not bring this Jordanian complaint to a vote. However," he continued, "whatever the legal position may be, there is no doubt, in view of the differing opinions, that the parade will increase tension and I therefore cannot support it."

The Israeli delegation then read its own summary, condemning the

Jordanians for creating tension by presenting the complaint, and for holding "Palestine Day" in the Old City of Jerusalem and the towns of the West Bank, where Arab speeches incited animus against Israel.

By the time the two speeches had been typed, attached to the protocol and signed by the various parties, the military parade had ended and its participants had begun to disperse.

The Night Tattoo

While this comic interlude, so characteristic of divided Jerusalem, was being played out, preparations for Independence Day events in Jerusalem were reaching completion. Because of the restricted size of the parade, the *pièce de résistance* was to be the military tattoo to be held on the eve of Independence Day in the Hebrew University auditorium. The first tattoo had taken place two years before to compensate Jerusalemites for having been deprived of their turn for the parade. Its great success prompted the decision to make the tattoo a permanent feature of the Independence Day celebrations.

But even this event was not free of problems.

Besides the torchlight exercises with infantry units participating, verses were read from a poem dedicated to the battles for the freeing of the Galilee during the 1967 "battle for the waters." With the help of the poet Haim Guri, a company commander in one of the battalions of the Jerusalem Brigade, we finally decided that a poem of Natan Alterman's written in 1956 best suited the occasion. It had been written at the height of the "Fedayeen" (marauder) attacks, forerunners of the Sinai campaign, and not about the Eastern Galilee, although it caught the tension rife in 1967 also, in the wake of the struggle for the Jordan River sources.

During the general rehearsal at the University auditorium a professor who heard the poem was so shocked that he telephoned a cabinet minister saying that it sounded like a call to battle. The matter was broached to the Prime Minister and the Chief of Staff and resulted in second thoughts and a general run-around. Telephone lines were tied up and military cars tore up to Jerusalem and raced back down to Tel-Aviv before things were resolved. As each side relaxed, the poem was confirmed for presentation with one changed verse.

The verse which so worried the Jerusalem professor reads:

Arab, think of what you do before's too late!
The knot doth weaken and may break!

You dream my hands are tied, my arms are bound!
You dream your rulers send me off to foreign ground!
Awake, oh do awake from dreams that futile be!
For this may be your final chance to see!

And the verse which replaced it was:

Arab, Arab, let not the die be cast
That for both of us twins sunny warmth to freezing blast,
Hold back your hand, oh stop it, we implore,
'Afore it slips the bolt on bloody war.
And glimpse the difference
'Twixt the indescribable and nameless malison
And peace that blesses and blooms on
The likes of which we Semite peoples ne'er did con.

In other words, a call for peace, not a warning against war.

The words now seem truly prophetic of an occasion only three weeks away. But who, on the evening of May 14th, thought about the morning of June 5th?

Shortly before the beginning of the military tattoo, all those to be on the reviewing stand in the auditorium gathered at the Prime Minister's office, where Zahal refreshments of tea or coffee, salt sticks and cakes were provided. We all felt the nervousness and tension that precedes a premiere. The balcony of the Prime Minister's chambers looked out upon the auditorium where the participating units had assembled. The audience filled the stands. Preparations were complete; the tattoo was about to start.

Two military policemen kicked the starters of their motor-cycles and we followed them slowly to the auditorium, driving once round the track. The car stopped in front of the reviewing stand. I took my place on it. Two minutes later the Chief of the General Staff arrived, followed by the Prime Minister. Then, with a group of mounted police cantering ahead, came the president. The officer commanding the event, Colonel Eliezer Amitai, faced him, saluted, and requested permission to start the tattoo. Its precision was superb. As men drilled, the small bulbs attached to their bare muscular arms combined with the movement of the drill to create a spectacular play of lights. Alterman's poem rang true and strong.

The president rose to speak and – a hitch no ceremony seems able to escape – the electricity failed. I had a small flashlight in my pocket, by whose beam the president managed to read.

The parade was over, the audience departed, and we gathered at the

Sherover home for the traditional Independence Day reception. During the evening, the Chief of the General Staff, Itzhak Rabin, received a phone call which he took in an adjoining room. He emerged a few minutes later deeply preoccupied. He had just spoken to Major-General Aharon Yariv, Director of Military Intelligence of the General Staff, and had been informed that the Egyptian army was advancing into the Sinai Peninsula.

A Divided City

For 19 years Jerusalem was bisected by a fence through its heart. Jerusalem is a naturally "difficult" city, a city of hills and rocks, a city of enclosed "quarters" and special communities, a city, since the end of the 1948 battle, with a population mainly of new immigrants, a city overburdened with problems of absorption and employment. To its natural problems were added the difficulties arising from being split in half, from having become a city with a frontier.

During those 19 years Jerusalem had interludes of frenzy, when, for example, an "unhinged" Jordanian officer pressed the trigger of his gun and set the boundary-line on fire. The expression "unhinged duty officer" came into use after this incident, on September 23rd, 1956. A Jordanian soldier stationed in the Arab Legion's position at the Mar Elias Monastery fired, with no provocation from us, a machine-gun point-blank at a group of archeologists attending a conference at Ramat Rahel. Four Israeli civilians died and 16 were wounded. The Jordanians later apologized, and said that the soldier was "unhinged." But we had no illusions. The soldier had become "unhinged" on orders from someone who had decided that the time was ripe to "warm up" the Jerusalem front...

Even in quiet periods, when the frontier was calm, the situation in Jerusalem was unmatched anywhere else in the world. Jerusalem was the capital of Israel, yet all its government institutions, the Knesset, the presidential residence, state offices, were in range of enemy guns.

During the lulls, when Israeli and Jordanian civilians conversed amicably across the barbed wire dividing their quarter, one could imagine Jerusalem always thus and always remaining so. But when things were at pitch, when a peaceful residential section was turned into a battle-field, old Jerusalemites agonized over why such a situation was countenanced, why the job had not been finished when it could have been in 1948. Some placed the blame on the leaders of the

1. Divided Jerusalem: a concrete wall next to Notre Dame de France

2. 1948. The Jewish Quarter in flames after its capture by the Arabs

State, who, they said, were bound from Mandatory times by special links with the Hashemite kingdom and wanted, at any cost, to come to terms with Jordan's King Abdullah. In 1948 we were not alone in wanting Jerusalem with our whole heart. For the Arabs, especially the Jordanians, Jerusalem was also the focus of ambition and desire. The Arab Legion concentrated most of its forces and resources on the Jerusalem front. Abdullah wanted the Eternal City for his capital, and the British, whose views were expressed by the Bernadotte Plan, supported him.

What was our strength compared to theirs? Two brigades fought for Jerusalem. The *Etzioni* Brigade commanded by David Shaltiel fought inside the city and defended some of its buildings; and the Palmach *Harel* Brigade, under Itzhak Rabin, fought for the road to Jerusalem and in the town itself. Both brigades were poorly armed, with few rifles, sten-guns, pistols, and light machine guns and still fewer light mortars. They had no heavy armaments whatever, no armor and no artillery. Battle experience was severely limited, particularly against regular armies, and there were shortcomings at the top. Little love was lost between the two brigades which fought for Jerusalem. The Palmach refused to take orders from Jerusalem headquarters, which, in their opinion, showed little respect for the Palmach men, who had more battle experience than they. But above all else was the terrible hopelessness and despair. Beaten, tired and depressed, weighted by the unbearable responsibility for the city's civilian population, not the fighters, nor the Yishuv as a whole, nor its leaders, could withstand the temptation of an armistice in order to make one more last-ditch effort – to free the whole of Jerusalem.

And so for 19 more years Jerusalem remained divided.

Perhaps – as several of my colleagues claim – it was fate. Jerusalem, they say, cannot be redeemed in one war. Nineteen more years of suffering were needed before the wheel turned full circle, before another generation was ready to complete the redemption.

Endless Trouble

I too suffered for 19 years from guilt that Jerusalem was divided, that no Jew remained in the Old City, that the Western Wall had fallen into the hands of strangers. For one night I held the gate to the city in my hands – but it was torn out of them.

It happened on May 17th, 1948 when I was deputy commander of the 4th Battalion of the Palmach. The day before, Battalion Comman-

der Joseph Tabenkin had been summoned to Palmach H.Q. in Tel-
Aviv, and before leaving had told me:

"The *Etzioni* Brigade together with forces of I.Z.L. and L.E.H.I.
plan to break into the Old City, to try and help the [surrounded]
Jewish Quarter. Etzioni [a Haganah unit] will break through at Jaffa
Gate, the Stern Gang from the New Gate and *Irgun* from Nablus Gate.
We have been given the job of creating a diversion to the south; we
must engage the Legion on Mount Zion, and, if possible, capture the
Mount. But that's secondary. Don't make too great an effort. If it
works, fine. If not, don't let it worry you."

Later I was summoned to *Etzioni* H.Q. for a briefing session on the
attack. It was agreed then with Brig. General Shaltiel that the 4th
Battalion would carry out the diversionary action toward Mount Zion;
if we succeeded in taking the Mount we were to be replaced
immediately by units of the Haganah from Jerusalem. Out of the one
thousand men of the 4th Battalion, who had been fighting ceaselessly
since they came up to the Jerusalem hills six weeks previously, only
120 were still in fighting condition.

That afternoon we moved from Kiryat Anavim to the Yemin-
Moshe Quarter, opposite Mount Zion, began the combined operation
around midnight and immediately came to grief. All three assaults
upon the city gates were beaten back. Just to be different, the "divert-
ing action" was successful. The tired Palmach men climbed the steep
slope and captured Mount Zion, although not without cost. One
company of the battalion's four was driven out of action.

Despite our agreement at the briefing session, there was no relief
next day. David Shaltiel phoned to ask me to exploit our success and
break into the Old City through the Zion Gate: the defenders of the
Jewish Quarter could not hold out much longer and unless we got to
them immediately, the Quarter would fall. And we were nearest...

By radio from the Old City defenders we heard the same story.
They begged us to help them.

Brigade Commander Itzhak Rabin agreed to deploy the battalion,
and I told David Shaltiel that, since only three companies were left,
we would be in urgent need of replacements after the breakthrough on
Mount Zion or a force to take over in our stead the responsibility of
manning the breach. I was sure that my men, weary though they were,
could manage the breakthrough. Indeed it was for just such an action,
the spear-head assault, that the Palmach was trained. But we were too
few and too tired to stand up to a protracted defensive battle. Shaltiel

promised, and asked, à propos, if I had flags to fly from the Tower of David once it was taken. In reply I suggested that a convoy of vehicles be equipped with ammunition and medical supplies for the Jewish Quarter, where there were many wounded and there was no plasma. I added that the convoy should set out as soon as we had taken Zion Gate, go up from the Hebron road along the track at the foot of the walls to Mount Zion, and from there enter the Old City. This he promised.

All day long the boys held Mount Zion. Towards evening they were deployed to attack. For the first time in the history of the battalion, volunteers for the assaulting platoon had to be called for, because none of the platoons could carry out the task on their own. Fatigue was a tangible presence. In the Order of the Day, prepared on the spot for the occasion, I said: "You stand facing the Fortress of Jerusalem. From this city the Jews were expelled 1,877 years ago. You are the first since the Destruction to mount this Fortress. Be strong and of good courage!"

After midnight on May 19th, the assault began, with Uri Ben-Ari as company commander. The spearhead platoon, commanded by David Elazar (Dado) captured the Gate and a second platoon raced through it down the narrow lanes, and reached the Jewish Quarter. The third platoon stayed back to secure Mount Zion.

I notified the area commander of our success, requesting that the relieving force and first-aid convoy be dispatched forthwith to the Old City. Meanwhile the corridor from Zion Gate to the Jewish Quarter was being held by a thin line of 25 men, so bone-tired that even though an Arab counter-offensive was momentarily expected they kept dozing off on their feet.

The convoy never turned up. In its place came a force of about 80 men, armed only with rifles and sten-guns, and very little ammunition. I was to learn later that they were not even an organic group, but had been collected at the last moment from various places, even from their homes. Although I requested the company to take upon itself the defense of the Gate and the Armenian Monastery opposite, it soon became clear that it could not carry out such a task independently.

During all this time the Arabs were making preparations in the adjacent lanes. I guessed that a counter-attack was imminent and was aware that my exhausted men would be unable to repel it and hold on to the Gate.

Finally, after much deliberation, when the horizon had turned red and dawn had broken, I brought the reinforcements into the Jewish Quarter and said to their commander: "Maybe you can recapture the Gate from inside," and withdrew my own men from the Old City and deployed them to defend Mount Zion.

Within the hour the Arab Legion recaptured Zion Gate. The Jewish Quarter fell and the walls of the Old City were sealed off completely.

There were other times during the 1948 War when an additional battalion, or even one more company, might have changed the course of history. But neither battalion nor company was available.

And Jerusalem remained divided.

The Story of the Jerusalem Boundary-Line

The so-called Jerusalem boundary-line, bisecting Jerusalem for 19 years, was established November 30th 1948 within the framework of the basic truce agreement. The fighting in town having ended somewhat earlier, Lt. Col. Moshe Dayan, who had replaced Brig. Gen. David Shaltiel as commander of the Jerusalem area, and the Jordanian commander, Lt. Col. Abdullah Tal, met in an abandoned building in no-man's land in the Musrara Quarter, where they spread upon the dusty floor a 1:20,000 scale map of Jerusalem and marked thereon the military positions of each of them. Using soft, waxy lead pencils, Moshe Dayan marked his positions in red, Abdullah Tal in green. The line on the map was 2-3 millimeters thick or 40-60 meters on the ground; beneath it were buried entire buildings and streets. As time passed the wax melted and, as the markings thickened, a greater area was covered. Neither commander paid particular notice to this, since both were convinced that the truce agreement would not last long. Israel hoped it would lead to a peace treaty and new boundary-lines; Abdullah Tal, who several weeks earlier had boasted to David Shaltiel that he would very soon enter Jewish Jerusalem at the head of his troops, riding on a white charger, believed it would reactivate the war. As it happened, neither came true. On April 3rd, 1949, an armistice agreement between Israel and Jordan was signed, and the map which had been marked in the abandoned Musrara house was adopted by all sides as the armistice map, red and green lines included. It was to be, for years to come, the root of many a problem.

The High Commissioner's Palace

Two sections of the line dividing Jerusalem were drawn even before November 30th, 1948: the high commissioner's palace and the Mount

2

3. No-man's-land at the foot of Mount Zion

4. Jaffa Street

Scopus bulge areas. Collectors of coincidences might find one in the fact that these areas were the first to see both the end of the 1948 battle and the start of the 1967 one.

The high commissioner's palace (or Government House, as it was also called when Britain held the Mandate) lies south of Jerusalem, between the Jewish Quarter of Talpiot and the Arab village of Sur Baher on a hill called, in Arabic, Jebel Mukhabar and in the New Testament the Hill of Evil Counsel. According to Christian tradition, the high priest Joseph Caiaphas lived on that hill, in the house where the priests decided to bring Jesus the Nazarene to trial before the Sanhedrin. It commands a beautiful view, to the north overlooking the Siloam Spring and the Old City, to the south Bethlehem, and to the East the Dead Sea. When the British chose the site for Government House, it was still outside the boundaries of the *yishuv*. Talpiot was a newly emerging community and Sur Baher a small wretched village, which, over the years, burgeoned across the slopes of the hill, just as Talpiot extended nearly to the palace compound. Later, Rachel Yanait Ben-Zvi built the Girls' Agricultural High School for New Immigrants along the fence of the palace, and the Moslem Higher Committee established the Arab college nearby.

Government House was the last British foothold in the Jerusalem region. On the morning of May 14th, 1948, the Union Jack was lowered. The last high commissioner, General Alan Cunningham, saluted the flag, folded it, left the palace to the music of Scotch bagpipes, entered a car and was driven to Kalandia Airport near Ramallah. The British gave the palace to the International Red Cross which, without Jewish or Arab objection, made it a refuge for civilians in flight. The girls' school was declared a Jewish refuge, the Arab college an Arab refuge. The palace itself housed Red Cross institutions to supervise these refugee cities.

On October 1st, 1948, without warning Israel, the Red Cross abandoned the palace and the United Nations established observer headquarters there, raising the light blue flag of the U.N. over Government House. No treaty ever confirmed this occupation.

The following year Moshe Dayan negotiated with Brig. Gen. Gundi about the partitioning of no-man's land, and, *inter alia*, about eliminating the Government House enclave. King Abdullah, however, was reluctant to sign an agreement which *prima facie* recognized the existence of Israel in Jerusalem, and the *status quo ante* obtained. This proved once again that in the Middle East nothing is so permanent as the temporary. For 19 years the palace enclave remained a demilitarized zone supervised by U.N. observers who were the sole occupants of the palace. It was a strange enough supervision. It expressed itself by complaining to Israel every time the water sprinklers of the agricultural school, where Jews lived, splashed the walls of the unoccupied house of the head of the Arab college next door.

The complaints were dealt with hour after tedious hour by the Mixed Armistice Commission, but the U.N. observers reacted not at all when the Jordanians put up buildings in the demilitarized zone or laid a by-road through it from old Jerusalem to Bethlehem. They closed their eyes when the Jordanians moved their Arab Legion positions in the "Sausage" redoubt to the eastern slope of the Hill of Evil Counsel, thus encroaching upon the demilitarized zone.

Mount Scopus

The Mt. Scopus enclave was determined at about the same time. The danger that the road to the Mount might be cut off in the event of fighting always concerned those responsible for the defense of Jerusalem. When the bloody riots of December 1947 broke out, after the November 29th U.N. decision about the partition of Palestine, Jewish buses en route to the Mount were increasingly attacked. The Arabs progressed from throwing stones to sniping, to mining, and finally to storming them. On April 14th, 1948, an Arab force ambushed a Hadassah Hospital convoy about 300 meters from the police college at Sheikh Jarrah. The dozens of armed policemen in the college and the British Army units nearby remained neutral while ambulances and buses were set aflame one after the other. Eighty-eight of the convoy's passengers perished, most of them lecturers and scientists on their way to the university or doctors and nurses on their way to the hospital. This was one of the worst massacres that ever brutalized Jerusalem.

From that day Mt. Scopus was in fact cut off from Jerusalem. On April 25th, 1948, a few days after the convoy slaughter, the 5th Battalion of Harel captured the Sheikh Jarrah Quarter. This time the British violated their neutrality. A British armored force arrived and its commanding officer informed Itzhak Rabin, Commander of the Harel Brigade, that if the Jewish force did not withdraw the British would open fire. The British gave as their reason that the Jerusalem-Ramallah Road was a vital communication link in their evacuation plans and fighting could not be permitted in its neighborhood. The

5. Government House

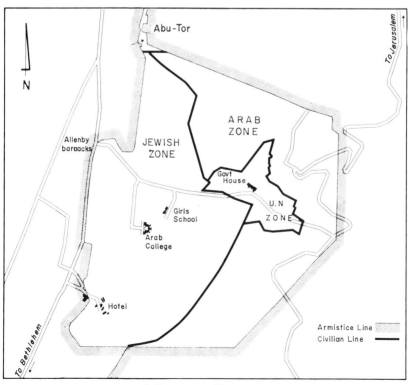

I Government House area

6. A Jordanian soldier throws a rock from his position

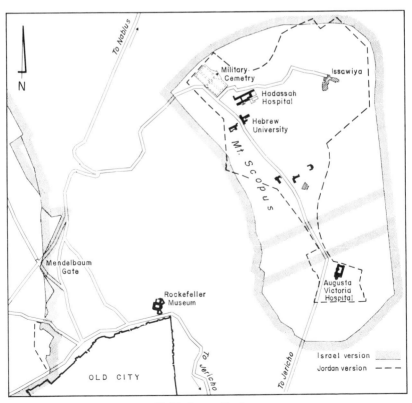

II Mt Scopus Enclave

Palmach withdrew and the Arab marauders returned to the quarter.

Until May 14th, the British provided the promised protection to Jewish traffic to Mt. Scopus. But after they evacuated Jerusalem, the Arab Legion occupied the Sheikh Jarrah Quarter and on May 17th Mount Scopus was cut off from Jewish Jerusalem.

At that time there were fewer than 100 defenders on the Mount and about 35 civilian employees of the university and the hospital. They held out under shell and siege until the first cease-fire on June 10th, 1948. Then the Society of Friends of the Hebrew University and Hadassah in the U.S.A. intervened. At their prodding, the U.S. Government approached the Red Cross and the consular committee (of France, the U.S.A. and Belgium), which represented the world in besieged Jerusalem. These, and particularly the French Consul, René Neville, persuaded Brigadier Lash, Commander of the Arab Legion on the Jerusalem front, to create a demilitarized enclave on Mount Scopus, encompassing the Hebrew University and Hadassah Hospital buildings, the almost deserted Arab village of Issafiya and the German-Arab hospital Augusta-Victoria. On July 7th, 1948, the agreement was signed by Brigadier David Shaltiel, Brigadier Lash, consul René Neville and Colonel Bronson, deputy to Count Bernadotte, recently appointed conciliator for the U.N. This, like all local agreements, was confirmed at Rhodes when the Israel-Jordan Armistice Agreement was signed and became an integral part of it. The agreement prohibited the maintenance of armed forces in the demilitarized enclave, but allowed a police force of specified size: 86 policemen in the Israeli sector (and 35 civilian, the number on the Mount when the agreement was signed), 40 in the Arab. It also permitted Israel to change half the garrison on the Mount once every two weeks. So that this could be done, Jordan agreed to a fortnightly convoy to the Mount, supervised by U.N. personnel. How the convoy was to be transported was not specified in the agreement but determined ad hoc; after much contention and many incidents, permanent arrangements were made.

If Mount Scopus Is Attacked

Through the years the destiny of Mt. Scopus was basic to the deliberations and considerations of Central Command. There was constant expectation of a Jordanian surprise attack on the Mount. And for good reason: Mt. Scopus is the highest spot in north Jerusalem and a key strategic point. Whoever holds the Mount commands the northern approaches to Jerusalem, the roads from Ramallah and Jericho, and overlooks and controls the Old City. Any Jordanian officer in the theatre would naturally want to uproot us from so dominant a position.

Mt. Scopus is a widely known historic site. If Jordan were to control it the whole world would know and the prestige of the Jordanian rulers would soar far higher than other military operations could send it. During the long years of Jordan's faltering prestige, its rulers were more than once hard pressed to withstand the temptation to capture Mount Scopus.

We never ceased preparing for such an eventuality. The Central Command archives are crowded with plans for the aid of Mount Scopus should it be attacked. Nor did the garrison on the Mount spare any effort in digging itself in, building redoubts and communication trenches. We were aware that the garrison lacked the strength to stop a planned regular army assault, especially supported by armor, in which event the lives of the 120 Israelis on the Mount would depend on how fast we could bring up our own armor. We particularly stressed this in our planning.

At the same time we took precautionary steps to prevent an attack on the Mount that might result from an incidental shooting which could snowball disproportionately. Standing orders to the garrison were strict and precise about shooting and opening fire, stricter than those about the municipal boundary line in Jerusalem. Each regional commander was obliged to confirm anew these orders, which read:

Under no circumstances shall fire be opened upon women, children or U.N. observers; on men trespassing the Israel boundary, fire may be opened, but only by shooting in the air. The only circumstances under which opening effective fire is justified is for the purpose of rescuing our forces, if attacked, and even then only upon the explicit order of the local commanding officer.

The agreement to demilitarize Mt. Scopus was intended to insure the status quo; in other words, to freeze the situation as it was on July 7th, 1948, and specifically to prohibit change in that situation. As with the Government House enclave, however, this primary condition was not to be applied equally on both sides.

Our first problems on the Mount began in the village of Isawiya, which had been unoccupied when the agreement was signed. Arabs began to settle there clandestinely and early in 1967 the inhabitants numbered almost two thousand.

Once they had settled into the village houses, they gradually took over the land, even that which was clearly within the Israeli enclave. This went on for years, encouraged by the Jordanian authorities. One fine morning, an Arab peasant appeared opposite one of our redoubts with a plough hitched to a bull and a donkey and began to plough. Our men shouted at him to go away, but he ignored them completely and carried on as if nothing were amiss. After several similar incidents, the highest echelons decided that if shouting were of no avail firing in the air might be, but no more than three rounds. Under no circumstances was firing to hit permitted.

The next time, therefore, that an Arab peasant turned up to plough in the Israeli sector, shots were fired above his head, and he abandoned his plough and fled. A few days later he returned, again tried his luck, and again we fired. This time he ran only as far as a nearby rock and when he saw that the shooting had stopped (the ration of three rounds having been used up), he returned to the field and the plough and was left in peace to till the land.

When the crop came in, burning was suggested. But we shrank from such a suggestion and the peasant eventually harvested his crop. The plot of land became his property by virtue of his perseverance and our inability to do anything about it. Field after field, dunam after dunam, was expropriated by the Arab peasants.

We lost hold in similar fashion of an olive grove on the edge of no-man's land. After having been abandoned and left untended for years, it was discovered one morning by a group of Arab peasants from Isawiya, who began to pick the olives. Although the soldiers shouted, they did not go away, and when the soldiers started to drive them away, our men were fired upon from the Arab Legion positions.

Now there were two possibilities: to return the Legionnaires' fire and risk a major incident – or give in.

And as always when we weighed a plot of land against possible war, the plot of land seemed puny. Our force withdrew and the Arab sector acquired another grove, thus diminishing, piece by piece, the size of the Israel enclave on Mount Scopus.

In the Arab sector exactly the opposite developed.

The Width of the Line

Faced throughout the years with the paradoxes arising from the terms of the Armistice Agreement, and with the problems of the armistice map marked by Moshe Dayan and Abdullah Tal, which had become the sole key to interpreting the partition of Jerusalem, we bit our nails

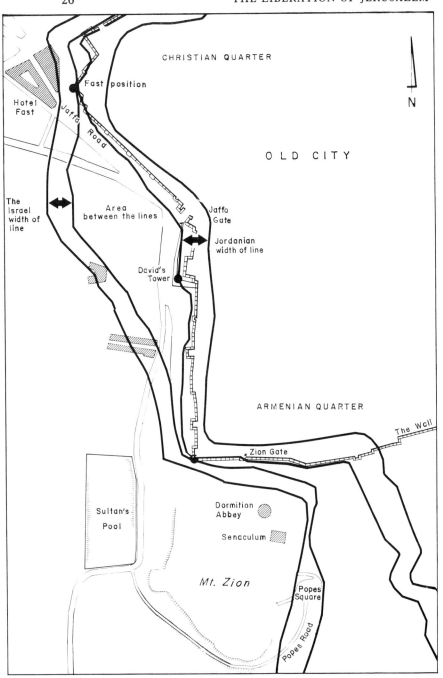

III "The Width of the Line"

in frustration and wondered how such intelligent people could so dismember a living city.

As I have said, I am convinced that Jerusalem was thus partitioned because neither officer believed for a minute that it would last forever. At that time, in November 1948, it could logically be expected that peace negotiations would soon begin and that the partition lines, so disturbing to the lives of its inhabitants, would be redrawn within the treaty framework. For this reason the lines had been drawn hastily and by hand. If here or there a line cut through a private house, what matter? After all, the house was empty. Sometimes, however, the line obliterated an entire building and years later we spent countless hours debating what to do about a house or even an entire street covered by the line markings.

Only very rarely did the U.N. observers take the trouble to intervene before something became a *fait accompli*, particularly if the situation was what was described as longstanding. The expressed objective of Zahal to establish Israeli sovereignty by its physical presence in each sector within our boundaries more than once created difficulties for the regional commander, and even crises of conscience. An outstanding example was the affair of the Old City wall on Mount Zion. When the defense map was drawn, our men held the Dormition Abbey, whose walls are but a few meters from the Old City wall, held by the Jordanians. The pencilled line passed through and obliterated the southwestern corner of the Old City wall, placing it in no-man's land. The Jordanians, who gave the map short shrift, built a strongpoint on the corner of the wall, which we were powerless to prevent except by a full-scale military operation. But we planned our patrol route to pass along the very bottom of the wall at this point. The patrols went on for years, and the area extending south from the wall in fact became Israeli territory. But one day in July, 1962, a "crazy Jordanian soldier on guard duty" opened fire on the patrol marching along at the bottom of the wall, killing Captain Avshalom Sela, the patrol commander.

The natural, almost instinctive, response of a Zahal officer in such a case is to continue patrolling the same route, to demonstrate that even death does not prevent our defending our positions. The patrol route was, after all, Israeli territory, and Zahal was bound to maintain its presence on every inch of it.

But instinct was quickly followed by thought. What if the patrol did not follow the identical route? At worst the place would be overgrown with weeds and thistles; the Legionnaires would never climb over the wall and physically occupy the slope. A bit more thought produced the question of whether, if we did not continue to patrol the same route, that strip of land would slip out of our hands for good, and, furthermore, would it be right, would we be justified in endangering yet more lives for the sake of one bit of land which was totally useless?

I struggled no little over this and similar problems, once in the province of Brigadier Joseph Geva, my predecessor, and now bedeviling me at almost every section of that municipal line.

Jerusalem Line Procedures

From Beit Safafa to the police college, an entirely built-up area, the Jerusalem line was about seven kilometers long, and was held by a reduced company of 72 men.

I remember that at a meeting of the Foreign Affairs and Defense Committee of the Knesset, General Zvi Zur, then C.O.G.S., disclosed the size of the force holding the Jerusalem line. The members were astounded and seriously concerned. The C.O.G.S. calmed them down by pointing out that the strength of our force at the line accorded with requirements and if necessary would be enlarged. Don't worry; Jerusalem will not fall, Zur told them.

Along the Jerusalem line, courage was not wanting; but fighting fitness and readiness to sacrifice oneself were not enough. Because of its sensitive aspect and because what happened in Jerusalem affected the world, every soldier sometimes had to be a diplomat. A platoon or defense-post commander in charge of two or three men on occasion had to decide, not necessarily from a military or strategic viewpoint, whether to open fire or answer the enemy's. He had to consider the outcome of his action and the repercussions from his decision at the Mixed Armistice Commission, in the newspapers, even at the Security Council.

To ease decision-making for the soldier, the Regional Command issued standing orders covering the defense of the line, doubtless the most complex and restrictive orders a military unit was ever faced with.

In case of enemy infiltration [this document read] it is permitted to open fire if the number of infiltrators exceeds two; and even then only with rifles and machine-guns.
If the number of infiltrators is two or less, they must be arrested or driven off with shouts. If they do not react it is permissible to shoot but only in the air. No shooting at all is permitted in no-man's land, where only shouts may be

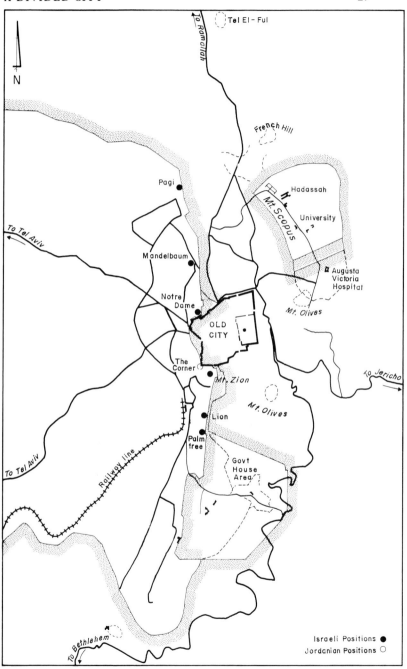

IV "The Jerusalem Line"

used. Any shot fired in no-man's land must first be authorized by the general
officer commanding the region.

If the enemy annoys you by throwing stones, the Brigade Commander may
authorize retaliation in kind. Any other action is permissible by order of the
regional commander only.

If fire is opened on our positions, the brigade commander is permitted to
order retaliatory fire by the same type of weapons. Artillery or tank action is
only permissible if confirmed by the Regional Commander.

In reality even the regional commander was not free to decide on his
own but had to get the consent of the Chief of the General Staff, who
received advice from the defense minister and the prime minister.
Such details cannot be included in standing orders intended for the
men in the field.

"Demilitarizing the British Ambassador"

The Jerusalem line began in Beit Safafa and proceeded along Ramat
Rahel to the Talpiot Quarter. In the '60's a large hotel, the Ganei
Yehuda, was built on the quarter's boundary and was later enlarged to
include a dining room and bar. Only after the new structure had been
completed was it noted that its eastern wall encroached about one or
two meters into the demilitarized zone of Government House, actually
putting a corner of the bar beyond the line.

One day I was host to British Ambassador, Michael Haddow, on a
trip along the Jerusalem Corridor which ended at the Ganei Yehuda
Hotel. I invited him to afternoon tea, but suggested that first we climb
to the observation tower above the dining room. The view is breathtaking, and I was only too pleased to share its wonders with my guest.
As we stood at the rail of the observation platform, I could not resist
saying, "Do you know, here we are standing in Israel, but when we go
down to the dining room, don't go too near the bar. The counter is in
the demilitarized zone."

Ambassador Haddow was a clever man with a sense of humor. He
raised his hat, listened to my explanation, judged the situation and
from the expression on his face made it clear that he would avoid a
confrontation with the demilitarized bar. Glancing at his watch, he
affected surprise at the lateness of the hour, apologized for having to
rush off, thanked me for my hospitality, entered his limousine and
disappeared.

"... and the Water Closet"

The Abu-Tor Quarter had always been one of the prickliest points on

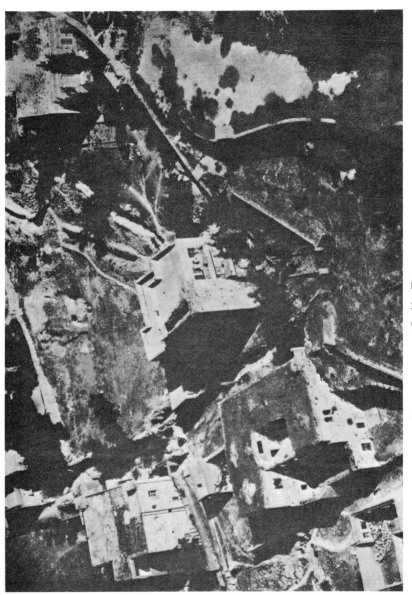

7. Abu-Tor

the line. Jews and Arabs lived in close proximity, separated by a courtyard or a lane, and sometimes only by a stone wall. Life went on in that special way peculiar to people living on a dividing line. Good neighbors had suddenly become bitter enemies. When things were quiet, after periods of undisturbed calm, housewives chatted across the barbed wire, comparing prices, sometimes exchanging food or clothing. A Jewish housewife, finding herself without bread, often called to her Arab neighbor across the line and received in response a *pittah* flying from one state frontier to the other. But if the Legion commander in the quarter were replaced by someone who happened to be a troublemaker, or if an incident in another sector of the line heated the atmosphere in this one, curses and stones, even bullets, flew in place of *pittot*. Then residents returning to their homes along the line would quickly take cover, dashing from post to post like sophisticated fieldmice. They would leave in the morning with heavy hearts, to spend endless hours worrying about the safety of their families at home on the line.

Of our nine positions on the line, two – the Palm Tree and the Lion redoubts – were in Abu-Tor because of its sensitivity. There was also an observation post. Even the Legion established positions inside the quarter, not more than fifty meters from ours. The years gave rise to many incidents here, and even more quasi-incidents, to occupy the time of the Mixed Armistice Commission. One such was the affair of the water closet.

In a miserable one-storey building in the quarter lived a poor family of evacuees from one of the *mabarot* (temporary camps for new immigrants). The house was virtually on top of the thick line and had a lavatory in the yard, so that whenever things got tense across the border, the family risked their lives going to the outhouse. One of the Arab Legion positions was only 50 meters away.

The family eventually got sick of running the gauntlet and applied to the municipality for permission to build a water-closet next to their house. After the usual consultation with Zahal authorities, permission was conditionally granted, conditionally because since the house was on the line, the Jordanians might object and the new structure might have to be demolished.

The man started work anyway, and Zahal took all the usual precautions concomitant with the possible occurrence of an incident. A command post was set up nearby, with an open telephone line to Brigade H.Q., Regional Command H.Q. and G.H.Q. The C.O.G.S. was in constant touch with the Prime Minister and the Defense

Minister; units were moved forward; others were placed on alert.

The first to complain was the Israel Ministry for Foreign Affairs, asking why we had authorized the erection of a building without consulting them. Then came the regular complaint from the Jordanians to the M.A.C.

The deliberations over the affair of the water closet filled a fairly fat file, one of whose documents, dated April 14th, 1966, is the protocol of the 420th emergency meeting called to deal with Jordanian complaint No. 91 (of the same year).

I shall quote verbatim:

Present: Lt. Colonel M.S. Stanaway, New Zealand Army, Chairman. Major J. Hussein on behalf of Jordan, Lt. Colonel Yair Biberman, Lt. Colonel Shmuel Gat and Major Tuvia Nevot on behalf of Israel. Secretary, S.I. Sarkassian.

Chairman: "Gentlemen, the time is eight minutes to four. The meeting is opened. I have convened this emergency meeting to discuss complaint No. 91 of Jordan which deals with so-called building construction by the Israelis in no-man's land in Jerusalem..."

Here the chairman quoted the Jordanian complaint:

at 15.30 hours Israeli workers and soldiers entered no-man's land and began to cast a new roof on a building the creation of which was commenced previously, in spite of assurances given on 9th February 1966 that the work would be stopped because of the gravity of the situation created by this Israeli action. Jordan demands an investigation and the cessation of the work.

The chairman suggested that the work be halted until conclusion of the investigation.

Biberman:"On no occasion did we promise to stop the work. If a citizen of Israel builds a lavatory for himself, there is no cause for tension nor does it have any bearing on the peace."

Later Lt. Colonel Biberman protested the chairman's calling an emergency meeting about this complaint. He said that on November 3rd, 1965, the Jordanians were asked to evacuate a redoubt they had built in no-man's land, and had not done so. The Armistice Commission had taken no steps. On November 4th, 1965, Israel asked for an emergency meeting to discuss Jordan's establishment of an army post in no-man's land; no meeting had been called. Nor had one been called on November 26th, requested in connection with shots fired by Jordanians at Israelis. On February 8th, 1966, an emergency meeting about shots fired in the Hebron area had been refused us, as it had on February 11th, 1966, when we complained that Jordanian peasants had crossed the armistice line. But over the building of a lavatory, an emergency meeting was considered necessary. Biberman suggested that the matter be turned over to a sub-committee.

Chairman: "We shall deal with each incident on its merits. There is no connection between this complaint and those mentioned by the Israeli delegate."

The discussion lasted several hours and was continued on March 8th, 1966, at which time the chief Jordanian delegate to the Mixed Armistice Commission, Lt. Colonel Muhammad Daud, was present. Said he, "The Israelis admit they built a room of blocks, described as a lavatory. They were prohibited from building this structure..."

Lt. Colonel Biberman: "True a lavatory was built but it has not been established that it was built in no-man's land. It was built in Israel; where does it say that building in Israel is prohibited?"

The M.A.C. held in all four meetings for a total of 18 hours during which the matter was discussed. The protocol covered 36 pages, ending with a decision condemning Israel. But the water closet remained standing.

The Incident of the Clod of Earth

From Abu-Tor, the line sloped down the Valley of Hinnom and climbed up to Mount Zion.

During those nineteen years Mount Zion was a sort of substitute Temple for the Jews, since it was not only the Israeli-held territory closest to the Western or Wailing Wall, but, according to tradition, contained the grave of King David. During the high holidays the area swarmed with pilgrims and people praying.

The city is holy to Christians, too. There in the Coenaculum, Jesus Christ partook of the last supper before his crucifixion. A large church was erected nearby and the burial grounds of several Christian sects lie roundabout.

The way to Mount Zion was a narrow dirt-track. While preparations were under way for the visit of Pope Paul VI to Jerusalem in January 1964, therefore, it was decided to widen the path and lay a proper road. The Pope had expressed a wish to pray at the Coenaculum; an improved road would make his journey more comfortable. The Jordanians did not object and the road was laid to within about 60 meters of the Coenaculum. At the end of the roadway, directly on the "Wide Line", a small square was laid out as a car park for the Pope's cortège.

After the Pope's visit, Mount Zion attracted so many Christian pilgrims that by the summer of 1966 there were beginning to be traffic jams. The Jerusalem Municipality and the Ministry of Tourism wanted to widen the road, and Central Command agreed. Earth-moving equipment was brought in and work began. We took care to restrict activities to the Israeli side of the line, but in spite of all precautions, when the bulldozer pushed a mound of earth down the slope and a few clods rolled across the line, the outcry was beyond belief. From their redoubt about 20 meters away, the Jordanians saw the innocent clods infiltrating their sector and immediately lodged a complaint with the Mixed Armistice Commission. When our Foreign Ministry heard of it, they complained to Major General Bar-Lev, then Chief of Operations ("G" Branch) at G.H.Q. One midday the general turned up to examine the situation himself. "We must not implicate the State, even with clods of earth," he said. "Yes, Sir," I replied. The corners of Bar-Lev's eyes wrinkled in a smile. The work was stopped.

At the Mixed Armistice Commission meetings a war of complaints was carried on, often coincident with the actual war that had broken out along the line.

We used to draw up a balance-sheet of condemnations, and even evolved a kind of tactical strategy during these protest wars. Our people sometimes refrained from lodging a single complaint and collected several to submit in one big batch on the chance of achieving a serious condemnation of the other side.

I, of course, was fully aware that the real decision would be made not at the debating table of the M.A.C. but on the line itself, where the number of hands raised for or against would not decide the issue, but the number of Israeli civilians living permanently on the line, earning their living there and raising their children. I will always remember a talk I had with a young officer early in my command. I pointed out to him that his patrol passed a part of the line in one of the mixed quarters.

"But we don't need to demonstrate our presence there," he said innocently. "The Jewish children playing near the fence demonstrate the presence."

Living on the Line

From Mount Zion, the line meanders along the wall towards the Sultan's Pool, passes through Chotzot Hayozer (east of the Yemin

Moshe Quarter on the Hebron Road) and reaches Beit Tannous opposite the Jaffa Gate.

Beit Tannous, a sizable apartment building, was captured by our forces on the night of the attack on the gates of the Old City. On the map the entire building is in our territory, but the line crosses its backyard. The garbage cans and the domestic gas cylinders were, so to speak, covered by the thick line, and whenever the garbage was removed or the gas cylinders changed, the Jordanians protested that we had violated the armistice agreement. Sometimes they even threatened to open fire. In spite of all this, and in spite also of the number of tenants wounded in one incident or another, the house was fully occupied until the outbreak of the Six Day War. Was it bravery, or that marvellous Jerusalem stolidity, which accepts what cannot be altered?

After a particularly dangerous shooting, a young female tenant said to me: "What can we do? We've nowhere else to go."

Normally the narrow streets of the quarters along the line were hives of children at play. There is not an empty lot in the area, not even a microscopic tuft of grass; the alleys served as playgrounds. The boys played football, the girls skipped rope, and their mothers hung the wash on lines stretched across the streets.

But suddenly a burst of machine-gun bullets would ricochet off the walls of a building, raise a cloud of dust, and the people's whole world changed. The war-wise children vanished; everybody hid in the safest corner of his apartment, stopped breathing, and waited. Either the shooting continued and became an "incident," or quiet was restored. Worried mothers tried to remember exactly where their missing youngsters had been when the shooting started and would shout from behind closed shutters, "Massouda, is my Nahum with you?" "Has anyone seen Rachel Mizrahi?"

And not a hundred meters to the west, town business went on as usual; buses ran their routes, cafes served pastries and cups of coffee, people went to work, strolled the streets, sat peacefully at home. Only here and there would someone stand quite still, every nerve alert, trying to pinpoint the direction of the shooting. These were the residents of Abu-Tor, or Beit Tannous or the Musrara Quarter, worried about their families who were living on the line.

Notre Dame de France

Opposite the wall in that sector is the monastery of Notre Dame de

France, built in 1887 by monks of the Order of the Augustinians of the Assumption. On May 14th and 15th, when the British had barely left, marauding Arab bands occupied the monastery and made it an armed fortress. A *Haganah* unit forced them out after a bitter fight. The next day, when the Arab Legion invaded Jerusalem from the north, captured the Sheikh Jarrah Quarter and reached the Nablus Gate, the monastery building with its thick walls assumed major strategic importance. It commands the approaches to Suleiman Street, the road leading from the Nablus Gate to the new city, and from it the Legion's armor began to advance on the morning of May 21st.

It was a decisive moment in 1948 on the Jerusalem front when armored cars of the Arab Legion began their assault on the Suleiman Street incline. I was at a Palmach base at *Ma'aleh Hahamisha* when my friend Brig. Gen. Amos Horeb, who was there, sent us an agitated message. "The Legion is advancing with armored vehicles! We are in the most urgent need of anti-tank weapons!"

I sent them one anti-tank gun out of the two we had, and the Legion, whether because of the gun or not, was stopped at the monastery. The Legion later took revenge on the monastery building, demolishing with cannon fire almost the whole of its northern side. But the rubble from the walls which piled up in the road became another anti-tank obstacle for the Legion's tanks. Two of their armored vehicles remained stranded in the roadway until the city was liberated.

From the north the monastery looks like a wounded gargoyle, its outer wall completely razed and its rooms exposed to view and gunfire. We set up a look-out on Nablus Gate. The gate and the square opposite were a barometer for what was going on in the Old City. On sensitive days like November 2nd (Balfour Declaration Day) or November 29th (U.N. Partition Decision Day) or May 15th (Israel Independence Day), the monastery served as a post from which to observe the crowds in front of the Nablus Gate. Their behavior could be anticipated by their numbers. Even on the days when the fortnightly convoy went up to Mt. Scopus, the observers on the roof of the monastery were of help to us. If they reported normal conditions at the Nablus Gate, we were not worried. But if they told us that the peddlers and taxi-drivers had disappeared from the square in front of the gate, we doubled our vigilance.

The Nun's False Teeth

Suleiman Street (now called Paratroopers Way), on the thick line, was completely blocked by demolished buildings, which we had piled on the roadway in 1948, and covered with barbed wire laid down by the Jordanians in case of sudden attack. To the best of my knowledge the barbed wire was opened only once in nineteen years, and then for exactly an hour. It happened in 1954, when a nun, leaning out of a window in the hospital wing of the monastery, coughed and dislodged her false teeth, which fell into the wire entanglements below.

The abbot appealed to us, and we to the M.A.C. Fortunately for the nun, the then Commission Chairman, a French officer, Commandant Carnot, realized that teeth were important and obtained Jordanian consent to our going between the lines. One morning subsequently, Commandant Carnot, Lt. Colonel Shimon Lavie, our delegate to the M.A.C., and a Jordanian officer opened the barbed-wire entanglements, and at the cost of a pair of trousers torn on a barb, recovered the nun's dentures. Jerusalem photographer David Rubinger immortalized the episode with a photograph published in *Life* magazine.

The Mandelbaum Gate

On the boundary between the Musrara Quarter and Beth-Israel is the Mandelbaum Gate, the official overland passage between Israel and Jordan during the first 19 years of independence and a place of undoubted and unusual importance.

The man for whom the gate was named, Rabbi Baruch Mandelbaum, came to Palestine from Poland in 1871, and settled in the Old City of Jerusalem. In 1927 the family left the walled confines and built, on the boundary of Musrara, a row of one-storey houses for themselves to use as a hostel for Talmudic scholars. They were called Mandelbaum's houses and were, in 1948, the scene of heavy fighting. Although they were destroyed right to their foundations, the name lived on. When Lt. Colonel Moshe Dayan and Colonel Abdullah Tal were asked to designate a crossing-point for the Mount Scopus supply convoy, they chose the area of the Mandelbaum houses at the end of Samuel the Prophet Street, a natural crossing to Mount Scopus.

The barbed wire fencing was broached, regulations were made for the crossings, and sentry posts set up on both sides. U.N. personnel began to use the crossing for their own purposes, and after them, all but hanging on their coat-tails, the Christian Arab residents of Israel, who were permitted across on their high holidays. When foreign tourists were allowed to cross from Jordan to Israel (but not vice-versa), the Mandelbaum Crossing was again pressed into service. To the military sentries, customs personnel and border-police were added a customs shed and a police post, making of the crossing a frontier-station. From our point of view, however, the chief activity around the crossing centered on the transit of the convoys to Mount Scopus.

The convoy, according to the agreement, was to relieve half of the garrison stationed on Mt. Scopus, take supplies and carry scientists and other university people to help maintain and safeguard the scientific equipment, instruments and books left there.

The convoy consisted of a number of supply trucks and two armored buses, one for the police, the other for the university people. So strict was Jordanian adherence to the belief that the armistice agreement was supposed to maintain the status quo as of 1948, that they insisted on the same buses as were used in 1948. I cannot overlook this opportunity to compliment our garage mechanics who succeeded in keeping those two vintage vehicles in running condition, kept them able to pant and grunt up the mountain road until the day we pulled down the barriers between Jerusalem and Mt. Scopus. Today they stand in a place of honor at the Zahal Museum.

On the day the convoy was due to go up, the two armored buses drove out of the garage after inspection and the passengers boarded. The convoy assembled in one of the lanes near the Mandelbaum Crossing and as departure time drew near, a general alert was declared in the sector. A redoubt close to the crossing was manned and used as the advance command post for the commander of the Jerusalem Brigade and the regional commander. From this position the convoy's progress could be monitored, and a force sent to rescue it in case of attack.

The convoy crossing set off numerous incidents, notably in June 1952. A Legion officer and a U.N. observer were checking the convoy as it assembled in the square of the Mandelbaum Gate, comparing the names of those going up to the Mount with the advance list we were obliged to submit. Then they checked the supply trucks, becoming suspicious of a sealed drum, whose contents were marked "Fuel" in the dispatch note. They asked that the drum be opened to prove that its contents were as described. The Israeli liaison officer replied that no clause in the agreement mentioned search or inspection of convoy contents. "If you won't let the barrel pass," he said, "it will be returned to the Israeli side as it is." The U.N. officer, who happened to be even more finicky and pedantic than the Jordanians, and who was clearly out to prove that the Israelis were not playing the game, did not agree. The convoy was delayed until a compromise was reached, specifying that the drum be placed unopened in a closed room in the hut of the U.N. observers (on the Israel side of the Mandelbaum Crossing), with an Israeli sentry on guard outside. Its fate would be decided by General Riley, then chief U.N. observer. The drum remained in the hut for several days, while Riley decided first that it should be returned to Israel and then ordered that it be opened. The Israeli officer said that he could not open it without permission from his superiors. A U.N. officer broke into the door of the room by force and photographed the drum and the Israeli sentry guarding it. An angry exchange of cables between the Israeli Foreign Ministry and U.N. Observer H.Q. ensued, Israel demanding the removal of the door-smashing observer. The drum was finally returned unopened to Israel.

Israel's stubbornness in this case paid off and established the precedent that neither Jordanians nor U.N. personnel had the right to examine the contents of the Israeli convoys: orders were then issued to convoy personnel to identify themselves to the U.N. observers, but under no circumstances to let the U.N. or Jordanian officers search them.

And then the Jordanians began to harass the convoy and provoke its passengers.

Cohen & Levy

On July 24th, 1958, the night before the convoy was due to go up, U.N. personnel had informed the Israeli liaison officer that the Jordanians would not permit two of the policemen (whose names, as required, had been given in advance) to go to Mt. Scopus, because they had criminal records. One was named Cohen, the other Levy.

It was a baseless allegation. The Jordanians knew very well that Cohen and Levy were the Smith and Jones of Israel, and that people could not be identified solely by such names. The Israeli liaison officer said that the convoy would not move without them.

We were deadlocked. The Jordanians refused to raise the barrier, and the armored buses spent the day on the square between the barbed-wire entanglements. Towards evening General Van Horn, Chief of Staff of U.N. Observer H.Q., arrived from Eilat with a compromise suggestion. The Jordanians would fingerprint Levy and Cohen to satisfy themselves that this particular Levy and this particular Cohen had no criminal records. We refused on principle and the buses remained between the lines throughout the night. In the morning the Jordanians gave in and the buses proceeded through the crossing.

For nineteen years, in times of tension and anxiety, of shooting and shouting, the crossing had never been closed, the transit area never affected, except during the Cohen and Levy episode. The Mandelbaum Gate, perhaps oddly, was always peaceful.

Shortly before I was appointed regional commander, I went up to Mt. Scopus in a convoy. I wore civilian clothes and a hat, sported a small mustache, and produced papers identifying me as a lecturer from the university, going up to Mt. Scopus to inspect its National Library archives.

The journey was uneventful. The convoy stopped at Hadassah Hospital, where we were greeted by Menahem Sharfman, for two years the "King of the Mount," who showed us the dugouts and trenches hewn out of the rock lying under the buildings. I studied the various plans of operation and read the standing orders. I was impressed by the tenacity of the diggers, who had truly turned the Mount into a fortress, but I was also extremely aware that it would be difficult indeed for the defenders to withstand an attack by Arab Legion armor.

When I took over the job of regional commander I began, as had my predecessors, to agonize over the question of what would happen if the Legion attacked Mount Scopus, or if the convoy broke down on the way. I pored over maps and aerial photographs, studied the negotiability by road, and pre-planned solutions for threats to the Mount and the convoys approaching it.

North of Mandelbaum Gate there was a large and empty piece of land called *Gan Abramov* (Abramov's Garden), and beyond it the *Poalei Agudat Israel* Quarter and the *Ma'abarot* Evacuees' Quarter. Since these were only a few dozen meters from the line, the eastern walls of the buildings had been especially reinforced and gun-apertures had been cut out below the ledges of the roof. Opposite the buildings was the police college established during Mandate times and used now as a food store for U.N.R.W.A. On the slope of the hill facing Jerusalem, the Arab Legionnaires had dug in. For nineteen years we watched the Legionnaires from our observation posts endlessly digging, camouflaging, covering, fencing and mining. The hill was considered a fortress in all our planning. Our war games in the Jerusalem area centered on the police college, which we sought means not only to overwhelm, but especially to bypass. Above the police college is a well fortified hill, later to be called "Ammunition Hill," from which the line wound north and west into a wadi, where it ceased to be the municipal boundary. It twisted and turned among uninhabited hills and wadis till it passed the village of Beth Iksa, following from there the mountain range overlooking the Tel-Aviv-Jerusalem Highway northwards.

That, then, was the municipal boundary. Seven kilometers of barbed wire, mines and forts which cut through Jerusalem, a handful of men guarding it with devotion, fortifying it jealously, and sacrificing their lives for it. Seventy-two soldiers and thousands of civilians, young and old, lived the life of the line. Some died on it.

Scouting with Haim Guri

Did we ever become reconciled to the line?

On the eve of Independence Day 1967, I reconnoitered the line with poet Haim Guri, a colleague and friend from my Palmach campfire days and the Negev campaigns. We went from one Quarter to the other, from one redoubt to the other and tarried a while at North Talpiot. Guri said: "Tell me, Uzi, how long will we go on educating our children on the Bible when most of the Land of the Bible is across the line and unavailable to us. Have we given it up?"

His question expressed that which had been eating away at my heart for years. I answered: "To a newspaperman like yourself, the regional commander cannot give an official reply, but *I can tell you* we haven't given it up. We aspire, we hope, we may even fight..."

However, the reality to be faced daily conflicted with our dreams. We were military men, with a mission to defend Jewish Jerusalem, to insure normal life there and to maintain full sovereignty over every inch of Israeli territory. And because we belonged to Zahal and knew that our defensive war would have to be fought in enemy territory, every shot from the rifles of "crazy Jordanian soldiers on duty" fired our conclusion that the place where shooting came from had to be captured! Whenever a convoy to Mt. Scopus was assembled and Zahal forces were placed on alert, we watched its progress to anguish from our command post in fear of the cry: "We are under attack!" We were ready to rescue the convoy if it were interfered with: one force would rush in from there, a second from here, a third from another place.

The day after Independence Day 1967, we gathered for a meeting of the General Staff, and were given, by the Director of Military Intelligence, full information about the headlines in the world's newspapers: "Large forces of the Egyptian Army cross into the Sinai Peninsula!" It did not then occur to me that the storm beginning to gather in the south would suck into itself the Central Command, Jerusalem and the whole of the land of Israel.

Operation "Rotem"

On Tuesday, May 16th, 1967, the newspapers and the radio reported that the Egyptian army had entered Sinai; some sources hinted that Israel had begun to mobilize its reserves.

I frankly admit that I was still not concerned, possibly because the festive atmosphere of Independence Day had not yet dissipated; more probably because I remembered an event in 1960 called Operation *Rotem*.

That year, after Zahal had soundly thrashed the Syrian army in a raid on the Taufik redoubts, panic broke out in Damascus. The Syrians spread the rumor that the Israeli raid was the forerunner of a general assault and turned to Cairo for help. At that time Syria and Egypt were united as a single State, and Gamal Abd el-Nasser, unable to avoid coming to the aid of the "northern regions" of his country, began to move his army forward and to issue threats against Israel.

Israel had to mobilize. When, after several days, the Israeli attack on Syria did not materialize, Nasser declared that thanks to the steps taken by the Egyptian armed forces war had been prevented. He claimed an easy victory for himself and enhanced his prestige in Damascus. Gradually he withdrew his forces from the Sinai Peninsula.

May 16th, 1967, seemed to me a repetition of Operation Broomstick. Even the background was unchanged. Tension on the Syrian front followed the April 1967 incident when six Syrian Migs were shot down and Israeli Mirages flew undisturbed in the Damascus skies, with Syria once more screaming: "Israel is going to attack!"

At first Nasser turned a deaf ear to Syria's appeals. His solution to
the Palestine problem was profoundly and significantly different from
that of the Ba'ath Government. The Syrians wanted an immediate
war, but the Egyptian soldiers to bear the brunt of it; Nasser was
determined not to become involved in a war until he was ready. And
when that would be, he would decide.

But the Syrians spared no breath in making warlike noises. Nasser
consulted his Soviet advisers, who confirmed the Syrian information.

That was the background for Nasser's decision to move his army
into the Sinai Peninsula. Perhaps he was not yet thinking in terms of
war. He may have believed that, as in 1960, if he moved his army into
Sinai the Israelis would abandon the plans of which he had been
informed. Egypt would gain another cheap and easy propaganda
victory and would again be acclaimed the savior and defender of the
Arab world.

At all events this can be assumed to have been his original intention,
which is why he moved his forces into Sinai in the way he did: in broad
daylight, with the wildly cheering populace of Cairo as witnesses. The
sight of that massive army, however, the endless stream of armored
vehicles crossing the Suez Canal, the enthusiastic acclamation given
his action by the Arab world, and, to no small extent, the demonstra-
tive support of the Soviet Union and France as compared to the
hesitation of the U.S.A., changed the Egyptian ruler's mind. He was
swept into the storm of enthusiasm he had himself aroused, inflated
with confidence in his skill and genius. Matters soon reached the point
of no return. Events took their course.

But on the morning of May 16th, the movements of the Egyptian
army were still considered, by us and the whole world, pure demonstration. The news of the military advance was being widely reported
at the same time that commentaries recalled that two weeks earlier
Nasser had declared his refusal to be dragged into war against Israel
until his army was ready, and his unwillingness to help Syria unless
she granted landing privileges to the Egyptian air force.

When the meeting at G.H.Q. was called to order on the morning of
May 17th, the atmosphere around the table was relaxed. Major-
General Itzhak Rabin prefaced his remarks by praising the fine Independence Day parade and thanked Central Command for their part in
it. Then he gave details about the size of the Egyptian armed forces
entering Sinai. In addition to the one armored division with 250 tanks

that had been stationed in the peninsula, hundreds more had moved in within the past two days. He said a few words about our own limited mobilization and told us that our armored forces in the Negev had been placed on alert. But the general attitude was that the whole military movement was only an exercise.

But even while we were sitting at the conference table, a basic change was taking place.

The previous evening, Indian General Rikhye, Commander of the U.N. Emergency Force, had received a telegram at his headquarters in Gaza from Egyptian Commander-in-Chief Muhammed Fawzy, demanding that the U.N. force be withdrawn from the Sinai frontier. The astounded Rikhye transmitted this information to U.N. headquarters in New York, and Secretary-General U Thant summoned the Egyptian delegate, Mohammed el-Kony, to tell him that the Egyptian request was rejected.

El-Kony informed Cairo, where a meeting of the government was called. On the morning of May 17th, after five hours of deliberation, a decision was made in Cairo, the gist of which was briefly cabled by Egyptian Foreign Minister Mohammed Riadh to U Thant.

"The Government of the United Arab Republic has the honor to inform you that it has decided to terminate the presence of the emergency force on the territory of the U.A.R. and in the Gaza Strip. Kindly take the necessary steps to withdraw these forces as soon as possible."

How will King Hussein React?

I still could not see myself as directly involved in what was going on. Whatever was happening down south did not affect my command, although on May 17th a state of alert had been declared in the Jordanian army. Jordanian Prime Minister Sa'ad Juma'a announced at a meeting of his government, attended by King Hussein and senior officers of the army, that "in the event of an Israeli attack on any of the sister Arab states, Jordan will not sit idly by."

This declaration seemed to us bumptious, boastful and insincere. Judging by the relation between Jordan and its sister states in mid-May 1967, nothing could have been farther from Hussein's mind than to go to their aid. While relations between Amman and Cairo could be described as very tense, between Amman and Damascus there was undisguised animosity. Diplomatic ties had been broken for a considerable time, and the air waves were filled with mutual recrimination; to the suspicious Hussein it was clear that the Syrian government had masterminded a number of attempts on his life.

What had engendered Sa'ad Juma'a's bombastic statement? When the war ended, I had the opportunity to talk with notables from East Jerusalem, important in the Jordanian administration and at court, who told me what had taken place in Amman in those tension-ridden days. Apparently Hussein, although outwardly tough and unyielding, felt, in spite of the bravado of his utterances against Gamal Abd el-Nasser, more than a little isolated, and longed to be restored to the bosom of the Arab family, not only to safeguard his throne against Egyptian or Syrian subversion, but also to show sympathy for the strong nationalism of the Palestinians and the young Beduin officers in the Jordanian army. Hussein could mock and slander Nasser as long as times were normal, but when Nasser marched his army into Sinai, and particularly when he ordered the U.N. forces to withdraw from their positions, his status in the Arab world was so exalted that Hussein felt obliged to conciliate him. It was, of course, a rather empty gesture, because Hussein did not really believe that war would break out. He was sure that the great powers would intervene to stop the saber-waving. On the other hand, however, Hussein did not want this round to end yet again in a prestige victory for Nasser, with Hussein idling on the sidelines. Hussein was to go on thinking and weighing and dilly-dallying until the last moment, when he was lured into the Arab web of overconfidence and could not extricate himself.

Zahal's Defense Doctrine

Signs of impending crisis and worsening conditions were evident at Central Command, but I was kept busy with the routine tasks of the Command. Within Central Command boundaries were Jerusalem and Tel-Aviv, Lod Airport and Ashdod harbor, the majority of the country's inhabitants, and practically all the nation's economic enterprises. The area of Central Command was vital to the country.

In its jurisdiction were the longest and most convoluted stretches of the frontier in all Israel. Hundreds of kilometers of Green Line separated Israel from Jordan, boundaries drawn after the War of Independence and the 1949 Rhodes Agreement. It came about as a reproduction of the purely fortuitous position of the front line on the day the cease-fire came into effect. Several amendments had been made after negotiations with King Abdullah. This boundary had all the drawbacks of a chance and temporary frontier: divided villages, landholders separated from their land, and settlements on the frontier with no possibility of defending their inhabitants. And from our (military) point of view, it had the topographical disadvantages of putting us in the plain and the Jordanians in the mountain ridges overlooking us.

The defense problems of Central Command were grave and not only because of the terrain. They were inherent in Israel's defense doctrine, as laid down by David Ben-Gurion: no withdrawal, not even for tactical purposes, and immediate transference of the war to enemy territory.

This doctrine had existed almost as long as Zahal itself. It was early decided that, should we be attacked, Zahal was to be deployed, in the initial blocking stage, by using regular armed forces only. In the second stage, after the reserves were mobilized, Zahal would counter-attack in order to transfer the battle to enemy territory. For many years afterwards, one of the main objectives of G Branch (Operations) of G.H.Q. was to seek ways of shortening the first stage and speeding up the start of the second.

In 1956, when Moshe Dayan was C.O.G.S., a new concept began to take shape. I remember a serious overall discussion in Zahal's war room early in 1956 when I was Chief of the Operations (G) Branch at G.H.Q. Present was David Ben Gurion, the Prime Minister and Minster of Defense, and taking part were the C.O.G.S. and all the brigadier generals. The focus of the discussion was Israel's defense doctrine and the establishment of objectives and priorities for it.

The maps on the wall made Israel's operative problems extremely obvious:
– The narrow bottleneck along the coastal region, and the ease with which the country could be cut into two;
– Jerusalem's position on the borders, and the possibility of blocking its connecting corridor to the coast;
– The threat to Tel-Aviv and other population centers in range of artillery fire from Jordan;
– The relative proximity of Gaza to Mt. Hebron, and the danger that an armored vehicle breakthrough from the Gaza Strip to Mt. Hebron or vice versa would cut off the Negev;
– The possibility of severing the Negev from Israel at Eilat or a little farther north;
– The need to mobilize, organize and move forces to the assembly areas near the borders, under air-observation and possible air bom-

bardment, shelling and the threat of a breakthrough by enemy armor;
– The danger to populated areas such as Rosh-Ha'ayin, Kiryat
Shemona, Shderoth and Mevasseret Yerushalayim, which an enemy
force could easily invade, causing numerous casualties, and withdrawing across the border before reinforcements arrived.

Even after so many years, I am not free to reveal what was discussed, but the subject never ceased to occupy the high command – until
the development of the concept so clearly brought to realization in the
Six Day War.

Another serious concern was which enemy to attack first in case of
an act of aggression against Israel. It was clear that Zahal would not be
allowed the luxury of a war on one front only, since war was likely to
flare up on more than one. Where, therefore, should the major effort
be directed? Theoretically Egypt deserved that "honor," as the largest
Arab state, whose president was the leader of them all, and the defeat
of whose army might intimidate the others and make them easier for
us to deal with.

But the more I thought things over, the less I was able to avoid an
opposite conclusion. I said to myself: Any war in which we have the
upper hand will be stopped by the U.N. and the Security Council
before our victory is complete. In the short time allotted us, we might
vanquish Jordan, but probably not Egypt.

Furthermore, victory over Egypt, including the capture of Sinai,
would give us only breathing space. The Egyptian Army would be
reorganized in a few years and Sinai would have to be returned. But
defeat of the Jordanian army would remove the direct threat to
Jerusalem and Tel-Aviv, enable us to form a defense line on the banks
of the Jordan and prevent both the Iraqis and the Syrians from
entering the West Bank. And most important of all, our historic rights
to Judea and Samaria would be honored and upheld.

The discussions, however, ended on a different note. I believe that
for a number of reasons, not necessarily operative ones, our attitude
towards Jordan became comparatively indulgent. Our reasons may
have originated in our unexpressed relations with the Hashemite royal
family, relations which were the cornerstone of our defense policy.

During the Sinai campaign (1956) no harm came to Jordan and in
spite of recurrent problems, our relations were at least superficially
satisfactory until the Six Day War. Even on the morning of June 5th,
1967, Israeli Prime Minister Levi Eshkol sent a message entreating
Hussein not to take part in the war. This attitude towards Jordan still
prevails.

The years have somewhat tempered the State's unwillingness to contemplate military action against Jordan. The process began in 1958, when the Arab world was inundated by a wave of fanatically nationalistic violence, which wiped out Hashemite rule in Iraq and joined Syria and Egypt in an alliance called the United Arab Republic. The tottering throne of Hussein was saved only by a British force flown into Amman.

If Hussein were Overthrown

In the discussions following this outbreak of violence, we could not evade the question of what would happen if, on the next occasion, the British did not rush to Hussein's support, or if their aid could not save his throne? What would happen, in other words, if such Arab extremists as Syria or Ba'athist Iraq or the Palestinians were to take control of Jordan?

Under such conditions Ben Gurion would agree to deliberate and to make decisions; in other words, were the status quo in the Middle East to change, were the Hashemite kingdom to fall, were foreign forces to march into the West Bank, Israel would feel free to act. Even the Defense Minister concurred in this in the Knesset.

We discussed at length the nature and extent of our operation should these possibilities be realized. Some thought that the entire West Bank should be occupied; others suggested advancing to the watershed line (the hillock from Jerusalem north to Ramallah and Nablus and south to Bethlehem and Hebron). But David Ben Gurion made the final decision: Only up to Mount Scopus, and that because we happened to have a valid argument: we must defend the Jews stationed there, because a new regime in Jordan might endanger them.

"We cannot justify the occupation of Jenin on the grounds of self-defense," Ben Gurion growled.

Once the decision was made and recorded in the minutes and the "G" Branch began planning its execution, the next question was how to create territorial continuity to Mt. Scopus? Logically by the shortest route, through Sheikh Jarrah, which, however, was even then, as well as the police college next to it, very well fortified. Better, perhaps, to bypass them. And who guarantees that if we break through at Sheikh Jarrah or launch an outflanking movement, the Jordanian army in other sections of Jerusalem won't intervene? It was clear that preventive and preemptive action must be planned in other sectors of the Jerusalem front.

A three-stage plan was therefore worked out: first, a breakthrough to Mt. Scopus via the Mandelbaum Crossing, Sheikh Jarrah and the police college, securing the corridor thus created; second, widening the corridor past Sh'afat and simultaneously capturing Abu-Tor, the southern passage of the Old City; and third, capturing the Old City itself. Although the first two stages were planned in detail and the necessary forces estimated, the third stage remained amorphous. We did not even know through which gates our forces would enter the city. It was stated only that the Old City would be captured according to separately provided orders.

Maintaining the link with Mt. Scopus was the first plan in the Command's Operation Manual, which may be why, when revisions were made, "Operation Mount Scopus" received the most frequent and detailed treatment.

Revision was necessary partly because of changes in the forces designated to execute the plans. On the assumption that "Operation Mount Scopus" might suddenly have to be put into effect after a change of government in Jordan during a period of relative calm, the planners earmarked regular army units for the operation. These were the Golani Brigade, a paratroop brigade, an armored brigade and elements of the Jerusalem Brigade. To be quite honest, although I was afraid to give reserve units so difficult a task as assaulting a fortified position, I sympathized with the rage and indignation of the men of the Jerusalem Brigade, who said to me in fury, "There'll be war in Jerusalem and I won't take part in it?" I was forced to give in. "Okay, you'll be in Stage II." The Six Day War proved how wrong I was. The Reserves were magnificent and fought like lions.

In any case, the officers of the various brigades came to Jerusalem, studied the plans and the terrain, prepared orders for their units and started to train them. And because they were Zahal commanders interested in improvement, they liberally amended the original plan.

As the planning manual of Central Command grew thicker, the scope of the plans broadened proportionally. Among them were Plan "A" which coincided with the original plan for maintaining the link with Mt. Scopus, Plan "B", which included the capture of Ramallah, Bethlehem, and other areas, and Plan "C", the most comprehensive, dealing with the capture of the entire West Bank in a joint operation of the Central and Northern Commands. Central Command to be aided by units placed at its disposal by other regional commands.

The Defense Plan of Central Command

But as long as Hussein was on the throne, and the status quo remained undisturbed, the defense of this vital part of the country fell upon the only three infantry brigades in the area, plus an armored brigade and an armored force belonging to the Command. "Egypt in any case is the main enemy. Syria gives us trouble daily, while the Jordanians create no problems," was the usual argument, sufficient reason for such a meager force.

The brigades were all named for famous exploits of the past. In the Natanya region the "Givati" Brigade, under the command of Colonel Zeev Shaham, was assigned in case of war, to prevent the severing of the country in two by a breakthrough from Tulkarem and Kalkilveh to the sea, a distance of 14 kilometers. It had to maintain a head-on defense, with no chance for maneuvering. The brigade's entire territory, including Kfar Saba and Natanya, was within range of the Legion's guns.

South of the "Givati" sector an infantry regiment under the command of Colonel Moshe Yotvat defended an area mainly of exposed hills overlooking battlefields where Zahal had suffered defeat in the war of 1948. To the rear, but also within range of Jordan's artillery, were the towns and villages of Rosh-Ha'ayin, Lod, Ramla and the Lod Airport, among others. Defending Jerusalem and its environs was a force which included the Jerusalem Brigade, commanded by Colonel Eliezer Amitai. Each of these brigades had artillery and mortar batteries, as well as a number of infantry battalions. All were Reserve units, with all that the word implies.

The Command also had its armored force. The No. 10 Armored Brigade was the "Harel" Brigade, famous in 1948, in which I fought at the time. It included one tank battalion, with about 50 out-of-date Sherman M-50's, heroes of World War II, and two battalions of armored infantry, whose complement of armored half-tracks was never filled. Another armored unit was at the disposal of the Command, with even more ancient tanks, the Sherman M-1's, whose prowess had been demonstrated by the American army in 1944. Zahal was probably the only army in the world still using them in 1967.

Of course, strategy can never be separated from political reality. The political circumstances caused us to assume that the Jordanian army of seven infantry and two armored brigades, equipped with American Patton tanks, would not attack us alone but within the framework of an all-out Arab assault. We assumed – both because of

the 1948 experience and because of the terrain – that the Iraqi reinforcements would be concentrated in the northern part of the West
Bank, the Jordanian army in the Jerusalem and Mt. Hebron sectors.
While the Jordanian army attempted to capture Jerusalem and attack
from the Latrun enclave towards Lod and Ramla, and perhaps even
Tel-Aviv, the Iraqi army would endeavor to split the country in two at
its narrow waist in the Natanya sector.

The Jordanian army was a good one, based on regular army troops
with English officers and British traditions. Its quality had deterio-
rated, of course, when British influence had been removed along with
Glubb Pasha in 1958. Even though the regular Jordanian army has
since been adulterated by reserve soldiers, it is still considered the
strongest and best of the Arab forces.

The Iraqi army which was supposed to have joined it was less
threatening, because of lower standards and internal dissension. Its
failure in the war against the Kurds is well known. But its numbers
were large, its vehicles many, and its artillery and armor considerable.
The expeditionary force it sent to fight against Israel was said to
include an entire armored division.

The Israeli tanks not assigned to the "Givati" Brigade were earmarked for reinforcing the Jerusalem Brigade and were stationed
along the boundary of the Jerusalem sector, beyond which maintaining armored units was prohibited under the terms of the armistice
agreement.

The 10th Brigade was the Command's entire operative reserve, to
seal up holes in our defense system, should such occur, and to launch a
counter-offensive when the time came. Within the framework of this
plan, the Brigade was to bivouac in the Ben-Shemen area, where it was
almost equidistant from all the sectors where it might have to operate.

These, then, were the forces at my disposal, with which I had to
carry out Israel's defense doctrine: to transfer the battle to enemy
territory as rapidly as possible. To fulfil that task against the superior
forces of Jordan and Iraq, I needed another armored brigade, without
which the task would almost certainly be too tough.

THE GATHERING STORM

The Situation Deteriorates

I believe that during the G.H.Q. conference on May 19th the serious-
ness of the situation developing in the south was recognized for the
first time. On the previous night, a partial mobilization had been
ordered, calling up some 60-70,000 men, particularly those in units to
be used as reinforcements for the Southern Command.

Although the morning newspapers reported that U.N. Secretary
General U-Thant had gone to Cairo to meet Nasser, this was the first
time since the crisis began that we stopped interpreting Nasser's
moves as "political exercises." There was an atmosphere of war in the
air, and the Southern and Northern Commands were ordered to
prepare for a possible offensive and for a speedy counterattack.
Besides full-scale war, there was the possibility of restricted warfare,
such as limited incursions or the closing of the Tiran Straits.

Also called up that night were several Central Command units,
especially anti-aircraft and civil defense. My orders were: "Central
Command on alert!"

The mobilization of the Command's anti-aircraft units turned on a
red light in my mind. The heart of the nation – two of its largest cities,
a concentration of its industrial potential, and the only international
airport in the country – were all within the boundaries of Central
Command. Even if Jordan did not enter the war, they would be the
selected targets of the Egyptian air force; Tel Aviv and Ramat Gan
were the two largest cities in the area. The following day, the Sabbath,
I went to the homes of Tel Aviv's Mayor Mordechai Namir and Ramat
Gan's Mayor Avraham Krinitzi and informed them of developments.

"I don't know whether war will break out, but if it does, don't
worry, we shall inflict heavy losses upon the enemy. I do not believe
enemy planes will succeed in getting into the greater Tel Aviv air-
space, but we are doing the best we can so that even if a bomb should
fall, sometime and somewhere, it will not cause heavy casualties. We

are in control of the situation, and the head of the Civil Defense Services in the Tel Aviv area, Colonel Yossi Haas, will be in touch with you."

I fear that my confidence did not infect them.

Central Command in the Cold

Even before I left G.H.Q. at the end of the May 19th meeting, I contacted Command headquarters and ordered that the command group be convened. By the time I reached camp they – my HQ team and the Brigade COS – were waiting for me. After telling them what had been said at the G.H.Q. meeting, I asked that the defense plans be brought up to date. I remember adding: "I doubt that at this stage Plan 'A' will even be allowed. All units are heading south and we've been left out in the cold."

The fact that we were out of the picture was more apparent to me later, when we were ordered to transfer units and equipment to the Southern Command. Fortifications there were going up at feverish speed and our engineering units and equipment were of great assistance. But their transfer down south weakened our entrenching capacity. When I asked G.H.Q. what would happen to us, I was brushed off with an impatient, "Nothing'll happen in your bailiwick!"

Indeed, in order to ensure that nothing would happen, the fortnightly convoy to Mt. Scopus was postponed for a week. But even though we were being bypassed, there was no feeling of business as usual at the Command. Men were constantly reconnoitering and updating plans.

Since the 1948 War of Independence, Central Command has been located in a former British army camp in the Ramla area, whose main buildings were built in Turkish times by members of a German religious sect. The central building, not unlike a monastery in appearance, was a long, two-story structure, with large rooms opening on a balcony which ran the length of the eastern wall. A pair of ancient cannon were mounted on both sides of the staircase. My office was at the southern end of the upper floor. In the corner was a desk, to which was attached a table where the staff officers sat during meetings. A large map of the Command area, protected by a nylon curtain, covered the wall. From my office a door led to the secretaries' room, which housed a telephone exchange, my adjutant, Captain Joel Herzl, and my secretary, Sgt. Ilana. To the right of the secretaries' room was that of the Command's Chief-of-Staff, Colonel Borka, and beyond it, the operations room, realm of the "G" branch officer, Lt. Colonel Arik Regev.

Arik was extraordinary: tall, broad and muscular, an Israeli warrior par excellence, with a superior capacity for work, black coffee and smoking cigarettes. Whatever Arik did, he seemed to do on a grand scale. In 1966, when I suggested that he join me as my operations officer at the Command, he was already deputy commander of a paratroop brigade, one of the young hopefuls of the force and possibly of Zahal as a whole. I had no idea how he would react to my proposal of cutting short his career in the paratroops, quitting life in the field and transferring to a staff job. To my delight he accepted.

When the alert was sounded and Central Command was bypassed, he undoubtedly regretted his decision. His former brigade, his own colleagues, were all somewhere in the northern area, preparing for the biggest war in Israel's history, and he was stuck at Central Command in apparent peace and quiet. But his disappointment was never allowed to affect his work. He went on energetically, equally enthusiastic about planning a "snatch" and resolving all of Tel Aviv's civil defense problems. He missed no opportunity to go down south and see for himself what was going on. Returning from one such visit – at the peak of a brutal *hamsin* in the Negev – he came agitatedly to see me. "The men are being boiled alive there!" he said. "The heat is terrible, and they don't get enough drinking water. They have no water-trailers." He begged me to lend some of ours to Arik Sharon's division, which had suffered particularly from lack of water.

"And what shall we do?" I asked.

"So far nothing is happening here," he replied, "and there they are parched. And if something does happen here, a water shortage can't be as serious as it is in the Negev." True, I thought, and sent some of our water trailers down south.

After the war, Arik Regev went back to the paratroops as a brigade commander, and was killed leading his men in a search for a band of terrorists. With him fell his faithful "G" officer, Captain Gadi Manella. His death cut short a brilliant military career and robbed Zahal of one of its most promising officers.

A few days before war broke out, Yaakov Sharett, the son of the late Prime Minister and Foreign Minister, Moshe Sharett, joined my staff. One day, when I ran into him by chance, he pleaded, "Save me! I have nothing to do and I'm dying of boredom!"

That same evening, after a meeting of G.H.Q., the general officer of the Southern Command, Shaike Gavish, asked in passing, "Will you be keeping a diary?" "No," said I, "I haven't even thought about it. And you?" "Certainly," he replied, "everyone is." At that point, Kobi came to my mind. Next day I phoned the Zahal spokesman's office, where Kobi was registered, and asked if he could be transferred to my Command. They agreed, and I appointed Kobi keeper of the war diary. From the first day of the war, he recorded all that took place. Thanks to his work, much was preserved that would otherwise have been lost, for, from the moment that war began until it ended, not a single written order was issued to or from Central Command whether from G.H.Q. to the Command, or from the Command H.Q. to the lower echelons. Everything was transmitted by telephone or radio-telephone. And because in Central Command the war took us by surprise, and not a single reporter or cameraman had been appointed to us, we were unable to record events. Even the historic broadcast from the Wailing Wall was made by a reporter, Raphael Amir, who was there by chance. The keeper of our history was Kobi Sharett, who recorded the great events.

Sunday – May 21st 1967

The tension seemed to ease slightly. Cairo Radio announced that Israel had concentrated nine brigades in the Negev, of which six had been brought down from the Syrian frontier. This was interpreted by some as preparation for trumpeting victory. "There you are. Israel had to cancel its plan to attack Syria, solely because the Egyptian army entered the Sinai Peninsula!"

The arrival of the Finnish prime minister on a friendly visit to Israel was also a sign of relaxing tensions, as was something else that happened on the same day and was interpreted by many as withdrawal from the war. In the village of Ramata, on the Jordan-Syrian frontier, a vehicle coming from Syria exploded. Fourteen people died, most of them Jordanian border police, and 28 people were wounded. The driver of the vehicle and a woman with him were arrested. It was rumored that the time bomb, which had exploded prematurely, was intended for King Hussein. Jordan closed its border with Syria, and although the Jordanian Minister of the Interior stated in Amman that "the gang of criminals in power in Damascus will not divert the minds of the Jordanian people from the Israeli danger," it was obvious that the chances of Arab unity against Israel were as remote as they had ever been.

The relaxed atmosphere persisted through the next day, May 22nd. Prime Minister Levi Eshkol presented to the Knesset a speech he had spent an entire day writing. Its contents had been scrutinized by all the Cabinet ministers, who had struck out any phrase which could possibly be considered provocative to Nasser. It was a most moderate and appeasing speech.

"I want to repeat once again to the Arab states that we have no intention of attacking anyone. We have no intention of threatening their security, their territories or their legal rights. We shall not interfere in their internal affairs, in their administration or in their relations among themselves... It is necessary to invoke international influence to its fullest extent in order to insure the maintenance of peace on the Israel-Egypt border ... We shall pay interested attention to the visit in the Middle East of the U.N. Secretary General ..."

And so on, in the same spirit.

On that same day the U.S. Sixth Fleet weighed anchor and set sail from its base in Naples to the eastern Mediterranean, and Moscow replied to an American cable that the Soviet Union also supported peaceful settlement in the Middle East.

A jarring note in the midst of general appeasement was heard in Paris, where a French government spokesman said that his country no longer considered itself bound by the 1950 tripartite declaration of the western powers guaranteeing the security of Middle Eastern boundaries.

Unknown to us, President Nasser, with his two deputies, Marshal Amar and Zakaria Mohieddin, the secretary of the Arab Socialist Union, Ali Sabry, Defence Minister Shams Badran, Air Force Commander Mahmoud Zadky and the commander of Egyptian forces in Sinai, General Mortagi, set out on an inspection tour of Egyptian army positions in the Sinai Peninsula. Towards evening he was to arrive at Bir-Gafgafa Air Force Base.

The Egyptians had also, apparently, stationed units on the Red Sea. Infantry and paratroop forces arrived in Sharm-e-Sheikh, and the "Palestine Liberation Army" of Ahmed Shukeiry was in the Gaza Strip, reinforced by some 30 tanks.

The First Meeting in the "Pit"

That same evening, at about the time that Nasser's plane landed at Bir-Gafgafa, a G.H.Q. meeting was beginning. For the first time since the onset of the crisis, the meeting took place not in the usual room but in the underground war room, the "Pit" as we called it. We were told of the latest developments and inferences and conclusions were drawn. When we left, the whole situation was still in question, with various developments possible.

The question-mark, however, was to be erased in a few hours, when Nasser got up – at the Bir-Gafgafa Air Force Base – and made a speech to the officers gathered in the mess. "Our forces," he said, "have been stationed since yesterday on Sharm-e-Sheikh; the Tiran Straits are our territorial waters. Not a single Israeli vessel shall again pass through them; we shall also bar passage to strategic materials to Israel on non-Israeli vessels . . . the Jews threaten to fight? We say to them: Ahalan we'Sahalan! Go ahead! We are ready for war!"

The speech was broadcast over Cairo Radio at 01.00 in the morning of May 3rd, 1967. The director of military intelligence, Major General Aaron Yariv, telephoned at once from G.H.Q. to the C.O.G.S.: "Itzhak, Nasser has announced the closing of the Straits."

"I'm on my way," replied Rabin.

Tuesday, May 23rd, 1967

At 4.30 in the morning, after hours spent discussing and constantly checking dispositions, the C.O.G.S. telephoned to the prime minister in Jerusalem, woke him, and told him the news of the Straits.

Eshkol left for Tel Aviv immediately.

That whole day was spent in perfervid consultation between the prime minister and G.H.Q. offices at 7.30, and afterwards at a meeting of the C.O.G.S. and the Ministerial Committee on Defense and Security in the prime minister's chambers. At 10 o'clock the prime minister, the foreign minister and the Chief of the General Staff met with delegates of the opposition parties. In the afternoon we were back in the "Pit" for another meeting. The atmosphere was somber indeed.

When the meeting was called to order, Major General Yariv briefly surveyed world reaction to Nasser's declaration. In almost every capital city of the world it was interpreted as a demonstration of Egyptian might against Israeli weakness. None of us disagreed with that interpretation. We were aware that blockading the straits meant that Zahal's image as a deterrent was shattered.

Israel had based its defense policy on that image for 11 years, since "Operation Kadesh" (1956), knowing that as long as the Arabs feared defeat at Israel's hands there would be no war. But the moment they no longer feared us, war would be inevitable and we would be attacked. When Nasser closed the Tiran Straits, much more than a sea-blockade was imposed on the southern gateway to Israel. From our point of view it was war, even though the guns were silent.

General Yariv added details about the movement of Egyptian forces towards their forward positions and the movement of Syrian armored units to the Golan Heights and the Israeli border. Then the C.O.G.S. rose to say, "The Government has decided to invoke to the fullest the American guarantees."

In that simple, characteristic sentence, Major-General Rabin summarized the decision taken in the morning at the meeting of the Ministerial Committee on Defense, held in the *kiriyah* (government offices). At that meeting Foreign Minister Abba Eban had read a cable received the previous day from President Johnson, requesting postponement of any military action for at least 48 hours, so that he could move diplomatically to get the Tiran Straits reopened. The foreign minister suggested an affirmative reply. He said that the United States had indeed in 1957 guaranteed to safeguard Israel's shipping rights through the Tiran Straits, but that if we intended to hold them to that guarantee we could not refuse a short postponement, even though it was clear that when the 48 hours were up further postponement would be requested.

In reply to questions from the ministers, the C.O.G.S. said that a 48-hour postponement would have no significant effect on the relative strength of the forces, but, on the contrary, would give Zahal time to organize more effectively. Postponement was therefore agreed to, and Abba Eban left for overseas to visit the capital cities of the great powers.

His statement having reduced the tension, the C.O.G.S. ordered a long list of reserve brigades, including those of Central Command, and paratroop brigades, including the 55th, to be mobilized that night. As we were leaving the meeting I caught a glimpse of the C.O.G.S. He was sitting alone, deep in thought, his face full of sorrow. I went over and whispered. "Itzhak, it looks serious this time, eh?"

He nodded heavily.

I left him. The burden of being Number One cannot be shared. Gloom descended on the country. With the closing of the Tiran Straits, every Israeli was convinced that war was coming. Israel would not suffer so barefaced a challenge in silence. The widespread mobilization during the night of May 23rd in large degree confirmed the opinion that Zahal was on the point of reacting.

But nothing happened. The Egyptian navy began mining the Tiran Straits – and still the camouflage nets over Israel armor bivouacked in the desert stayed in place. Abba Eban went hastily to Europe and the U.S.A., and the Security Council in New York was about to hold a conference in which nobody placed hope. President Johnson issued a condemnation of the sea-blockade at the same time that he called for self-restraint and patience.

In Jerusalem the prime minister met with the leaders of the opposition, Menahem Begin of Gahal and Moshe Dayan of Rafi. Dayan, who no longer served in the army, came to the meeting in khaki, having spent two days among army units in the Negev. He was rumored to be a candidate for the job of commander of the southern front. The general public increasingly clamored for the establishment of a national government, in which Dayan, or perhaps Ben Gurion, was often put forth as candidate for the defense portfolio. On the other hand it was announced that the Alignment heads had turned down the proposal for an emergency cabinet. Depression deepened.

In the Arab countries the atmosphere was radically different. Nasser's boldness in closing the Tiran Straits was received jubilantly, and when Israel failed to react the trumpets of victory seemed to sound. All restraints on eastern imagination and ebullience were apparently lifted, and spirits grew wilder as the reins were loosened. In Cairo tens of thousands shouted:

"Nasser! Nasser! Lead us to war!"

In the Gaza Strip, armories were opened and arms distributed to cheering Palestinians, who believed that within a day or two they would land in Tel Aviv. A new hit tune was broadcast ceaselessly from every Arab radio station, whose refrain was "Slaughter! Slaughter!" (*Atbah! Atbah!*). Obviously the wild refrain hypnotized not only the Arab masses but their leaders as well. Nasser seized the opportunity to extricate himself from the lengthy, ill-starred Yemen war, and ordered the Egyptian expeditionary force brought directly from there to the Sinai Peninsula. This gesture of Arab fraternity gave rise to flamboyant promises from Algiers, Iraq and Kuwait to send troops to Egypt. Saudi Arabia declared its "complete" solidarity with Nasser. Hussein could not but join the merrymaking, and announced over the radio that he had decided to allow Saudi and Iraqi army units into

Jordan to fight Israel. Since the birth of the Arab Nationalist Movement at the end of the 19th century, there has, I believe, been no finer
hour for the Arab people.

As for myself, I was not partner to the despair of the Israeli people,
including several of my Zahal colleagues. I was optimistic, not
because I had a short-sighted view of reality or because I lived in a
fool's paradise, but because I knew the Israeli man-in-the-street, the
reservist, the civilian-in-the-rear, and I knew how much devotion he
was capable of. I knew Zahal, its corps, its branches. I knew its
officers, and I knew what they could do. And I had known the Arab
enemy for years, and believed with complete faith that we could defeat
them again this time.

Wednesday, May 24th, 1967

On May 24th, the C.O.G.S. fell ill and the head of "G" Branch,
Major-General Ezer Weizman, chaired the meeting in the "Pit." It
lasted about three hours, and discussion went on as though war would
break out the next day. General Weizman ordered Southern Command to be in a state of alert as of the morning of May 25th.

At Central Command, as at Southern Command, plans for a variety
of missions had been amassed over the years, among them one for the
capture of the Gaza Strip and another for an offensive along the coast
to El-Arish. There were plans for continuing the assault along the
coastal axis to the Suez Canal, and for the capture of the whole Sinai
Peninsula.

I was not satisfied with taking the Gaza Strip only as far as El-Arish,
since I had no doubt that Zahal could overrun the Gaza Strip with very
few casualties. But I wondered what would happen if, after we had
taken the Strip, the Egyptians still refused to barter and to open the
Tiran Straits in exchange for our withdrawal. We would have
hundreds of thousands more Arabs under our administration, which
might sow more evil than good and the Egyptian army would remain
in Sinai in full strength, and continue to threaten our existence. What
then would we do, and how long could we hold out if there were a
general mobilization? I was convinced Zahal should not accept half-
measures; it must force the whole Egyptian army into submission.

When the discussion ended, the prime minister, Defense Minister
Levi Eshkol and Deputy Defense Minister Dr. Zvi Dinstein joined
us. They had been invited by the chief of operations, perhaps to
convince them that Zahal was all set and ready to go.

I was pleased that they had come: it was important that they be aware of the confidence that we felt. We began to discuss the prospects and objectives of war, an endless subject, because the decision made the previous day, to give President Johnson every possible chance to move diplomatically, was still in force.

Bar-Lev Returns from Paris

That same night Major-General Haim Bar-Lev returned from a study-furlough in France. When the state of alert was announced, Bar-Lev cabled the C.O.G.S. from Paris on the 17th of May: "From here the situation seems worrying. Want to return to any job, even commander tank team."

Haim Bar-Lev had been my friend since our Palmach days. We had met originally during an officers' training course of the Haganah in 1944 in Juara. In the struggle against the British we were both platoon commanders in "H" Company in Ramat Rahel and at Beit Ha'arava, and met again in the Negev Brigade during the War of Independence.

When that war ended we were both instructors in a battalion officers' course, which Bar-Lev was chosen to direct when Rabin was transferred to another post. At that time he, Zwi Zamir (who later headed the Israel equivalent of the C.I.A.) and I lived in Jerusalem and shared a jeep. We drew lots every morning to see who would drive it to the Zriffin army camp, and every evening to see who would keep it overnight. When the course was over we went in different directions, but kept in touch, as did our families.

I knew him well and knew also his remarkable composure under stress, heightened by his slow, deliberate way of speaking, which inspired confidence even in the midst of furious action.

When I learned of his arrival that evening, I was so pleased that I decided to stay a little longer at G.H.Q. and wait for him. Major-General Aaron Yariv, Director of Intelligence, was as pleased as I.

"At this time of insecurity," he said, "Haim Bar-Lev is security." We were sure that his imperturbability and capacity for diffusing calm would serve Zahal well at such a time.

Itzhak Rabin recommended that Major-General Bar-Lev be appointed his deputy; confirmation was published on June 1st.

At the G.H.Q. conference, during which we were told of Bar-Lev's appointment as deputy C.O.G.S., I congratulated him and invited him to our home in Zahala. There we found my father-in-law, David Hacohen, M.K., who had come straight from a meeting of the Foreign Affairs and Defense Committee of the Knesset and was very upset about what he had heard. We sketched for him the preparations and strength of the defense forces, clearly demonstrating our confidence in the outcome of any military test. Unusual though this was, David Hacohen sat and listened, speaking only when we had finished. "If that's the situation," he said, "it's a pity the government isn't aware of it..."

The state of alert continued, and with it the tension and worry. I felt vividly that it was incumbent upon us, the officers of Zahal, not only to strengthen the army but to let the people know how strong it was. When I talked with people I realized that they were concerned chiefly with the casualties war might inflict. Even those closely involved with the defense establishment, even senior officers, thought that casualties would be heavy, and that urban population centers would be mercilessly bombed. Some quoted figures: "Twenty thousand dead," I heard somebody say.

Thursday, May 25th, 1967

I have, however, jumped the gun. It is still May 25th, the day of the massive mobilization of reserve units.

The previous day U Thant had met Nasser and had left as he had come, empty-handed. Nevertheless his statement to the press held a modicum of optimism. Abba Eban was received by De Gaulle at, according to early reports, a satisfactory meeting. From Paris Eban went on to London for a brief meeting with Harold Wilson, who was about to depart for Moscow, and who promised to persuade the Kremlin to try to ease the tension. The Security Council debated for six hours about the closing of the Tiran Straits without arriving at a decision. But the most important news to us at Central Command was:

"A Jordanian spokesman confirmed that his government has authorized the entrance into Jordan of the Iraqi Army. Jordanian Independence Day celebrations have been cancelled, and general mobilization has been declared."

Amman's statement was not given much credence. Because we at Central Command still did not believe in the war, all our military strength was not called up.

On the evening of May 25th, a meeting of reserve brigade officers was held at *Beit Hayal* in Tel Aviv. The men were furious at not having been mobilized, and the apprehension and lack of confidence had spread to the streets and to the people. The reserves feared that their not having been called up meant that we were not going to fight, and I spoke to them briefly: "I don't know if there will be war. But if there is, 72 hours will not have passed before we take the entire West Bank." I promised them that they would be mobilized before war was declared.

On Friday, May 26th, I issued instructions on orders from G.H.Q., to set the defense plan in partial operation throughout the Command's area. The same day, in Washington, the fateful meeting of President Johnson and Abba Eban took place. Just as Eban had anticipated, the President requested a further postponement of Israeli military action. This time he asked for several weeks, during which period the U.S. would be able to make plans for joint action with the maritime nations, consummated by ships sailing in convoy, protected by warships, through the Tiran Straits.

That night the text of a speech by Gamal Abd el-Nasser at a conference of the Egyptian Professionals Association was published. The Egyptian ruler abandoned all diplomatic posturing and pretense and said unequivocally, "Our objective is to destroy Israel. This will be an all-out War!"

I was occupied not only with current affairs but also with a personal problem whose solution was to affect the Command directly. A day or two earlier, Col. Uri Ben-Ari, deeply depressed, had come to see me. "We're about to go to war," he said, bitterly, "and I am left behind." I had known Uri since 1947, as his instructor in a platoon commander's course of the Haganah in Juara, and later as his commanding officer in the "Assault" Battalion of Harel Brigade. There he was known as the "Ace Invader." He took part in all the battles, in every one of which he was the leader, moving straight into the line of fire.

When I was transferred from Harel to the Negev Brigade he replaced me as deputy commander of the "Assault" Battalion. Several months later he was also transferred to Harel and served as my deputy in the 7th Battalion. We took part together in the capture of Beersheba and in "Operation Horev," at which time he replaced me as battalion commander. Some time later he joined the armored corps. In "Operation Kadesh" he commanded the 7th Brigade, which bore the brunt of the fighting in the central sector of Sinai. Soon afterward, at the age of 32, he was appointed commander of an armored regiment. Then he left the army. We had seen little of one another, but the deep ties which had bound us in the days of Harel and the Negev were strong and abiding.

I had no way of consoling him. Not a single job in the Command was available and I told him that. "But hang around," I said. "Come with me on inspections. Perhaps something will turn up."

The next day Major-General Israel Tal, commander of the tank corps, contacted me. "Say, Uzi," he said, "you've got to help me; we're getting new equipment and there are enormous technical problems. Let me have Mendi. I need him."

Colonel Mendi was commander of the 10th Brigade, an able tank man by any standards. At that same instant it flashed across my mind that this was the solution to Uri's problem.

On the evening of May 31st, before a G.H.Q. meeting, I cornered General Rabin and said, "Talik has asked me for Mendi. I want Uri Ben-Ari in his place." Rabin frowned, hesitated and agreed.

I telephoned to Ben-Ari immediately. Although it was late and I woke him, he was delighted with the news that he had been appointed commander of the 10th Brigade and that he must report the following day.

The next morning he was in my office, virile and confident. In his high tankman's boots, carrying a riding-crop with which he impatiently slapped his thigh, he was the familiar Uri Ben-Ari. He went at once to the Ben-Shemen Woods, where his brigade was assembled, and took command. At four o'clock that afternoon I went to see him at a meeting of the brigade's officers held in the Modiin Amphitheatre. It was clear that the brigade had gained a leader. Among veteran tankmen, in other units and other services, the return to the army of Uri Ben-Ari aroused much rejoicing.

At that officers' gathering in the Modiin Amphitheatre, I said: "The easy stage has come to an end. Now the hard part begins. Actually, in plain words, the position is – Meanwhile No! And both words bear the same emphasis. There is no knowing when 'meanwhile' will end or when 'no' will become 'yes.' When it happens, it will surprise the enemy. But not us! We must be ready for even the most extreme changes in Zahal's objectives, by which I mean a constant state of alert and a high morale. I have confidence in you and in your men."

Saturday, May 27th, 1967

In the small morning hours came a telephone call from G.H.Q.: "Meeting at 7.30."

When I entered the war room in the "Pit," I could feel the tension. Decision was in the air. The C.O.G.S. reported that the government had decided to postpone its meeting until the evening, after Abba Eban's return from the U.S.A. I wrote: "The talks with the Americans are worthless. If we do not look after ouselves, no one will do it for us." Reports were made, followed by questions and answers. I made a note of my remark that Hussein is not to be trusted. I think I wrote that in response to somebody who said that he thought that this time, as in 1956, Jordan would stay out of the picture.

I waited until the C.O.G.S. managed to extricate himself from the generals and then went into his office. I was chiefly concerned about the Iraqi tanks in the West Bank, and I felt that I could not be without armor. I decided to be adamant in my demand for an armored brigade. It was obvious that the C.O.G.S.'s thoughts were entirely in the South, and he told me that, when the time came, the problem would be attended to.

The foreign minister arrived at Lod Airport at 10 p.m. and went at once to the *Kiriyah*. The cabinet meeting lasted until very late at night, with the C.O.G.S. and Generals Haim Bar-Lev, Ezer Weizman and Aaron Yariv in attendance. They stressed that further delay would allow the Egyptians to settle in more solidly, giving rise to heavier casualties when the inevitable war finally broke out. The foreign minister took a different view and supported the suggestion that President Johnson be granted his request for further postponement. No decision was made. The prime minister decided that it was too late and the ministers were too tired to decide so crucial a matter. Another meeting was called for the next day.

Sunday, May 28th, 1967

Nothing. Not a thing. We needed no telephone call from G.H.Q. to know that action in the south would not begin today. The morning papers reported the sensational visit of opposition leader Menahem Begin to the home of David Ben Gurion, the man who, till yesterday, had been his bitterest opponent. The differences between them had never been resolved, but the enmity had vanished, a significant sign of the times. Although the papers capitalized on the foreign minister's journey, they had no reliable information about the meetings with the United States President, but the evening papers were able to report that the U.S. had finally decided not to use force to break the Tiran

Straits blockade, and that the President had asked Israel for more time so that a diplomatic solution might be found. In exchange he promised Israel oil and military equipment.

A G.H.Q. meeting was called for 8 p.m., since Rabin thought that the senior officers should meet the prime minister for a direct exchange of views.

Two hours earlier, at six o'clock, Prime Minister Levi Eshkol made his famous broadcast to explain to the nation Israel's reasons for delay, and to strengthen the national morale. The results were the opposite. I did not happen to hear the broadcast, but when I arrived at the G.H.Q. meeting shortly before it began, some of those who had heard the speech were seriously disheartened by it.

The Prime Minister had insisted on a live broadcast in spite of two sleepless nights: on Friday night the Russian ambassador had wakened him with a cable from Kosygin and on Saturday night the long late meeting of the Cabinet had taken place. It was a great mistake. While reading the handwritten speech, he stumbled on a word, stopped, and tried to cover up by using another word. Actually a minor mishap which under other circumstances would have made people smile, but in the nerve-racking tension of the moment crushed their already wavering spirits.

The G.H.Q. meeting started late. We waited interminably for the prime minister. Tension mounted. At last Eshkol turned up with his political secretary, Adi Yaffe, Minister Yigael Allon, the Director-General of the Defense Ministry, Moshe Kashti and the Prime Minister's military secretary, Israel Lior.

The meeting was held in the conference room close to the war room. Levi Eshkol in an open-necked shirt sat at the head of the table between the C.O.G.S. and Yigael Allon, just back from Moscow. Only the generals were in the room. No refreshments were served. Unmarked maps hung on the walls. The air was heavy, emotion and cigarette smoke almost equally tangible. The faces were pale under the new lights, but the Prime Minister seemed palest of all because of his terrible fatigue. He began by recapitulating his radio speech. I wrote in my notebook:

Eshkol: The danger to Israel from the concentration of Egyptian forces in Sinai and the blockade of Israeli shipping in the Red Sea are grave matters. Our reply: maintain the state of alert and increase our efforts. The government praises Zahal and the people and decides: The blockade of the Straits is an act of aggression, and we shall defend ourselves against it when the time comes. [I underlined "when the time comes."]

There is a willingness in the world to act diplomatically and the government will continue to encourage those statesmen to act. Tomorrow there will be a debate in the Knesset. Last night the government almost decided to move today, but meanwhile several things were revealed at the diplomatic level which necessitated postponement for a long period, perhaps forever.

Then Eshkol told us of the visit of Soviet Ambassador Dimitry Tzubachin early the previous morning. The Prime Minister observed the Sabbath in Tel Aviv, staying at the Dan Hotel. At 2.00 a.m. Adi Yaffe, his political secretary, who was sleeping in the adjoining room, was awakened by the secretary of the Russian Embassy, Bykov, who said that the ambassador wanted immediate audience with the Prime Minister. Yaffe suggested either postponing it until morning, or arranging a meeting with the ambassador and the director-general of the Foreign Office, Arieh Laviv, who was also spending the night at the Dan Hotel. The Russian insisted, and added threateningly, "Do not take upon yourself the responsibility for postponing the meeting."

Adi Yaffe woke the Prime Minister and Arieh Laviv, and it was decided to receive the ambassador, who had an urgent cable from the Prime Minister of the Soviet Union.

Eshkol read the contents of that cable: "From reports reaching us, tension in the Middle East is mounting, and in Israel the feeling is that there is no solution other than war.

"It is dangerous when weapons begin to talk.

"The Union of Soviet Socialist Republics calls upon you to take every measure to avoid military confrontation so as to keep it from becoming a new focal point for war in the world.

"The more complicated the situation appears to be, the more essential it is to seek peaceful means for its solution.

"It is easy to light a fire, but difficult to extinguish it. Israel must do everything to prevent the fire's being lit."

Eshkol told us that a discussion lasting one-and-a-half hours took place, in which he, in his dressing-gown, tried to convince the ambassador that Israel was not an "agent of imperialism." Tzubachin was not to be persuaded.

Eshkol asked if a similar cable had been sent to Nasser. Tzubachin replied that it hadn't. What, in Tzubachin's opinion, Eshkol asked, should Israel have done that it had not done already? The ambassador avoided replying.

Eshkol then told us that a message had come from Johnson last night: "I have received word from the Soviet Union to the effect that Israel is about to start a war. The Soviet Union suggests relieving the tension by peaceful means and requests you take all measures to avoid a military conflict. According to them, the Arabs do not want war, but if Israel opens fire the Soviet Union will support the Arabs. As your friend, I ask you not to carry out a preemptive action. In my reply to the Soviet Union, I shall deal with the international status of the Tiran Straits. Barbour [the U.S. Ambassador to Israel]," he added, "who brought me the message, told me that the United States was preparing to move an armed international fleet through the Straits, in order to keep them open to all flags of the world. Hence Israel must not take independent action. The Americans have invited Canada, Holland, France and India to participate in the flotilla. Israel might also be requested to send a warship. The assembling of the fleet might take about three weeks. In all events, the President of the U.S.A. is determined to open the Straits, and if necessary, the 6th Fleet will be used for the purpose."

The Prime Minister ended by saying that at the Cabinet meeting it had been agreed almost unanimously that it was impossible to ignore either message and therefore no operations were to begin. The United States must be allowed to do what she could by diplomatic means. This decision had been passed on to the Foreign Affairs and Defense Committee of the Knesset. When the Prime Minister had finished, the discussion began. It became heated, the speakers arguing about the situation and the consequences of not taking action.

The neon lights picked up the lines of worry on the faces of the speakers, fearful for the nation whose fate, most of us believed, depended upon our initiative. There was a suspicion that the Russians might intervene. Memories of the end of the 1956 Sinai Campaign came to mind, when Bulganin and Khrushchev cabled Ben Gurion that unless Israel withdrew the Russians would show their hand. At the same time they took care to feed the news media with reports of Red Army troop movements and a state of alert beyond the Caucasian Mountains.

I recalled to them the story of Colonel Monat (a Polish Jew who had deserted to the West), who had been military attaché in Washington in 1956. He described the actions of the military attachés from the Eastern bloc. Throughout the U.S. capital, they spread false stories, which were believed, of Russian preparations for intervention against

Israel, an example of psychological warfare par excellence; the world bought the stories, and Israel withdrew. I thought that we must not be fooled a second time.

Monday, May 29th, 1967

The government decision to comply with President Johnson's request to postpone all activity for two to three weeks found its way into the newspapers, which dropped the security aspects of the matter and considered only its economic consequences. They speculated wildly about the Prime Minister's garbled speech the day before, going so far as to express their lack of confidence in him and his leadership. The clamor for a national government increased.

At 3 o'clock in the afternoon there was another G.H.Q. meeting. The frequency of these meetings interfered considerably with our regular work, but they gave me a chance to meet my colleagues and find out the mood among the Zahal rank and file and the problems of the other commands. The Egyptian military build-up in Sinai had intensified enough to augur a surprise attack without the requisite preparations which serve to warn us ahead of time.

It was now clearer to me than ever that the main problem was the lack of government confidence in Zahal's ability to win quickly and decisively.

Naturally, the indifference of everyone to the needs of Central Command annoyed me. One might have thought that Hussein had given a guarantee that if war broke out he would stay passively on the West Bank and not intervene.

Hussein goes to Cairo

King Hussein surprised the entire world, Israel not excepted, when he flew to Cairo for a meeting with Nasser. Nothing that reached our ears about Jordan gave indication of such a development. Only a few days earlier Cairo and Jordan had exchanged insults and abuses, accusing each other of treason, and Radio Damascus had broadcast a call to the "brave masses" in Jordan to rise up against their government. "The administration of blood and crime in Amman should not prevent you from fulfilling your duty in the battle of honor for which all your Arab brethren are preparing..." And only a few days before that, Hussein had sent the Chief of his General Staff, General Amer Hamsh, to Cairo where he had been most coolly received and all but told outright that Egypt wanted nothing to do with him.

What then had happened in Amman to turn things so topsy-turvy? There are several answers.

After the war I discussed this with East Jerusalem notables who were close to Hussein. One of them, Anwar El-Khatib, Governor of East Jerusalem until June 7th, 1967, told me that King Hussein had felt most uncomfortable in the isolated position in which he found himself after Nasser became the hero of the entire Arab world by closing the Tiran Straits on May 23rd. He tried to break through the isolating wall by sending Amer Hamsh to Cairo to revive the Joint Arab Command. General Hamsh found the doors closed at Egyptian Supreme Command Headquarters. Finally he managed to get to the Commander-in-Chief, Field Marshal Abd el-Hakim Amer, who also refused to talk without Nasser's explicit instructions. Hamsh did not succeed in speaking to Nasser.

Hussein seemed to have accepted the situation. A few days later he began conferring with dignitaries and senior officers, all of whom urged him to climb on the Egyptian-Syrian bandwagon, on the grounds that, even if he did not, Israel would attack Jordan when war broke out, in which case he would get help from nobody. The officers went even further and said the troops would revolt if Syria and Egypt went to war while Jordan sat on the sidelines.

According to Muhammed Abu-Zuluf (editor of the East Jerusalem newspaper *El Kuds*), the Jordanian army officers demanded a meeting with Hussein, which took place at the Mafrak military base, where they protested loudly, insisting that Hussein join Nasser should war break out. Following that meeting and, in the opinion of Abu-Zuluf, as a result of it, Hussein called for a top-level conference on May 28th in his chambers at Amman. Participating were Prime Minister Sa'ad Juma'a, several ministers, the Chief of the General Staff, and the Egyptian ambassador to Amman. At that meeting Hussein expressed his desire to go to Cairo and meet Nasser. Everybody approved, and the Egyptian ambassador promised to bring Cairo's reply within 24 hours.

In his book Hussein says that he was certain war would break out any moment and Jordan would be dragged in willy-nilly. He did not, he says, believe that Egypt and Syria alone would defeat Israel. "Although they did have a certain edge in arms and equipment, I did not believe in their ability to achieve total victory." He was sure that Jordan's joining the axis (with a promise of military aid from Iraq) would enhance the Arabs' overall chances, and certainly those of

Jordan in holding out against Israel.

Hussein set forth. Awaiting him at the Al-Maza Airport were Nasser, his four deputies, the Egyptian Prime Minister, and the Chief of the Joint Arab Command, General Ali Amer. At first the atmosphere was restrained and cool, Nasser even asking ironically: "What would happen if we arrest you?" But at the discussion table at the Kube Palace the chill evaporated.

It was agreed that, since Syria objected to collaboration with Jordan, she could not be included in the Egyptian-Syrian alliance, but there was nothing to prevent an Egyptian-Jordanian alliance similar to that with Syria. And so this was agreed.

Nasser at once ordered the deputy Chief-of-Staff of the Joint Arab Command, General Abd el-Monaim Riadh, to go to Amman and take command of the eastern front. He also informed Iraqi President Aaref of developments. Ahmed Shukheiry, chief of the Palestine Liberation Army, who but a day or two previously had issued a call over the radio for the overthrow of the Hussein regime, was at the Kube Palace during the deliberations and was told to make peace with the Hashemite king and accompany him to Amman.

When Hussein's plane took off for the return flight to Amman, immediately after a festive luncheon at the Kube Palace, Cairo Radio removed the blackout on the king's journey and broadcast complete and dramatic details of the signing of the military alliance, thus giving the people of Jordan the news of their king's flight to Egypt.

We learned of the dramatic developments in Cairo a short while before the broadcast. G.H.Q. ordered full implementation of the defense plan throughout the Command. All my anxieties of the past fortnight, evaluations, plans, and yes, even my secret hopes, were suddenly and astoundingly realized.

Hussein's alliance with Nasser at once gave added meaning to the statements from Amman, which until now had sounded hollow, about opening Jordan's frontiers to Iraqi and Saudi Arabian troops. From this point on we could expect them to reach Jordan, and quickly, possibly joined by Egyptian forces. Then we would have to face not only the nine regular brigades of the Jordanian Army, but an Iraqi and Saudi Arabian force of unknown strength. To the small Jordanian air force, previously of no particular concern to us, would now certainly be added fighter and bomber squadrons of the Iraqi air force, equipped with Russian planes.

After the Jordan-Egypt alliance, there was rejoicing in Amman.

The masses believed in victory. The king himself and a few close associates may have comforted themselves with the hope that war might not break out, but they too were confident that, war or no war, a great diplomatic victory was assured the Arabs.

Muhammed Abu-Zuluf told me about a typical evening (either on the 2nd or 3rd of June) with General Muhammed Ahmed Selim el-Betnia, at Jordan Army H.Q. in Bittin on the West Bank. The general, tall, pleasant, and not particularly popular in East Jerusalem because he was not considered sufficiently extreme, entertained, as was his custom, the notables of the area and officers close to him. They spoke of the war to come. General el-Betnia thought that there would be no war, because the great powers would not allow such a deterioration in the situation. But should war come, he said, the Israelis had not the slightest chance of crossing the green line. "The line is so fortified, that even a bird could not get through..." He pointed to the horizon in the west, where a sort of halo of light shone over Tel Aviv in the distance, and said: "Perhaps in a few days we'll be there..."

Colonel Mohammed Dauer, head of the Jordanian delegation to the Mixed Armistice Commission, was much more optimistic. On the morning of June 5th, he promised his secretary Ibrahim a house in Tel Aviv.

Wednesday, May 31st, 1967

Everyone talked about the Jordanian-Egyptian alliance and its implications. There was profound concern among the general public, some of them blaming the indecision and vacillation of the Israeli and U.S. governments for having pushed Hussein into Nasser's arms.

Other reports, too, were pessimistic. Moscow had rejected France's suggestion of a meeting of the Big Four to draft and possibly enforce a peaceful solution for the Middle East. Friends in the Foreign Ministry pointed out that France was no longer the friend of Israel that she had been, and that the meeting between De Gaulle and Abba Eban had not been as friendly and warm as early reports had indicated. In addition, the newspapers reported endless meetings of the Security Council, from whom no help, apparently, was to be expected.

During the morning, I held a staff meeting in my headquarters at Ramla. I began, as usual, with a review of the situation, emphasizing that even though Central Command seemed to have risen in rank so far as priorities were concerned, thanks to Hussein's trip to Cairo, this heightened status still lacked practical relevance. We had received no additional forces or equipment. This introduction notwithstanding, however, the men's spirits remained high, since in fact they had at last become part of the general effort. Arik Regev actually glowed.

We got down to work. Arik reported that the laying of minefields the previous night had been too slow but was progressing. That night Zunik would begin laying mines in his sector. My thoughts were concentrated on Zunik and his armored unit opposite Natanya. It was clear to me that whatever forces I might succeed in mobilizing would be used on the Jerusalem front, and that Zunik, whether the Iraqis joined the battle or not, would have to manage on his own, at least until we were free to come to his aid.

Arik reported that the O.C. Jerusalem Brigade had asked whether to lay mines opposite the Jordanian position of Sheikh Abdul Aziz, where, if we went to war, mines might interfere with our advance in that direction. I finally decided that, on balance, the mines should be laid.

Again my thoughts turned to the armored brigade I did not have. If it did not materialize, the Command would have to make do with the 10th Armored Brigade of only 50 tanks on a front stretching from the outskirts of Hadera to the outskirts of Beersheba. Furthermore, as soon as the south was alerted, Gush Lachish would be transferred from Southern to Central Command. And what if the Jordanian army chose to strike from the Hebron mountains southwards, towards Beersheba, or westwards, in an effort to connect with the Gaza Strip via Ashkelon? How would I rush reinforcements to Gush Lachish? And where would they come from?

I discussed this with Uri Ben-Ari of the 10th Brigade, and asked him to split his brigade into two, part remaining where it was, in the Ben-Shemen Forest, and part in the Hulda Forest. From Ben-Shemen it could deal with problems south of the Command area, in the Natanya to Petach Tikvah sector, while from Hulda he could quickly reach Gush Lachish. And from both bivouacs he could, if necessary, race to Latrun.

Uri acknowledged receipt of the instructions. Although his voice rang with confidence, I knew it would not work. The 10th Brigade alone was not enough. I needed another armored force. My efforts to obtain such reinforcements for the sake of the area continued until the moment the Command entered the war – and achieved nothing.

On June 4th a company of Centurions arrived as reinforcement, but had too few technical crews, tools and spare parts. The company was

8. Arik Regev

added to one of the battalions of the 10th Brigade, whose crews were trained to handle Shermans. During the war, when the Centurions began to slip their tracks on the difficult hilly terrain to Beit Hanina, they could not be repaired and within a few hours most of them were out of action.

Dayan Visits Central Command

Toward midday Moshe Dayan came to visit the Command, as I had been informed he would by telephone from G.H.Q., I think by the C.O.G.S. himself, who said, "Moshe's coming to see you. Tell him everything."

The information did not surprise me. Actually Moshe Dayan was only one of the one hundred and twenty members of the Knesset even if he was a major-general (Res.). At that particular time he had been assigned no other activity, but he would obviously not remain inactive long. It was impossible to ignore his leadership qualities or the confidence people placed in him.

He arrived in khaki, without insignia, and a peaked cap. I received him at the camp gate and brought him to the war room, where, with Arik Regev and two of our "G" Branch (Operations) officers, Nehemia and Kimmel, I spread out the maps and explained the Command disposition and our defense plan. We sat for about two hours. Dayan, always impatient, never stopped fidgeting.

I maintained that, since G.H.Q. thought the trouble would start in the south, most of our resources were concentrated against the Egyptian army, leaving Central Command insufficient material to contend with whatever might develop in its own area, to say nothing of defeating the enemy.

Dayan listened, he was interested, he asked questions. But I was disappointed, because all his questions centered on our defense plans and the enemy's estimated strength, suggesting that he wanted to be sure that we could defend ourselves with our own force, without assistance. He took no interest whatsoever in our assault plans.

I invited him to lunch, but he explained that he had a previous engagement, arranging, however, to return next day to inspect the Jerusalem sector, which, even in Dayan's opinion, was the most sensitive area of any in the Command's territorial responsibilities.

His "previous engagement" was a meeting with Prime Minister Levi Eshkol in the Dan Hotel in Tel Aviv, where Dayan's future role was decided upon.

At a Cabinet meeting that evening, Eshkol announced that he had offered Dayan a Cabinet seat, but that he preferred a military appointment. Eshkol's recommendation of Alon for the Defense Ministry roused strong objections from the ministers of the religious parties, who were the main sponsors of a national government and feared that without Dayan a government could not be formed. A committee of five ministers was appointed to bring concrete suggestions to the Cabinet the following day, June 1st. The 10 p.m. Cabinet meeting was held at the same time as our G.H.Q. meeting.

In spite of all that we had to consider, our thoughts were with the Cabinet, where an important decision was about to be made. Just before our meeting broke up, Lt. Gen. Gavish told me that he had just had word that everyone favored Allon.

I was immersed in my own problems, still believing that Hussein would not embroil himself in an all-out war but fearing that, since he knew that our strength was concentrated in the south and north, he would try to carry out some incursions.

Towards the end of the meeting, I raised the question of the convoy to Mt. Scopus, which, because of the tension, had been postponed until Wednesday, June 7th. Throughout this nerve-racking period, with all the mobilizing, arming, equipping and deployment of command units, the Mt. Scopus convoy alone kept us on a "business as usual" basis and we never stopped dealing with it. But now I felt that handling the convoy was taking too much of our time and interfering in the consolidation of plans. I feared that dispatching the convoy to the Mount, under the tense conditions in Old Jerusalem, would set the torch to the powder keg, and therefore suggested not sending it, even though exchange of the garrison was two weeks overdue. With the agreement of the C.O.G.S., it was decided that the convoy would not leave on June 7th.

Dayan at the Castel

Thursday, June 1st, 1967

I went to the Castel, the place we had deliberately chosen for the meeting with Moshe Dayan. The Castel, which rises to a height of 799 meters (about 2,000 feet) above sea level, is one of the highest ridges west of Jerusalem. Since ancient times it has been a strategic fortification on the way to Jerusalem, its importance recognized by the Romans who built a fort on its peak, from which its name derives: *castellum* = fort.

Colonel Eliezer Amitai, O.C. of the Jerusalem Brigade, waiting at the foot of the mountain, was joined a few minutes later by Moshe Dayan. We climbed up the goat-track to the top, and ensconced ourselves on the roof of *Beit Hasheikh* (the Sheikh's house), the only house still standing in the Arab village, the capture of which in April 1948 had been my first battle experience with the "Assault" Battalion of Harel Brigade.

At the beginning of April, 1948, I went to Jerusalem from Tel Aviv at the head of 200 fighters of the 4th Battalion of Harel Brigade in order to secure the passage of a convoy carrying the entire 4th Battalion on its way to fight in Jerusalem. We came to the mountain ridges north of Sha'ar Hagai and fought there throughout the day against a gang of Arab marauders. Afterwards we withdrew to Neve-Elan and to Ma'alei Hahamisha. As the 4th Battalion's convoy became mud-bound that morning at Hulda and was unable to proceed to Jerusalem, my 200 warriors and I stayed at Ma'alei Hahamisha with nothing to do.

I reported to Jerusalem Commander David Shaltiel, who told me that Arab gangs had settled in Castel and were threatening the Jerusalem highway. I asked for permission to capture the Castel with my men, received it, and we took the Castel. A few days later the Arabs counter-attacked, and recaptured the village, in the course of which action Abd el-Kadr el-Husseini, their revered commander, was killed. Our forces organized and captured the Castel anew and destroyed its houses.

Now we stood on the top of the Castel at the same spot where 19 years earlier I had announced, "The Castel is ours."

An intelligence officer spread a map on a concrete slab, a remnant of the half-destroyed house, placing stones on the map's edges to keep it from being blown away by the ceaseless strong winds. Dayan, however, as usual, preferred to look at the area itself, rather than a map, and we, therefore, gazed out at the magnificent scenery before us. We were surrounded by silence so peaceful that even the hum of motor-cars at the bottom of the mountain could not disturb it. On the slope of the mountain grazed the herd of one of the nearby settlements, and now and then the throaty sounds made by the shepherd reached us, or the tinkling of the bell of the bellwether.

This time we looked with military eyes at the sloping terraces planted with fruit trees, to see whether infantrymen could climb them with their loads and how armored vehicles could negotiate the rocky terrain, which defied anything with wheels.

One after another we pinpointed the settlements and the fortified points – ours and the enemy's – in the scenic panorama. Opposite was Mevaseret Yerushalayim, with dozens of small houses, complete with kitchen gardens, only a few hundred meters from the frontier. Although there were defense posts, trenches and shelters along the border, they would not seriously deter the enemy.

Above Mevaseret Yerushalayim, actually overhanging it, was a Legion redoubt at Sheikh Abdul Aziz, and beyond, Radar Hill, the radar camp and redoubt. This grouping of enemy fortified heights – how much bitterness it had caused us 19 years ago! How much blood of our brothers-in-arms had been spilled on its approaches!

Northeast, with the mosque rising high in its center, lay the Arab village of Nabi Samuel, which also poignantly recalled the days of 1948, when Harel Brigade tried to take it and was driven back. Eastward, along the horizon, Tel el-Ful, on top of which Hussein had begun building his palace, and to the north, Ramallah. The aerials of its broadcasting station, built during the time of the British Mandate, rose so high that they could be seen clearly from where we stood. Farther eastward lay Mt. Scopus.

Dayan shifted the binoculars from ridge to ridge, redoubt to redoubt, and then swung back to Sheikh Abdul Aziz. From here, above the Castel, Mevaseret Yerushalayim appeared at the mercy of the Jordanian position, and Dayan put the landscape's message into words.

"You've got to take good care of Mevaseret Yerushalayim," he said, "what force do you have there?"

"One company," I answered.

"And what if the Legion attacks, captures Mevaseret Yerushalayim, and from there cuts the Jerusalem highway in two?"

I explained how our forces were deployed for defense, pointing to the place where two battalions of the Jerusalem Brigade were concentrated, and the camp where the company of tanks were bivouacked. I said we could, without difficulty, mount a counter-offensive that would push the Legion back across the border.

But, thinking of the effect on morale if the Jerusalem highway was severed even for a short while, he said, "And what if you don't succeed? Imagine how our prestige would suffer if the world learned that the road to Tel Aviv was cut and Jerusalem was again under siege."

I thought, "You're right," and on the spot instructed Eliezer Amitai to widen the belt of land-mines between Mevaseret Yerushalayim and the frontier. (On the morning of June 6th these mines delayed the tanks of Uri Ben-Ari on their way to capture Sheikh Abdul Aziz.) But I said, "Moshe, I can take their positions before they attack Mevaseret Yerushalayim."

He did not seem enthusiastic. "Don't get yourself involved in a battle with the Legion," he said. "You'll have to stop them by defensive tactics only."

But I refused to give up, and said, "Moshe, it's clear what will happen if the Jordanians take Mevaseret Yerushalayim and cut the highway: we'll throw them back in a counter-attack. But what if they take Mt. Scopus?"

For 19 years we had lived with that nightmare. I repeated my question, and added, "Moshe, imagine what it would do to our prestige, to public morale and to the Jewish people everywhere! No El-Arish or Abu Agheila in Sinai," I added forcefully, "could compensate for the loss of Mount Scopus. Nobody's ever heard of the places in Sinai, but the whole world knows of Mt. Scopus!"

He looked at me. "Therefore," he said, "you must not get involved in forays or anything which would complicate or disturb Israel's position vis-à-vis Jordan. You must not drive the C.O.G.S. crazy with demands for assistance."

"And what if the Jordanians attack without provocation from us and take the Mount?" I doggedly persisted.

"Well, then," he replied, "we'll bite our lips and hold on. When we've finished with the Egyptians and reached the Canal, Zahal the 'Great' will come back and get you out of the mess."

"Just a minute," I expostulated. "You say that if the Jordanians capture Mt. Scopus I'll have to wait until Zahal arrives. But who can guarantee that Zahal won't be bogged down in Jebel Libny or somewhere else, while the Jordanians are making havoc in Jerusalem?"

"Don't worry," he replied, "we shall smash the lot of them and reach the Canal and Sharm el-Sheikh and then the whole Zahal will come and rescue you."

I was not pleased with what he said. Even though I agreed that we could beat the Egyptians, I could not accept his attitude towards Mt. Scopus or the idea that Central Command should sit by and do nothing or that we should wait for others to get us out of the mess. But I did not continue arguing.

We folded the maps and went down the mountain, with Dayan, as always, walking ahead, marching down the slope pensively, his feet carefully exploring each step, like a person who, despite the difficulty of judging distance and changes in height, nevertheless negotiates the terrain quickly. When we reached the waiting cars, children had already gathered and were applauding.

We drove to Jerusalem and went up to the roof of Beth Hahistadruth, where a special emergency room had been installed for the Jerusalem Brigade C.O. From there, when the time came, he would be able to direct his forces. In a strongly reinforced room, communication lines and the bases for aerials for field telephones had been installed.

The north and east of the town were visible from the roof of the building. From there one could pinpoint the important buildings and know what was happening in Jerusalem across the municipal line.

We descended, but, at Dayan's request, delayed in the cafeteria opposite to drink a glass of tea. The elderly owner of the cafeteria was so excited by the honor done him that he refused our money. People gathered outside and applauded Dayan when we left. There was no doubt that the man had become a symbol in the eyes of the public.

We made a quick tour of several positions on the municipal line, but Dayan was impatient. His political fate was at that moment being decided in Tel Aviv, and, indeed, during the tour, the adjutant was informed by our car radio that Mr. Dayan must report to Tel Aviv at once.

He left immediately, arriving at Eshkol's chambers in Tel Aviv at 4.15 p.m. The Prime Minister offered him the post of defense minister in his government. Dayan accepted.

Later Eshkol invited Bar-Lev to come and see him, and appointed him deputy Chief-of-Staff.

With the Cabinet in the "Pit"

A national government was formed under the leadership of Levi Eshkol, with Dayan Minister of Defense. All around me, at Command H.Q. and among the units, there were sighs of relief and happy faces. Morale shot sky-high. If that had been the only outcome of the newly-formed national government, it would have sufficed.

The news of the expanded Israeli government also caused an enormous reaction from abroad.

Gamal Abd el-Nasser threatened to close the Suez Canal to all

4

participants in the international flotilla the United States was trying to send through the Tiran Straits. To Amman came Egyptian General Abd el-Monaim Riadh, Commander of the Eastern Front, and his H.Q. staff; Jordan radio announced that Jordan would attack if Israel started a war. Iraq decided to join the United Arab Command, and Nasser gave his blessing to the decision, saying, "We are fanning more than burning embers in our hopes of fighting Israel. Such a war will show the world who the Arabs are."

Ahmed Shukeiry, who was living in East Jerusalem and had reopened the offices of the P.L.O. (Palestine Liberation Organization), closed since January, boasted at a press conference, "If the war is slow in breaking out, perhaps we shall fire the first shot ... it will not be a war of half-measures. We shall not be satisfied with less than the liberation of the whole of Palestine!" And as to the question of the fate of the Jews living in the country, he replied, with an arrogant smile, "If war breaks out, no Jews will remain in Palestine."

At 9 o'clock in the morning the G.H.Q. officers were called to the war room for a conference with the new Cabinet. General Rabin briefly welcomed and congratulated the new Cabinet, remarking that he was pleased to be able to sit with them and present to the government details about the enemy's forces and ours. After the information was presented, a discussion ensued, which closed with a summary by Eshkol, which sounded as though we would go on waiting. When the meeting ended and the Prime Minister and his entourage had left, I went into a small empty room adjoining Rabin's chambers. I sat and thought about what had just happened. My heart was with Eshkol, whom I liked and who seemed to have been in distress. He knew too little about Zahal's capability, and it was therefore hard for him to decide to act. He remained cool, and managed to control the State in this critical time of enormous Russian pressure, dubious American innuendo, French animosity, our growing isolation from most of the countries of the world, and the countless obstacles within his own group and outside of it.

Rabin announced that he would visit Jerusalem today, meeting us near Tzuba at 10 a.m. At a short H.Q. meeting at the Command, I had word of an incident in the Ben Shemen sector on the previous day. During the meeting another report arrived, this time for Jerusalem: a stone had been thrown at one of our soldiers on the municipal line. Standing orders in such cases are to respond in kind. But, given the situation, should they react?

I told them not to, but ordered all brigades to operate a larger number of ambushes that night and to continue laying mines. Then I set forth for Jerusalem to meet Major-General Itzhak Rabin.

Rabin visits the Jerusalem Brigade

Our first tour stop was a camp in the Jerusalem area where the Jerusalem reconnaissance unit and a tank company earmarked for Jerusalem were stationed. It was a very hot day, characteristic of that entire summer, but at that hour the sun was not at its strongest and a light and caressing breeze blew in the Jerusalem hills.

The recce unit, a very special one, most of whose men were Jerusalem academics and students, were on parade awaiting our arrival. Instead of army caps, they wore red *kova tembels*, on which "PEACE" was written.

Rabin wanted to find out about the alertness and morale of the troops. After his brief speech the men shouted the traditional *kifak!* (bravo), flung their caps in the air, broke ranks and gathered around us. They were a noisy lot, ebullient and brimming with confidence. "No flap," they promised, "whatever we're told to do will be done." Their self-confidence reassured us enormously.

From there we moved on to the tank company, under the command of Captain Raphael Yeshayahu, which demonstrated, at the request of the C.O.G.S., their "enter battle" exercise. The tanks, covered with camouflage nets, lined up their crews in front of them. Within two minutes the nets were off, the engines revving and the tanks in motion.

But what tanks were they? Although we marvelled at the agility of the crews, I could not forget that these Shermans were older than most of the men operating them, that their finest years had been during World War II. What would happen when they confronted the new Pattons, younger by a generation? Would the superiority of the men compensate for the inferiority of the tanks?

Not far from there, near the Tzuba quarries, we visited one of the battalions of the Jerusalem Brigade, commanded by Lt. Colonel "Zwicka" Ofer (killed in a chase after terrorists in December, 1968). The rendezvous was a success and Rabin addressed the troops briefly with a "don't worry ... things will work out" speech. Here we witnessed a moving scene, an expression of the kind of solidarity that exists nowhere in the world except between the civilians in the hinterland and the soldiers of Zahal. From one of the nearby settlements came men and women carrying bowls of cholent to the batallion's lager, near the village, to share their Sabbath meal with the troops. That may have encouraged several of the men to approach the C.O.G.S. with a request to go home for a few hours' break. They all came from the surrounding settlements, Beth Shemesh, Hartuv and so on.

"Leave camp? – No!" said the C.O.G.S. "But there's nothing to stop your families from visiting you here."

The news spread with the speed of a bird in flight, and soon the whole neighborhood had heard. We had only just left the battalion's lager when civilian-filled vehicles began to appear carrying mainly women and children, bearing goodies of all sorts. The "big picnic" of the eve-of-war had begun.

How many Shells for Jerusalem?

On the way to Jerusalem we called on a mortar unit in an olive grove in the Valley of the Cross. The mortars were to be used in defense of the city, and because of their limited range could not be stationed farther away. In the same grove was the H.Q. of the Jerusalem Brigade's artillery unit. We entered a tent between two ancient olive trees, set up, like the whole encampment, with an eye to avoiding damage to the hundreds-of-years-old tree roots. The C.O.G.S. was given an explanation of the Jerusalemites' artillery plan.

But to use the term "artillery" was to make a mockery of it. To defend the whole of Jerusalem all we had were twenty-four 100mm mortar tubes and eighteen 25-pounders. The ammunition situation was even worse. I told the C.O.G.S. that one of the missions of the artillery – in case of a Jordanian attack on Mt. Scopus – was to lay down a curtain of fire between the Mount and the Jordanian attackers. But a curtain of fire must be continuous to be effective, and we would need an enormous number of shells.

"How long can you maintain the curtain with the ammunition on hand?" I asked the commanding officer.

"A few minutes at the most," he replied, adding, "but besides that, not all my guns can reach Mt. Scopus."

I shot a glance at the C.O.G.S. who said nothing. The number of guns and the quantity of ammunition were ridiculous by any criteria. I began to realize more acutely that I would have to find a solution to the Mt. Scopus problem other than the curtain of artillery fire.

Two days later we received an extra allocation of ammunition and some heavier guns: three 155mm guns on caissons and three 160mm mortar-tubes. Relatively speaking, they were a considerable addition to our Jerusalem fire-power, but not much vis-à-vis the siege of the sector, the importance of Jerusalem and the fire-power of the Jordanian artillery assembled against us.

We reached the Jerusalem Brigade H.Q., where the O.C. showed us on the map how his troops were deployed, immediately after which we set out for a quick visit of the municipal line. On our way to north Jerusalem to check the air-raid services, Mayor Teddy Kollek joined us. On this Sabbath, bearded religious Jews were filling sacks with sand and digging ditches. They stopped working to cheer us and applaud, and immediately resumed their task. I was well aware of the spiritual sacrifice these people were making.

I had known Jerusalem in good times and bad. I lived and fought there in her glorious hours of 1948, when she was under siege, when she was hungry and thirsty, ceaselessly bombarded but never surrendering, never despairing, as though clenching her teeth and drawing from deep within her the strength to hold on. Yet I think Jerusalem went through no more glorious period than the fortnight preceding the 1967 War. As though the town knew, and her residents felt, that redemption was about to come, and that they were sanctified by it.

Jerusalem, like other population centers in the country, was empty of males. But the Jerusalem hills were not like those of other towns. Jerusalem was a frontier town. From the suburbs of Musrara, Abu-Tor, and others could be seen the barbed-wire entanglements of the line, the rusty signboards warning "Caution – Frontier Ahead!" and the positions of the Arab Legion opposite. The coming of night meant the coming of fear. Without the stabilizing presence of their men, women had to soothe their children at the same time that they worried about their husbands' safety and wondered whether there would be enough to eat the next day. But there was no panic and nobody fled the border suburbs.

"...Within Six Hours"

We went into the overflowing dining-room. Major Amos, the "G" Branch Officer of the Brigade, sat at our table opposite Ezer Weizman and reminded him of their recent meeting when Amos was a cadet at the Staff and Command College, and Ezer, still O.C. of the Air Force, came to give a talk. He was asked how much time the Air Force would need to destroy the enemies' air forces. Instead of replying directly, Ezer turned to an Air Force cadet and said, "You can answer that question. How long do you need?"

The Air Force man squared his shoulders. "Six hours, sir," he said. "That's what you taught us to say."

Reminding him of that conversation, Amos asked, "Ezer, will you keep your word?"

The Chief of Operations answered seriously. "It might last eight hours, and our Air Force losses might reach 50% – but we'll wipe them out completely."

After the meal, General Rabin waited at the door and said to the officers around him, "Friends, we fought here in 1948 – and were not very successful. I hope you'll be more successful than we were."

That same Sabbath, at midday, King Hussein called a press conference at his palace and issued the following announcement:

"President Nasser has just informed me that Iraq has also signed a mutual defense pact with Egypt. Iraqi troops will take over the sectors along the Israel-Jordan frontier designated for them."

During the morning the two Jerusalem armored brigades, the 40th and the 60th, were ordered to cross the Jordan to the West Bank.

The Countdown Begins

Sunday, June 4th

The beginning of the new week gave no hint that the hour of decision was approaching. On the contrary. The newspapers were full of Defense Minister Moshe Dayan's first press conference the previous evening, and headlined some of his remarks: "We are not living with a stop-watch in hand," which was interpreted as war was not imminent.

A spokesman for the French government declared in Paris that his country would impose an embargo upon whichever side opened fire, a statement accepted as further strengthening the resolve that Israel would not initiate war, because France was its main source of military supplies. To complete the no-war picture, the newspapers reported that thousands of reserves, home on week-end leave, filled the country's beaches.

In reality, the decision about a preemptive war to begin the morning of June 5th had begun to crystallize the previous evening at a Cabinet meeting. The formal decision was made during the day, on Sunday.

At 9 a.m. I arrived at G.H.Q. for a meeting headed by Rabin. "Dado," Commander of the Northern Command, and I presented our plans, "Dado" operating towards Jenin with a force of two brigades. I enthusiastically presented mine: getting to Mt. Scopus with the Jerusalem or the 10th Brigade. In his summing up, the C.O.G.S. tried to temper my enthusiasm by stressing that we were not interested in opening another front in the east and would initiate no operation against Jordan. Several times he repeated, "Don't get involved."

I returned to Command H.Q. with mixed feelings, on the one hand pleased that the government was at last overcoming its doubts and hesitations, but on the other jealous and a bit wry. Here we were, going to war: my colleague Gavish, in the south, would sit on the banks of the Suez Canal and paddle his toes in the water; my friend Elazar, in the north, would plant his feet on the Hermon; and I would go on patrolling the fences at Abu-Tor, looking out on the square at Nablus Gate from Notre Dame, and frittering away time in intellectual clashes with Messrs. Stanway and Muhammed Daoud of the Jordanian Armistice Commission.

I went into my chambers. It was very quiet. "No important telephone calls," said my secretary Ilana. Joel, the adjutant, reported on the organization of the command group. I contacted the battalion commanders several times. But most of the day I sat alone in my room, facing the map of the command area which covered the wall, and analyzed the situation. Had everything possible been done to defend the area, each section of which I saw in my mind's eye? I tried, from the position of the Jordanian commander, to weigh how I could launch an offensive, even with the tiny forces I possessed.

The Final Session at G.H.Q.

Towards evening I went to a meeting called by Rabin. As soon as I entered the conference room I noticed the absence of the Commander of the Southern front and his aides. And when I saw the face of Rabin, I knew that this was it. He was clearly exhilarated.

The meeting lasted only thirty minutes. I left with Dado. "Well?" I said.

"Well, well!" was his reply.

We wished each other luck. I did not know when I would need those good wishes, for we were actually still awaiting developments.

The Final Briefing at Command H.Q.

I contacted Arik Regev and instructed him to call a 9 p.m. meeting of the Command group. I wanted to take advantage of this last opportunity to check the Command's anti-tank defense plans against possible attack by Jordanian and Iraqi armored units. Also I wanted to brief the brigade commanders, because as of tomorrow morning each would be committed to his sector and duties, and we might not meet again until the battle ended.

One of the long walls of the rectangular war room was the map wall, part of which was curtained. The required map was moved on rails from behind the curtain. There were rows of seats, the first row for the unit commanders, the remainder for their various aides.

On one side of the room were batteries of communications equipment, so that those present could maintain contact with the command units. Opposite were a number of cubicles used by operations and intelligence sergeants to learn what was going on in the field and thus bring the maps up-to-date.

The Command intelligence officer presented his assessment of the enemy forces:

Until May 23rd the Jordanian army had been at ease. Two of its infantry and two armored brigades were bivouacked east of the Jordan River at their permanent bases. The five infantry brigades on the West Bank kept only a small part of their strength along the demarcation line, their main strength at their rear bases.

On May 23rd the Jordanian Army moved into emergency deployment. The West Bank was reinforced with an additional infantry brigade, and the permanent brigades reinforced the front line. They dug trenches and settled in. Reserves were called up. Reserves who had completed their service during the preceding 3-4 months were returned and posted to their previous units.

On the morning of June 4th, the approximate deployment of the Jordanian army was:

North of the Jordan Valley was the 36th Brigade, with two battalions on the line and a third in the rear, in the Jiftlick zone;

North of the Triangle, in the Jenin sector, was the 25th Brigade, also with two battalions forward and a third in the rear, at Kabatiya. This Brigade was reinforced by two batteries of 25-pounder guns and by the main elements of the Command armored battalion, two companies of which were laagered in the rear.

These two Brigades were deployed opposite the forces of Northern Command.

In the region where our Northern and Central Commands met – in other

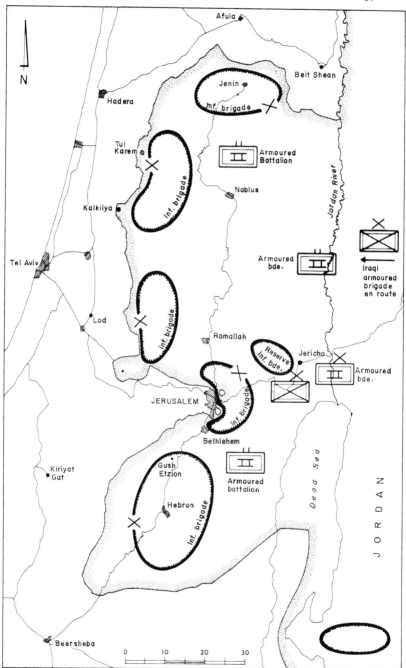

V Jordanian Deployment, 4th June 1967

words, opposite Zunik's Brigade – the 1st Jordanian Brigade was deployed, with one battalion forward, in Kalkilya and Tulkarm, and two in the rear, south of Nablus.

The Latrun enclave, south and east, was in the hands of the 2nd Brigade, which was also responsible for the strong-points along the Jerusalem Corridor to Beit Hanina. One of its battalions was posted in the Latrun enclave, another in the Corridor strong-points, and the third was used as reinforcement and was stationed at Tira camp.

The Jordanian 3rd Brigade, which was to give us the most trouble, was the equivalent of our Jerusalem Brigade. It was reinforced by a battalion of field-guns and maintained an infantry battalion in the north Jerusalem positions at the police school and Sheikh Jarrah. A second battalion was in fortified positions along the municipal line in the Old City; and a third was at Neve Yaacov. The Brigade commander was Zayim Ali Ata, with headquarters at El Ram.

The 27th Brigade, which had crossed the Jordan from east to west a few days before the war, was bivouacked at Ma'aleh Ha'amudim on the Jericho-Jerusalem highway and kept in reserve. On Saturday night, June 3rd, one of its battalions was moved up to occupy the Abu-Dis ridge east of Jerusalem. As a matter of fact, the entire brigade was to be used to reinforce the Jordanian deployment in the Jerusalem area.

The sixth brigade of the Legion, the 29th, was permanently stationed at Mt. Hebron. One of its battalions was deployed between the Mar Elias Monastery and Hussan Village, south of the Jerusalem Corridor, a second at Gush Etzion, and the third south of Mt. Hebron. It was reinforced during the alert by two infantry companies composed of the staff of the Jordanian army's training base, a battery of field guns and two companies of Centurion tanks.

The two Jordanian armored brigades, the 40th and 60th, also left their bases on the East Bank that Sunday, crossed the river and laagered in the Jordan Valley. The commander of the 60th was Sharif Zayid Ben Shaker, a Beduin, and a relative of King Hussein.

Those were the forces against which I fought mentally while sitting opposite the large map at Command H.Q.

When the intelligence officer had finished, Command operations officer Arik Regev spoke, repeating and briefly defining the sectors and tasks of the brigades, emphasizing anti-tank warfare. While they were speaking, my eyes drifted across the faces before me: serious faces, attentive; some worried, some, like that of young Lt. Ehud Shani, a paratroop officer who commanded a unit of armored half-tracks, impatient. He sat on a table, legs dangling like a schoolboy's, clearly thinking about the many times he had listened to briefings, and for what, when even the newspapers said there would be no war. Ehud Shani died on the second day of the war, bravely commanding his unit in the battle at the foot of Tel el-Ful. I was tempted to tell him and the others the secret I knew.

Arik finished speaking. The brigade commanders rose in turn and went over their brigade objectives. I closely followed what they said. Uri, his silvery hair cut very short, exuded the self-confidence of his "No problems." Eliezer Amitai, bright-faced, blue-eyed, spoke slowly and restrainedly, an introspective man. Was there an undercurrent of worry in his voice? No, only caution. And Zunik, friendly, a little awkward, but unworried, his thick mustache outlining the smile permanently on his face. And Moshe Yotvat – tall, erect and quiet, organized and methodical, who had worked hard during the alert and deployment stages to increase the fitness of his brigade and dig them into the terraced and sloping terrain of his sector. Lt. Colonel "Yousouff," C.O. of the Command's armored force, had been one of the Jerusalem warriors of 1948 – a brave lad who during the battle on Radar Hill had, single-handed, attacked a Jordanian armored vehicle and destroyed it with a Molotov cocktail. I was confident he would not disappoint us this time either. Major Z., Commander of the reconnaissance unit, was the type to whom, in the Palmach tents, we referred as "the finest of youngsters." Actually it was true of all of them that, given the opportunity, they would prove themselves.

My summing up once again expressed confidence in their ability to defeat the enemy, but stressed that until such time difficult hours lay ahead for some, perhaps all, of us. Whatever happened, we must, at any cost, prevent the capture of any position or strong-point or a surprise incursion by the enemy anywhere.

Again I went over with the brigade commanders the question of *khapps* (surprise raids) if opportunity presented itself. These were to be carried out by specific orders only. Tunik's Brigade would be on the alert for a Kalkilya and Tulkarem *khapp*, Moshik's for a *khapp* at Abd el-Aziz and Sur Baher. The 10th Brigade would wait to *khapp* into Latrun, Radar Hill and Abd el-Aziz. "That's the lot. Good night boys. See you!" They got up, jumped into their waiting cars and were gone.

I stayed behind a minute to instruct the Command chief of staff to go to Tel Aviv in the morning and check the alert in the air raid defense services. "Why tomorrow, all of a sudden?" asked an interested Borka.

"It's always wise, and especially tomorrow," I replied, but did not explain further.

Later Zunik telephoned to ask if he could mine another sector of the line, near Yad Hannah. He had mines to spare and sappers available, but the snag was that the crop in that particular field had not been harvested. I decided that mining was more important than the crop at this point.

Eliezer Amitai also telephoned to know whether he should lay mines near Ramat Rahel. "Mines! Better more than less."

Command headquarters was quiet. My driver came in to ask if I were going home or sleeping at H.Q. I thought that if I behaved differently tonight than on other nights, the secret would be out. "Home," I said.

FIRING OPENS IN
JERUSALEM

June 5th, 1967: The Die is Cast

I got up early, full of the excitement of the day ahead, but calm and controlled. Whatever possibly could have been done had been done.

I glanced at the morning paper. "Iraq Joins Arab Defense Pact," said the headline. This had a distinct bearing upon the central front, but gave no hint that the hour for which the last twenty days had been preparing would strike today. I kissed my children and my wife Esther. If she noticed something in my expression, she asked no questions. From our home in Zahala we look out upon the Judean hills, with the sun rising above them, red and flaming, as on every other day in the month of June, instead of a sun of a different calibre that I had somehow expected today. I knew that soon the first wave of our planes would take off to the south, and I very much wanted to see them fly overhead.

Eleven years earlier I had stood on the runway of an air-field when a flight of 16 Dakota planes had taken off, carrying a battalion of paratroops to the Mitla Pass, when the Sinai Campaign (Operation *Kadesh*) began. Then, as deputy chief of "G" Branch, I had taken an active part in the campaign. Now, as G.O.C. Central Command which had no part in the simmering war, I was nothing but a sort of onlooker. At least, I could feel a modicum of involvement in what was about to take place by watching planes flying towards their objectives.

My disturbing thoughts were completely at odds with the pastoral silence all around. Zahala was an apparently unembattled quarter. An abundance of greenery hid the shelters which the local youngsters had dug in backyards during the past days. And perhaps because so many of its inhabitants were military men, the quarter was quieter than usual. Most of the men had been away from home for the past weeks.

I delayed a moment to pick up Koby Sharett, who lived in the neighborhood, and drove off. The road through the sleeping town was empty. Mobilization had been general. Now and then we saw a single vehicle or a milkman on his route, but of army vehicles there were none. 07.30 hours. We slowed down at the railway crossing near Ramla. A tremendous roar overhead drowned out the hum of my car engine. I put my head out of the window – and there they were: dozens of planes, Fuga-Magisters, flying southwards.

That was it. The die was cast.

When I reached Command H.Q. and entered my office the telephone rang. It was Haim Bar-Lev. "Uzi, Yerachmiel will visit you today," his voice quiet and his speech slow and confident as usual. "That's good," I answered.

I contacted Arik Regev, who was still fast asleep after his late night. "Arik, the war has begun. Get here on the double." He was wide awake in a jiffy. "I'm already running." he exulted, like a veteran war horse.

I woke up my chief-of-staff. "Don't go to Tel Aviv," I told him, "the war has started. We've work to do."

Arik came in, still unshaven, his uncontrollable forelock falling across his forehead. "What's going on?" he called out from the doorway, incredulity and jubilation shining from his eyes.

I said, "The air force has taken off to bomb Egypt," and at that same instant another flight swept over our heads with a tremendous roar. "Run and prepare the war room. Alert all units and call a meeting of the H.Q. staff."

Did he run!

A few minutes before 8 o'clock the C.O.G.S. telephoned the first reports from Egypt. "The first wave went into action," he said, "and scored bulls' eyes. We caught them on the ground. Egyptian losses are heavy and our planes are O.K." While he was speaking I could hear the Ramla air raid sirens. There were warnings throughout the country that morning, against enemy air force activity.

Central Command at Alert

The staff officers gathered in the war room, where I repeated what the C.O.G.S. had told me, adding that two planes trying to intervene had been shot down. The men clapped each other on the shoulder and embraced, but their joy was tempered by the unvoiced question: What about us?

"We are on the defensive," I said. "For the time being. We must go into full deployment and organize for war. Keep maps up-to-date, get your duty-rosters arranged, check telephone lines. And make sure that all standing orders, procedures and prepared plans are meticulously carried out."

I asked to be connected with the brigade commanders, starting with Colonel Eliezer Amitai, C.O. Jerusalem Brigade. "Eliezer, the war's started. For the moment we're on the side-lines. But," I added, "be careful. Jerusalem is your baby. Avoid all provocation!"

The next was Uri Ben-Ari, the 10th Brigade. The noisy exuberance around me began to settle into the more organized sounds of a war room preparing for war. The staff was trained and ready for it, psychologically and practically; even I began to think in terms of war. The 10th Brigade was the mobile reserve of the Command, yet entirely deployed within range of the Jordanian artillery.

"Uri," I said, "you are our main armored force. Look out for their artillery. Be prepared to move within five minutes of the warning signal."

I contacted Moshe Yotvat, whose brigade was deployed opposite the Latrun enclave, and Zunik, in command of Israel's narrow waist opposite Tulkarem and Kalkilyeh.

Then I prepared a series of orders for the staff officers:

– Move armor in the Natanya area to permanent, pre-arranged defensive positions.

– Declare a state of emergency in all air raid defense units throughout the Command's area of operation.

– Alert the armored half-track company at Gush Lachish to be ready for a possible move to Jerusalem.

– Concentrate the border police at Lod Airport and the West Bank H.Q. (of Lt. General Herzog) at Ramla.

–Most important of all, call up the home guard.

It worried me that most of the Command's home guard battalions had been released five days previously and their positions in line fortifications taken over by the infantry. In essence it meant that the latter units were not using their spear-heading capabilities, and their best men were tied down to defensive duty action along the whole frontier. If they were called to action, therefore, it would be many hours before a unit could assemble. According to G.H.Q. planning, the home-guard units were to be mobilized by open proclamation, broadcast at 10.00 hours. I offered up a silent prayer that they would return to their positions before the infantry was needed.

Arik asked about the train to Jerusalem, and I hesitated before replying. The railway lines to Jerusalem passed alongside the Jordan frontier. What if they attacked? All the same: "The railway will operate as usual," I said.

For a few moments there was a break in pace. The command machinery was getting into gear, was beginning to digest, execute and transmit the orders coming to it. Joined by Didi Menussi, who had been posted to the Command, I exploited the moments to summon Moshe Shamir, editor of the Command bulletin. We agreed that from then until the end of the war the bulletin would be issued as a daily war report, for whose first issue we composed the first order of the day:

From the General Officer Commanding Central Command
   OUR TROOPS STRIKE IN EGYPT
   WE ARE CAPABLE OF STRIKING OTHER ENEMIES ALSO
   WE ITCH FOR ACTION
   WE ARE CONFIDENT OF VICTORY!

                                         Maj. General Uzi Narkiss
                                         G.O.C. Central Command

I wanted to tell the troops more of what was happening in the south, and what we anticipated would happen, but that order of the day would have to do. It said everything.

I called Teddy Kollek. During the past couple of years more than one crisis had involved us both, in all sorts of incidents on the municipal lines, and a close friendship had developed, whose common denominator was our love for Jerusalem. "Teddy, the war has started and everything's fine."

King Hussein's Call To Battle

It was 09.20 hours, almost the same moment at which King Hussein, with a nod of his head, confirmed the order of the Egyptian commander of the Jordanian army, General Riadh, to start the war. In his book Hussein writes that he began his day in the company of his wife, breakfasting and reading the newspapers. At 08.50 hours he was still at the table when his adjutant, Colonel Jazi, telephoned: "Radio Cairo has just announced that the Israelis have launched an assault upon Egypt."

Hussein immediately contacted headquarters, where the news was confirmed. A coded order from Marshal Abd el-Hakim Amer to General Riadh stated:

1. Israeli planes began bombing Egyptian airfields and 75% of the enemy planes were destroyed or put out of action.

2. A counter-attack by the Egyptian air force has begun. In Sinai, ground-fighting has broken out and the Egyptian army holds the initiative.
3. Marshal Amer has instructed the Supreme Commander of the Jordanian front to open a new front and carry out assault operations according to plans confirmed the previous day.

"Without finishing breakfast," Hussein relates, "I jumped behind the wheel of my car and raced to army headquarters. In the command post, in the basement of the building, I studied the message from Amer by the light of a pale neon lamp and took counsel with Riadh as to our next moves.

"Riadh told me he had ordered our artillery to take up positions at the front, and the air force to attack Israel – and also had ordered a battalion of the Imam Ali Brigade (27th Infantry Brigade) to take Mt. Scopus in Jerusalem."

Mt. Scopus was in no-man's-land. The H.Q. of Norwegian General Od Bull, chief of the U.N. supervisors, had occupied this isolated spot ever since the beginning of the Israel-Arab dispute in 1948.

"It was captured by our troops shortly afterward."

In actual fact enemy action only commenced about ninety minutes later, the length of time the Jordanians needed to move their guns into positions. Hussein recounts that they were also delayed by having to wait for the Syrian and Iraqi air forces, in order to bomb Israel together. Iraqi bombers finally arrived, but the squadron of Syrian fighter planes never did turn up, and so it was decided to take off without them.

Jordan "Captures" Jebel Mukhaber

The first ground operation – the capture of Government House by the Jordanians – did not take place until more than four hours later. Great confusion accompanied the enemy's announcement of this attack for a reason revealed many months after the war in Hussein's *Diary*. In the English edition, Hussein speaks of the capture of Mt. Scopus, but in Arabic of Jebel Mukhaber (Hill of Evil Counsel), the hill on which Government House stands. Radio Cairo's broadcasts on the morning of June 5th referred to Mt. Scopus.

The contradiction caused us hours of anxiety, but in retrospect can be considered a miracle. I now think that the ambiguity or error of the Arab announcement was a major factor in the Israeli G.H.Q.'s decision to counter-attack on the Jordanian front. It also decisively influenced my decisions and deliberations.

What caused this confusion? Had the Jordanians really intended to capture Mt. Scopus, and attacked Government House by mistake or impulse? This question, not answered in Hussein's *Diary*, baffled me for a long time. Only after the war, after conversations with East Jerusalem authorities, and the discovery of the Jordanian battle plans for the Jerusalem front, does the explanation seem to have been found.

The "father" of the plan for the capture of Jerusalem was Jordanian Brigadier Aataf Majali, a member of one of the most influential families in Transjordan, and thought to be one of the ablest, and most radical, of the Legion's officers. He was a believer in violent reaction against Israel, and was one of the group which, during the state of alert, pressured King Hussein to straighten out his differences with Nasser and join the all-Arab alliance. Nevertheless, in spite of his aggressiveness, he had no illusions as to the outcome of such a war, saying openly that in direct confrontation between the two armies the Jordanians would be defeated and thrown back from the entire West Bank. He therefore recommended concentrating the entire Jordanian army along the Jerusalem front, even at the risk of sacrificing the other sectors of the West Bank, and throwing all their resources into the effort to take Jewish Jerusalem. After the shooting stopped, under pressure of the Great Powers, Jerusalem could be used as a pawn for which Israel would withdraw from whatever territory she had taken. According to his plan, the Jordanian army would strike from the north, from the Sheikh Abdul-Aziz redoubt towards Mevaseret Yerushalayim, cutting Jerusalem off from the coastal plain, and occupy Government House, Ramat Rahel, Beit Zafafa and Hadassah Hospital, thus tying a noose around Jerusalem.

The key to the entire plan was the speedy occupation of Mt. Scopus, which Majali saw as the kingpin to any operation north of the city. "Whoever holds Mt. Scopus," said Majali, "holds the key to Jerusalem."

The Egyptian Supreme Commander of the Eastern Front, Abd el-Monaim Riadh, did not approve Majali's Jerusalem plan. Instead of concentrating troops in a narrow sector, Riadh preferred an offensive operation all along the line, paying particular attention to southern Jerusalem and Mt. Hebron, for the purely Egyptian reason of threatening the Zahal flank deployed in the Negev and forcing us to transfer some of our strength from the south to the east. Riadh, on the eve of the war, therefore ordered the 40th Jordanian Armored Brigade, laagered in Jericho, to move up and occupy positions on Mt. Hebron. Similarly, the 60th Armored Brigade, laagered near the Damia Bridge as reserve for the Samarian front, was ordered to replace the 40th in Jericho.

From Riadh's point of view, the key to the operation on the Jerusalem front was not Mt. Scopus, but Government House. The capture of that area by Zahal might cut off Mt. Hebron from the Samarian heights and the eastern bank. Occupation of the palace by an Arab force would eventually open the way for an operation in the southern sector of the city and provide a twofold threat from Mt. Hebron upon Beersheba.

The fact that Government House was in no-man's-land and was used as the headquarters of the chief U.N. supervisor did not at all deter the Egyptian general. If the U.N. forces could be withdrawn from their positions in Sinai and the Gaza Strip, why not from Jerusalem? In this spirit the operational orders were agreed upon, drawn up and approved, and confirmed and distributed on June 4th. First Government House, then Mt. Scopus. After the War I was told by the secretary to Colonel Daoud, chief Jordanian delegate to the M.A.C., that the force designated to take the two objectives – a battalion of the 27th brigade – was brought forward from Ma'alei Ha'adumim to Abu Dis. On the night of June 4th, as the battalion was beginning to occupy its assault positions, the secretary was ordered to keep the U.N. people busy and prevent their noticing the battalion's movements above Wadi Joz.

So much for the plan. But when it came to execution, or, more precisely, to the news-reporting phase, everything went wrong. The Voice of Arabia broadcast from Cairo announced the capture of Mt. Scopus three full hours before Government House was taken. In Israel we heard the broadcast and were shocked. Although our fears were soon allayed by the garrison on the Mount, which assured us that it was a cock-and-bull story, from then on anxiety over Mt. Scopus, ceaselessly in my thoughts, intensified until it was vented at G.H.Q. That anxiety resulted, to a great extent, in the plan which, within 48 hours, was to liberate all Jerusalem.

But on that morning, this was a secret that the future would divulge.

Evil from the South

Meanwhile, the war room at Central Command buzzed with activity.

Telephones rang; girl clerks shouted, "Repeat, I can't hear you"; operations sergeants reproduced the latest reports on the huge wall map. And conducting it all was Arik Regev, his forelock unkempt and his face unshaven, but wide awake and full of the joy of activity. He stood at his desk, in the middle of the room, one leg on a bench, a long pointer in his hand, and every now and then let out a roar which temporarily silenced the signals officers of the brigades seated at their own table at the end of the room. When they had nothing else to do they talked loudly among themselves. At Arik's table his two aides, Major Nehemia and Major Kimmel, were bending over maps, and the operations secretaries, Ophry and Dana, were rushing between Arik's desk and mine with the dispatch register. Since everyone except myself chain-smoked, the room was blue. I sat opposite the map-wall, my eyes riveted on the map of the Command, trying to clarify developments from now on.

09.27 – all doubts vanish. The intelligence officer announces that Hussein has just broadcast a call to arms to his people, with no attempt to mince words. It was war!

"My brothers, Arab citizens," Hussein began.

Now is the time when each of us is called upon to do his duty to achieve the objectives we have set ourselves! At this fateful hour the nation stands as one hand and one heart in the face of the Israeli enemy and those behind them. I have placed the armed forces under the command of one of the finest of Arab officers, Farik-Awal Abd el-Monnaim Riadh.

Rest assured that our armed forces and our people and all the Arab nation will prove itself and achieve its objective.

We are at the beginning of the decisive battle and hope that an early conclusion will bring the victory we have awaited for many long years. We are determined to live in honor or die with honor, defending that which is dearest to every Arab wherever he may be!

I reacted by telephoning Eliezer Amitai, C.O. Jerusalem Brigade. For superseding all my plans, my dream to remove Mt. Scopus from isolation, and complete the tasks left undone in 1948, was concern for the city, surrounded on three sides by enemies.

We spoke briefly. I reminded him that he was still not to move the tank company at his disposal from its present positon: "Keep an eye on Sheikh Abdul-Aziz and Government House." These were the two trouble spots at the moment – Sheikh Abdul-Aziz because it threatened Mevaseret Yerushalayim and because it was a vantage point from which Jerusalem could be severed from the coastal plain; and Government House, because as long as our forces had no hold in

the area it was the Achilles heel of our defense dispositions south of the
town, opposite the U.N. enclave. I added: "Be careful! The evil could
also come from the south."

Mobilizing the Home Guard

I was restless. What else should be done? My eyes scanned the large
map on the wall. Somewhere in the mountainous region beyond the
Green Line were the Long-Toms, the long-range, Jordanian artillery
to which we had no reply. At that very instant they might be moving
up to firing position, or had perhaps already moved and were training
their long barrels on – on what? On Tel Aviv? On Ramla? Perhaps on
Lod? What could I use against them?

I ordered the commander of the reconnaissance unit, Major Z, to be
ready to carry out a night foray on the Long-Tom somewhere in
enemy territory, probably the Rafa'at region. Attacks on air fields,
particularly Lod Airport, could be expected. With Arik I rechecked
the map. From which spot could the Jordanians shell it? The Latrun
enclave was the nearest. The artillery of Yotvat's brigade in the plain,
poor as it was, would have to deal with them with the help of the heavy
mortar battalion of the 10th Brigade which would have to be transferred to the plain. I still hoped that all the artillery in the region would be
at the disposal of the 10th Brigade; and until then it would be impossible, at the very least, to exploit the fire-power of our mortars.

09.55 hours – My anxiety about the safety of Jerusalem increased
and I spoke again to Eliezer Amitai. He told me that all was quiet, but
I said, "Quiet or not, move the tanks towards the city."

He complained that his infantry battalion was tied down with guard
duties, which was true. I bit my lips as I recalled that two battalions of
the home guard had been sent home only a few days ago. The plans for
the defense of Jerusalem, meticulously drawn up over many years,
called for the home guard to man the line fortifications. And now that
we were going into battle, all the planning was treated as though it did
not exist. Instead of the home guard, part of an infantry battalion sat
along the line. "At 10 o'clock there will be a radio call-up of the home
guard," I told Amitai. "Try and equip them and have them release the
men on the line quickly."

At ten o'clock, the Voice of Israel began broadcasting a long list of
code names, designating different Zahal units. The men reported
immediately, but it was too late. By the time they reached the assembly points, by the time the quartermaster stores were opened and

equipment distributed, the Jordanians had opened fire. One of the home-guard battalions, outfitting themselves from the stores at Allenby camp, received a direct hit during the bombardment. Many of the battalion's men, including C.O. Bill Aaronson, were injured. Deployment of the battalion was delayed. The shelling made it more difficult to carry out the daylight exchange of units along the line, because their positions were all within sight and range of the Jordanians opposite. Only after dark could the changeover be completed and the Jerusalem Brigade revert to its planned strength.

A Question of Tanks

In the war room the tumult went on, with me in the middle, but somehow detached from it. Arik came back and asked again about the train to Jerusalem. I stuck to my earlier decision of operation as usual, but without passengers.

And then came a report: The Jordanian army had withdrawn the farmers from their lands along the border with Israel. Arik: "Fine, we won't pick tomatoes on our side today either."

An order from G.H.Q. demanded immediate expediting of the plan for protection against commando infiltrations of airfields throughout the Command. Arik ordered the border guards to settle in at Kfar Vitkin, and the reconnaissance company of the Givati Brigade at Lod.

I inquired from G.H.Q. about developments on the southern front. Since the report that the tanks of Major-General Tal's division had gone into action, nothing had been forthcoming, but at that moment a savage battle was developing on the outskirts of Khan Yunis and Rafiah, and the G.H.Q. people had no spare time to report to onlookers like myself. I instructed the Operations N.C.O. to pull out the map of the southern front. I knew it well. I was well acquainted with both the plan code-named "Red Sheet" and the officers in charge of its execution.

"At this moment," I said to the staff officers, "Gorodish and his Centurions are beginning to attack. I know him and his pals. They're an angry lot. The Egyptians won't stop 'em. The Centurions will crush the Egyptians and force them to run away, and by 16.00 hours, Gorodish will reach El Arish. You'll see!"

Thinking about Gorodish's tanks racing along, crashing their way through every obstacle, may have made me connect the whole thing with Uri Ben-Ari's tanks. I was gnawed by the thought of Jordan's 60th Brigade with 100 Patton tanks: Where was it? Last night it had been somewhere in the Jordan Valley, near Jericho. Was it still there? We had no independent intelligence, not even one miserable reconnaissance plane. We were dependent upon G.H.Q. for everything, and just now their eyes were riveted southwards. Did anyone care about the movements of a Jordanian armored brigade?

What if that brigade had already moved from where it had been and suddenly turned up on the outskirts of Jerusalem? The thought alone was enough cause for serious alarm. Against a possible concentrated armor attack, our handful of men on Mt. Scopus didn't stand a chance. I contacted Uri Ben-Ari, who was in the middle of a briefing for taking Latrun. "Uri, you might be summoned to Jerusalem. I don't yet know why, but be ready for a quick take-off. When the time comes we shall transfer civilian traffic to the Caessalon road and keep the main road clear for you." He simplified things for me by not asking questions, but simply saying, "Roger."

And to my quartermaster officer, Lt. Col. Menahem, I said, "If the 10th Brigade is moved up to Jerusalem, we shall have to close the road from Sha'ar Hagai for its sole use. Please take care of it."

So far not a single shot had been fired.

The First Shots

The first shots on the Jerusalem front were fired at about 10.45 hours. Close to the Italian hospital, a woman was killed and a number of passers-by were wounded. A few minutes later a burst of gun-fire hit our position on Mount Zion, and the sergeant in charge was hit in the neck. Gradually the shooting encompassed the entire city.

The report was late in reaching me. Well afterwards, the operations officer of the Jerusalem Brigade, Major Amos, reported scattered shooting by light weapons at various places in town, but not about the casualties, because he knew nothing. Arik gave Amos telephone instructions: "For each of their shots, reply with a barrage." That was his style. In actual fact the standing orders were still valid, that we respond to Jordanian fire by shooting back with the same type of weapon. Rifles against rifles, mortars against mortars. "Barrage" only meant that from now on we would not underplay the gravity of a shooting incident. The response to Jordanian shooting would be in kind, from all available weapons.

11.30 – a report from the Jerusalem Brigade: The Jordanian fire is increasing, but is still from light weapons only.

To Eliezer Amitai: "Have they fired mortars?"

He replied that they had.

"And now?"

"Firing 81 mm. mortars."

"Then respond. Watch the southern side."

11.41 – to the C.O.G.S. "The Jordanians are firing mortars. We are replying."

11.42 – Arik tells me that an artillery bombardment has been launched on Mt. Scopus and Ramat Rahel.

And the red light which had been blinking in my brain since morning turned on full and permanently.

Aaron Yadlin, deputy Minister of Education, contacted me to say that the Ministry of Education building in the Musrara Quarter, in the heart of the Jordanian bombardment, was being heavily shelled. All the office staff, himself included, had taken shelter in the basement. He had contacted me because he was worried about Jerusalem's children, who had gone to school that morning. Should he instruct schools to close and the children sent home? I said that he should consult the mayor, but that from my point of view the safest places were the school buildings, provided they had shelters.

Confirmation was received from G.H.Q. for the use of explosive charges in Jerusalem. I ordered Eliezer Amitai to use Laskovs (explosive charges specially adapted for the defense of the Jerusalem line) all along the line. "Have you brought the tanks in? Against mortar fire, use mortars. Against artillery – ask me first!"

12.05 – The C.O. Jerusalem Brigade said that someone was "driving him nuts about a cease-fire." And Jerry Bieberman, our senior delegate on the M.A.C. in Jerusalem, informed me that it had been agreed with the approval of the C.O.G.S. that a cease-fire in Jerusalem would come into effect at 12.15 hours.

I (bursting): "A cease-fire is my sole prerogative!"

But it turned out not to be.

Diplomacy

Eliezer Amitai gave me the first hint of the extensive diplomatic activity in Jerusalem since the morning – first, to prevent the entrance of Jordan into the war, and later to extricate her from it. It was strange that until mid-day nobody had taken the trouble to inform the General Officer, Central Command, of these efforts. In fact, any information that I possess reached me not via normal channels but in private conversations after the war was over.

The endeavor to prevent Jordan's entering the war followed a political decision made at the highest level. As a result, Foreign Minister Abba Eban telephoned Arthur Luria, deputy Director-General of the Foreign Office, from Tel Aviv at 08.00 hours on June 5th, and dictated a message which Mr. Luria was to bring to the attention of the chief U.N. supervisor, General Od Bull, as an official statement of the Government of Israel. "We are in the thick of a defensive war in the Egyptian sector. We shall take no action against Jordan unless Jordan attacks us. Should Jordan attack Israel, we shall direct all our might against her."

Luria asked one of the senior officials, Michael Pragai, to invite Od Bull to the Foreign Office. Pragai did so at 08.10 hours and Bull promised to come at 10.30. But Pragai stressed the importance of the matter, and it was agreed that the General would come right away. Accompanying him was his deputy, Colonel Johnson, of the U.S. Army.

Arthur Luria received them in the chambers of the Director-General, and without undue formality read the message, adding that Prime Minister Eshkol asked that it be brought to the attention of King Hussein. Colonel Johnson asked that the last sentence be repeated for his proper understanding and General Bull asked what sort of battles were being waged down south. Pragai replied that they were tank battles, to which Bull commented that it was strange that fighting should have broken out just when Nasser had sent his deputy, Zacharia Muchy e-Din, on a peace mission to Washington. Luria did not reply and the two men departed. The meeting had lasted about 15 minutes.

At 10.35 Od Bull telephoned from Government House and informed Mr. Pragai that the message had been sent to Hussein, but that no reply had as yet been received.

According to Hussein's *Diary*, the king received Od Bull's message by telephone, a little after 11.00 a.m., while he was at Jordanian Air Force H.Q. in Amman. Hussein explains that "by that time our forces were already fighting in Jerusalem and our planes had taken off to bomb airfields in Israel. I told Od Bull that they had begun the war and would receive our reply by air."

General Od Bull does not confirm receipt of the king's reply. At 5 p.m. after our forces had recaptured Government House, Pragai again asked Od Bull if any reply had been received from King Hussein and was told that none had come.

Still earlier, after shooting began in Jerusalem, further efforts were made to bring about a cease-fire, this time via officers of the M.A.C. They were not brought to my attention at the time, and I finally learned about them from Eliezer Amitai.

At 11.25, as shooting increased in Jerusalem, Colonel Stanaway contacted Lt. Colonel Jerry Bieberman, the Israeli senior delegate on the Israel-Jordan Armistice Commission: "There is shooting, apparently by the Jordanians, not far from the Commission's building. I asked Jordan for an immediate cease-fire. I believe you are not shooting, but if you are, you must stop at once!"

Bieberman replied: "We are not shooting."

At 11.40 Stanaway got in touch once again. "Muhammed Daoud [the Jordanian chief delegate] is ready to cease firing at 12.00."

Bieberman contacted Lt. Colonel Shmuel Gat (chief of the armistice branch at G.H.Q.), who passed the report on to his superiors. Bieberman was ordered by Gat to reply in the affirmative and request that the cease-fire begin at 12.15 hours.

With his affirmative reply, Bieberman asked Colonel Stanaway to give Colonel Daoud the following message: "I wish to bring to your attention certain information – that the Egyptian air force has been wiped out."

Daoud's secretary confirms that the colonel received the message, but cannot recall whether it was transmitted to Amman. He remembers quite well that Daoud, influenced by the Cairo broadcast, treated the message with contempt. "We shall soon be in Tel Aviv," he said.

The cease-fire did not become effective at 12.15. The Jordanians said that they had taken Mt. Scopus. I contacted the C.O. Jerusalem Brigade to ask if it were true that the Jordanians had taken Mt. Scopus or Government House, but was told that there was no information. I ordered him to check it, and in a moment he told me that our observers at Government House reported all quiet there, but that Mt. Scopus was still being shelled.

The cease-fire did not become effective at 12.15. The Jordanians went on firing, and so did we. At 12.20 Major A.H. Hagerty telephoned and suggested a cease-fire at 12.30. Again Bieberman agreed, but the Jordanian fire did not stop. An hour later, Hagerty phoned to say that the chairman suggested a cease-fire at 13.30, and that our forces were firing machine-guns from Mt. Scopus.

Major Tuvia Nevot, who took the call in the absence of Jerry Bieberman, indignantly replied:

"And make a laughing-stock of myself? How can we agree at 13.32 hours to a cease-fire at 13.30 hours? I'll contact my authorities. Meanwhile refer the matter back to the chairman and ask for a later time."

A short while later came the news that Jordan had captured Government House.

"Saut El Arab": The Voice of the Arabs

At mid-day, when the U.N. administration began to try to effect a cease-fire, war had already broken out along the entire front. In Jerusalem we heard of heavy bombardment centered mainly on the Schneller Camp, as well as bombardments and air raids, mostly in Zunik's territory in the Sharon. Kibbutz Bahan and Kibbutz Ayal were bombarded; Ramat Hakovesh and Kfar Saba were shelled.

"12.10. To the deputy C.O.G.S. Four Laskovs have been used with good results. There are dead and wounded in town, and I think we must take action, that even if the Jordanians are shooting only to fulfil an obligation, we should fix them. I suggest we take Latrun, Abdul-Aziz and Government House."

One of the signals officers at G.H.Q. informed us that Dado (David Elazar, General Officer, Northern Command), had been given the green light to attack Jenin and destroy the Jordanian artillery deployment which was shelling the Ramat David air-field. The news shook me. Why should Northern Command be permitted to cross the green line to defend Ramat David when Central Command, defending Jerusalem, had its hands tied?

Even more annoying was the talk of a cease-fire (Lt. Colonel Bieberman had meanwhile informed me that a cease-fire in Jerusalem had been agreed upon, at 12.15 hours), with which I did not agree, but was told that the C.O.G.S. had confirmed. Having no option I instructed Eliezer Amitai to stop shooting, but if they continued, to answer with all he had. To myself I thought that we were hearing the same old story of the Jordanians doing whatever they wanted, shelling Jerusalem and causing heavy casualties, and then promising to be "good children," and being forgiven by everyone ... or worse: attacking and taking Mt. Scopus (which was being increasingly heavily bombarded), with Hussein declaring that he would be content with its capture, would advance not one foot further and would graciously agree to a cease-fire. Was there a guarantee that such an idea would not meet with government favor, since it was so keen on avoiding a clash with Jordan now that Zahal was fighting the Egyptians? It would pay the price – Mt. Scopus – which eventuality I had to do everything to prevent. Mt. Scopus must not fall.

12.45 hours: Intelligence says they have recorded a broadcast of *Saut el-Arab* from Cairo in which a Jordanian spokesman in Amman reported the capture of Jebel Mukhaber by Jordanian forces. In the English translation it was said that Mt. Scopus had been taken by the Jordanians.

When news of the broadcast reached the Foreign Ministry, Michael Pragai telephoned to ask Colonel Johnson at Government House if the Jordanians had seized the palace. Johnson said no, but, with diplomatic caution, added, "You never can tell." He hoped that both sides would keep their earlier promise to respect the neutrality of the supervisors' headquarters.

In the war room, where reports chased each other, my attention was needed for a report from Jerusalem and news of fighting in Lachish; to instruct Arik to stop all railway traffic to Jerusalem, and to Eliezer to use his snipers. But throughout, my brain was weighing the broadcast from Cairo. If the Egyptians announced the capture of Mt. Scopus, there might be a plan afoot to seize it, since the Arabs tended to put the cart before the horse, at least in their reporting. During the Sinai Campaign and earlier, during the War of Independence, Egyptian H.Q. had issued orders to carry out an operation and afterwards treated it as a *fait accompli*. So they might indeed try to seize Mt. Scopus.

In response to a telephone call from G.H.Q., I reported Jordanian Hunter aircraft over the Sharon and shelling all along the line, and was told that the air force would soon deal with the Jordanian airfields.

I ordered that the weeds on the Lachish frontier be set on fire to interfere with the Jordanian gunning of our forces, and that the company of light tanks, which had been down south, be moved up to Faluja.

To Tel El-Ful

In my chambers I studied the area maps to see what operational options were open to the Jordanians. An intended attack on Mt. Scopus would presumably be by combined infantry and armor, for which they would have to move infantry from Ma'aleh Ha'adumim and the 60th Brigade from the valley to the hills, a 6-8 hour journey of 20-30 kilometers. If the 60th Brigade set off immediately, it might reach the hills by dusk. But as Arab armies were not accustomed to attacking at night, we would have a breathing space till dawn. By 5, or even 4 a.m., however, we would need a tank force in the hills, where we could frustrate a Jordanian armored assault on Mt. Scopus.

I noticed the name Tel el-Ful, a high-point north of Jerusalem, about a kilometer north of Shua'afat, and decided that the Israeli tanks should meet the Jordanians there. But how would they get there?

At 13.15 I told Uri to come up to Jerusalem, ready to attack enemy positions south of the main road, to break through between Ma'aleh Hahamisha and Beit Iksa to reach the El-Ram area. I reminded him of the cowshed at Ma'aleh Hahamisha, which the Arab Legion forces reached in '48, below which was a twisting path to Katna, our western boundary. If he could break through, he would reach the Kubeiba road and an open route. The Radar axis was another entrance which he would have to take, to the place where the British half-tracks had been when they attacked the people coming back from Nabi Samuel.

I told him that a third axis was at Abdul-Aziz, the road up from Mevaseret Yerushalayim, about where his company's line started before the capture of Koloniya. Uri remembered the place, as well as the one where the armored car with the Davidka got stuck during the attack on Beit Iksa. I suggested that he might try the path there from our highway into the groves and up to Beit Iksa, from which point a road went to Nabi Samuel. Perhaps he could also open that axis. I finished by telling him to move to the wooded area (Martyr's Forest and Ma'aleh Hahamisha Forest) and await orders there, and added that Northern Command had received confirmation to go down to Jenin. "This is our chance to take Jerusalem."

He had only one request: "Please don't stop me at the Green Line. I want to go straight in from moving up to attack." I agreed.

I could not give Uri specific orders, because G.H.Q. had not agreed to the attack, but I hoped to convince them of the feasibility of my plan, in which case moving the 10th Brigade at once would save valuable time. Even though the plan of moving the 10th Brigade to Tel el-Ful via Abdul Aziz and Nabi Samuel was already formulated, the quickest way to help Mt. Scopus was still the direct route through Sheikh Jarrah and the police school. I did not want to get bloodied at that redoubt, described in our intelligence bulletin as a veritable fortress, but time was vital. By 4 a.m. we had to be at Tel el-Ful.

I wondered whether the tanks attached to the Jerusalem Brigade could, with two battalions, advance on Sheikh Jarrah while Uri outflanked it from the left. At 12.54 hours I got in touch with the C.O.G.S. and discussed the problem, requesting his consent to my plan to move the 10th Brigade to the hills south of Jerusalem to defend Mt. Scopus. The C.O.G.S., however, handed the receiver to Dayan, who was, after all, the Defense Minister.

It turned out that my problem also worried the high command, that my nagging about the danger to Mt. Scopus, my earlier talks with the defense minister, the C.O.G.S. and his deputy, and the idea of bringing the 10th Brigade to help Jerusalem had all done their bit.

General Igal Yadin, who during all that time had been in the war room at G.H.Q., told me after the war that my nagging had forced G.H.Q. to think increasingly about Jerusalem, and to discuss, with the C.O.G.S. and the defense minister, the possibility that there might be no cease-fire and that there would be war in Jerusalem. It had been agreed that the 10th Brigade be moved to the capital to get to Mt. Scopus, but not how to do it.

I told Dayan my dilemma. If the 10th Brigade made a flanking attack or a frontal assault on Sheikh Jarrah it would suffer heavy casualties because the objective was so well-fortified.

He said: "If there is danger to Mt. Scopus, act as you think best. The flanking idea appeals to me."

"But it might be too drawn out," I said, "and they might not get there in time."

Nothing was decided. Arik tried to encourage me by telling me that with a lot of tanks and all the Jerusalemites on Sheikh Jarrah, we would take it. I tried to be equally optimistic, and added that Eliezer Amitai had to be ready with the tanks so that he could begin the moment Uri arrived.

Arik began to organize artillery support for the 10th Brigade's attack and I contacted Uri, who was just moving his brigade from the Ben-Shemen Forest. "You must reach Tel el-Ful by dawn tomorrow; you have three movement axes at your disposal. You can choose any one of them, or come in on all three – but get there."

At that moment Eliezer Amitai reported that the Jordanians were advancing from the Mar Elias Monastery in southern Jerusalem.

"Use what you have against them," I said.

At 13.30 the plan took detailed shape in my mind. I told Eliezer,

"Uri is coming up to Jerusalem. Be ready to attack towards Mt. Scopus. The operation will be along two axes. Uri is responsible for the sector from Sheikh Jarrah northwards."

Eliezer: "That's tough."

I: "If so, don't capture it. Just move the tanks forward and blow up redoubts. If it's easy, enter the college and move on to the hill next to it. That's the plan for the time being."

I understood his misgivings. Who knew better than the commander of the Jerusalem Brigade how strong and powerful were the fortifications at Sheikh Jarrah? If he was not sure of capturing it, I could not force him.

When Moshe Dayan telephoned a little later, I told him that Uri would take Abdul-Aziz and move from there to Tel el-Ful, and that we would make a feint at Sheikh Jarrah, taking it from outside and not from within. Dayan said that I should do as I thought best.

The Paratroops Are Coming!

Within minutes the picture had changed. When I phoned G.H.Q. for authorization of my plan, Colonel Itzhak ("Haka") Hofi, head of "G" Department, replied that one battalion of the 55th Brigade was to be placed at my disposal and asked where I wanted it. "Jerusalem," I said, and immediately asked to speak to G.H.Q. again. Major General Ze'evi, assistant chief of "G" Branch, answered, listened to my plan for the Jerusalem Brigade to operate on the right axis with a battalion of the 55th, and authorized it.

I felt easier, since I knew the men of the 55th well. They were the ones to have been parachuted behind the enemy's lines at El-Arish to facilitate the advance of Major-General Tal's division. It was a very fine brigade even though it had not yet "consecrated its standard," a Zahal tradition whereby all reserve brigades undergo a series of back-breaking exercises over a period of years, climaxed by a large-scale brigade maneuver. After its successful completion, the brigade receives its colors – the ceremony of "Consecrating the Standard" – and becomes a full-fledged unit. Its men were all battle-experienced and its officers veteran paratroopers of whose ability to storm Sheikh Jarrah I was convinced.

The brigade, whose equipment was already in parachute sacks, was waiting on the tarmac at an airfield, ready to take off for the southern front. The message informing them that the operation had been

cancelled because of the rapid advance made by the armor of Colonel
Gorodish (Gonen) was received with great anxiety, a mood unchanged
even after receipt of the order to transfer one battalion to Jerusalem.
The paratroops thought this meant defense duty, and to avoid the
battalion O.C.'s complaints about injustice, the Brigade O.C. decided
to select the battalion for Jerusalem by lot.

The task fell to the 66th battalion, but before they set out they
received an order to send a second battalion to Jerusalem, corrected
later to "send the whole brigade."

I asked the C.O. to call in at Command headquarters on his way to
Jerusalem to receive my orders.

Tel el-Ful by Dawn

At 14.05 Colonel Uri Ben-Ari reported, having, an hour earlier,
received my telephoned orders to move his brigade up to Jerusalem.
At the time the brigade had been preparing to attack Latrun, and he
was briefing his men on its capture when the new orders arrived.
Within the hour, the brigade, with all its vehicles, was on its way
eastward. The vanguard had already reached Lod when Uri left the
convoy and raced to Command headquarters for his orders. He
walked into the war room in green battle-dress, his black Armored
Corps cap thrust under a shoulder strap. "Well, Uzi, what's doing?"

"Come and see," I said.

We went into my chambers, the Chief-of-Staff accompanying us. I
spread the map on the table.

"Look. Here is Tel el-Ful and you are to get there by dawn with the
maximum number of tanks, in order to neutralize a possible armored
attack by the Legion on Mt. Scopus.

"The limits of your sector are from Ma'aleh Hahamisha in the west
to the police college in the east. Opposite you is the 60th Armored
Brigade with about 100 Pattons. I don't know where they are, and I'm
not the only one who doesn't. They might already be on the move. I
suggest you get up to the operational area along the main road, by the
Martyr's Forest axis or by any other way. All the routes are at your
disposal. You must take the positions at Sheikh Abdul-Aziz and
Radar, but also try to break through at the 1948 Davidka Trail. And
there's one other route, which Gorodish once suggested to me: the
Khirbet el-Borg. See if it's negotiable. Clear?"

"Absolutely clear."

Uri again asked not to be held up at the green line but to be allowed to move straight in from advance to assault. I promised him it would be so.

As he got up to go, Borka, the Chief-of-Staff, who had been sitting quietly, interrupted.

"Sir," he said, "look." He bent his forearm to his shoulder and pointed at his hairy elbow: "Here are the ridges. Here is Tel el-Ful. The Jordanian armor is in the Jordan Valley and to reach the ridges all they have to do is drive along the road, their own territory, whereas we have to break through enemy strong-points. Think of them: the Radar, Abdul-Aziz, Nabi Samuel and all the rest. You know their strength. And even after we take them, if we do, we have to continue moving along difficult hilly mountain trails till we reach Tel el-Ful. Everything is in their favor. They'll anticipate us, and you understand what that means! Think of all the exercises we've taken part in together. In every one, the lesson was the same: He who reaches the ridge first fixes the other. Isn't this the place for a classic tank-ambush? The Jordanians will get there first! As our tanks struggle up, they'll be fixed one by one. We won't have a prayer! And, remember, we have Shermans to their Pattons. I beg you – I was your Chief-of-Staff in the division, and we went through a lot together on maneuver exercises – don't do it!"

For a moment I hesitated. Borka was a veteran tank man who spoke from great experience. And there was no arguing with the logic of his words. Was I being rash? I considered seriously. There was an element of danger in my plan, but a calculated one. Furthermore, there was no other solution, no time to spare, and a decision had to be made now. I glanced at Uri, who stood frozen-faced. My glance asked for his opinion.

"No flak" he said with a wink, and that was all. His quiet confidence dispelled my doubts.

"Right; off you go!" I shook his hand; he saluted and was gone.

The Jordanians Seize Government House

For the second time that day plans were changed. At 14.10 came a report from Eliezer Amitai that a Jordanian company had seized Government House and were nearing the agricultural school.

I: "What forces do you have there?"

He: "At the moment only an observer."

9. Jordanian soldiers occupy Government House on June 5th, 1967

I: "And what of the company that was supposed to settle in at the school?"

He: "Apparently not there yet."

I: (to myself: The hell with it! So what's to stop them entering Allenby barracks, the railway station, Katamon?)

"Are you in contact with the observer? What are the Jordanians doing?"

I could visualize a Legion force breaking through from Government House to the Allenby barracks and seizing the railway station, from which the way to Katamon is wide open. There are only women and children left there. I reported the Jordanian movements to Major-General Ze'evi at G.H.Q. and suggested a counter-attack that would also take Sur Baher. Air cover would be needed, I told him.

"Gandi" asked when we would be ready to start and I said in 1-2 hours. "I'll attack Government House first."

"The Egyptians and Jordanians threatened in their radio broadcasts to seize the palace and, sure enough, they've done it. Now it's clear they'll try their luck on Mt. Scopus too." He handed the instrument to Haim Bar-Lev, to whom I repeated the report and from whom I requested authorization to counter-attack.

"I also request authority to bring up the 10th Brigade between Ma'aleh Hahamisha and Sheikh Jarrah and to let the paratroops enter Sheikh Jarrah at the same time."

Bar-Lev: "The 10th Brigade agreed. You can move it to Jerusalem, but stop it at the green line."

Apparently G.H.Q. were still afraid to grapple with the Jordanians. But, as I saw it, from the moment the Jordanians had taken Government House, the war had begun and nothing could stop it.

At 14.20 Arik reported after a talk with the Jerusalem Brigade that Eliezer would be ready to attack Government House in another five minutes.

At 14.25 an attack on Government House was authorized and transmitted to the Jerusalem Brigade.

At 14.27 G.H.Q. announced that two planes would bomb Abdul-Aziz and the Radar, and two others would support the counter-attack on Government House. I said that the 10th Brigade would begin attacking at 16.00 hours and would need aerial support. As for the palace, the attack was expected any minute.

Arik Regev informed me, having apparently heard it from Jerry

Bieberman, that General Od Bull and his people were still in the seized palace.

"If so, an air raid on the palace is out of the question. They'll attack without air support."

Another talk with G.H.Q. My plea since mid-day had been fruitful: the Air Force was ordered to seek out and attack the 60th Brigade somewhere in the region of Jericho.

The last page of the operational diary of the Israel-Jordan Armistice Commission reads as follows:

1134   COS phoned Stanaway who was talking to Daoud trying to arrange cease fire. Firing was going on close to Machouse.
1136   COS talked to Pragai requesting a cease fire. Pragai took notes.
1138   COS talked to Daoud who said *ready to cease 1200 LT*.
1144   COS talked to Pragai informing him that Jordan accepted cease fire.
1145   COS talked to Daoud informing him that Israel accepts cease fire at 1200 LT.
1155   COS phoned Pragai. Privilege of GH area.
1155   COS phoned Daoud. Him out.
1209   Firing still going on. Arrangement between Jordanian government north and south of agriculture school.
1211   COS phoned Daoud and talked with him. He mentioned cease fire 1230.
1214   COS phoned Stanaway and confirmed cease fire for 1230.
1217   COS phoned Pragai who accepted cease fire for 1230.
1300   COS phoned Pragai who promised to send this message to Commander Rabin.
1355   COS called Pragai.

Od Bull's Delaying Tactics

Rafi Efrat, aide-de-camp to the C.O.G.S. (Efrat died in January, 1971, while serving as military attaché in West Germany), said that the defense minister wanted to go to Jerusalem. I suggested that he travel by the Bar-Giora axis, which is not as prone to shelling as the main highway, and ordered two armed jeeps to accompany him from Ramla to Jerusalem. The jeeps were delayed en route, but the impatient minister of defense refused to wait and ordered his driver to proceed without an escort.

At 14.50 I notified G.H.Q. that the Jerusalem Brigade was beginning its assault on the palace, to which they shouted, "They are not to attack without prior authorization!"

Meanwhile another attempt to stop the war in Jerusalem was under way, initiated by Od Bull. Sometime after 14.00 hours he had phoned

Mr. Pragai of the Foreign Ministry and Lt. Colonel Bieberman and announced that a Jordanian force had seized the grounds of the palace and all the U.N. observers were assembled in one wing of the building. He added that he had been in touch with the Jordanians and hoped to arrange the withdrawal of their forces. Bull asked Israel to desist from all military activity. Bieberman transmitted the message to Shmuel Gal at G.H.Q., who passed it on to General Rabin.

A few minutes prior to that, the Supreme Command had learned of the Jordanian seizure of Government House. The Defense Minister ordered an immediate counter-attack, and at 14.25 hours I was authorized to begin operations.

After Bull's announcement, I was told that, according to C.O.G.S., a counter-attack would broaden the war on the Jordanian front to no purpose and that General Bull should be allowed to try in his own way to get the Jordanians to leave Government House. The Defense Minister agreed, emphasizing that if no general cease-fire were achieved, the efforts to join with Mt. Scopus were to continue. The C.O.G.S. therefore ordered Lt. Colonel Gat, liaison officer with the U.N., to tell General Bull that Israel was agreeable to a cease-fire in Jerusalem.

I was, therefore, not to attack the palace, but to await confirmation. At Jerusalem Brigade H.Q., Operations Officer Amos told me that the Brigade C.O. had left to join the forces attacking the palace. "Can you stop them?" I asked.

"No," was the reply. "We have no direct contact with them."

"Try to get to them and stop them."

Contact was not made, and the palace was captured.

The Evelina de Rothschild School

From the brief reports sent by the Jerusalem Brigade, it was impossible to learn about events in town or the difficulties faced by the Brigade. Jerusalem had been under fire for upwards of three hours. Soldiers and civilians from one end of town to the other were wounded. The heaviest bombardment landed on the Schneller Camp, which the Legionnaires knew well, training their artillery and mortars dead upon it. The camp was blasted into a shambles. Dozens of shells fell on it, telephone lines were shattered, the electricity was cut and roofs were splintered.

The Jerusalem Brigade had prepared an emergency Command H.Q. in advance, in the basement of the Evelina de Rothschild

School, but did not move there until mid-day, at which time it was discovered that communications equipment and telephones had not yet been installed, and personnel to complete the arrangements had to be hurriedly mobilized. There were no telephones, but Amos took the initiative of sending his men to neighboring houses to requisition instruments, which were installed at H.Q. Communication with Brigade H.Q. was therefore limited.

When the order to prepare to counter-attack the palace was received at the improvised Brigade H.Q., the operations officer went over the list of units at his disposal. His eye lit upon the infantry battalion commanded by Lt. Colonel Asher Dreizin. Two of its companies had gone into the line to replace Home Guard battalions and the rest were deployed along defense positions in the southern part of town. He ordered Dreizin to transfer one company immediately to Allenby barracks and to be ready to attack Government House, telling him that he would reinforce Dreizin's unit with everything he had.

But with what? The Brigade reconnaissance company was rushed to southern Jerusalem.

Another force – six tanks of an armored company – was placed at the Brigade's disposal. Commanded by Company Commander Major Aaron Kamra, they were moved to the Russian Compound when the shelling began, from which they could hurry to wherever they were needed. Now need had arisen, but the tanks could not be contacted by radio because they were stationed between high buildings, which made radio contact impossible. Amos, the G. 3, summoned police officer (and football referee) Otto Fried, who was liaison between the Brigade and the Jerusalem Police, and asked if he was in touch with the commander of the Jerusalem Police, whose office was in the Russian Compound. Fried said that he was.

"Tell him to send someone to the officer commanding the tanks parked near his office, and order him, in the name of the Brigade C.O., to move at once to Allenby barracks and report to Lt. Colonel Dreizin." And so the job was done.

When all the commanders reported "Ready," Eliezer Amitai informed me that he would be ready to counter-attack in five minutes. It had apparently slipped his mind that Lt. Colonel Dreizin's battalion lacked transport facilities. The reconnaissance company was stationed west of Jerusalem and had to cross the entire town at the height of the shelling, so that almost an hour passed before the force was fully assembled and ready to counter-attack.

I knew nothing of this at the time, and I did not understand why I could not get through to the O.C. Jerusalem Brigade or why it was having difficulties contacting its units deployed to attack the palace.

Other problems awaiting decision began to pile up. The first was that the paratroop brigade under Colonel Motta Gur was on its way to me.

My immediate objective, as confirmed by G.H.Q., was to join our small force on Mt. Scopus and bring the armored force to Tel el-Ful before the enemy got there from the Jordan Valley and began an assault on the Mount. How this could be achieved had undergone several metamorphoses in my mind since morning. At first I tended towards a combined operation between the Jerusalem and 10th Brigades. But, in view of the developments at Government House, I decided in favor of a flanking operation by the 10th Brigade and restricting the Jerusalem Brigade to blasting the Legion's strong-points at Sheikh Jarrah, without storming the Quarter. Now another brigade – paratroopers – was at my disposal.

I was confident that the 10th Brigade could overcome the obstacles en route and reach the ridges. But, wondering when it would arrive, I remembered the rocky, difficult terrain the Brigade would have to negotiate and force a passage through. By any military definition, it was unsuitable for armored warfare. I was fully aware of the enemy's massively fortified strong-points, and was sure that the Brigade would overcome them, but had no idea how long it would take. And the time factor was now decisive. At dawn the enemy's armor would appear, to threaten Mt. Scopus. And the shortest posssible distance to Mt. Scopus was undoubtedly via Sheikh Jarrah.

I decided that the paratroops would get the Sheikh Jarrah assignment, in addition to and parallel with the flanking movement of the 10th Brigade.

"Bear Right to Rockefeller"

At 15.05 Motta Gur arrived with his staff intelligence, operations and Brigade communications officers, and asked Arik Regev about the Brigade's assignment. Then he came into my chambers. He was all warrior – steel helmet covered with a camouflage net, properly belted and accoutered, paratrooper boots, and an "Uzzi" sub-machine gun – his whole being eager for action.

A few days earlier, at one o'clock in the morning, I had visited him in an orange grove in the plains where he had set up his H.Q. The

Brigade commander and his staff sat in the H.Q. tent around a field table illuminated by a small lamp with a dim light, busily planning their jump behind enemy lines at El Arish. It was a daring and dangerous mission and the men of the Brigade were delighted with it. They commiserated with me for being condemned to the sidelines in a war which might develop into one of Israel's greatest campaigns. And now things were reversed. Their dangerous mission had become redundant and been cancelled and they were a G.H.Q. reserve transferred to that same Central Command which a few days ago had been sitting on the sidelines.

"Mt. Scopus is in danger," I told them. "Your job is to capture Sheikh Jarrah and the police college and get to the Mount. The southern boundary of your assault sector is the Mandelbaum Gate. From there on the Jerusalem Brigade operates. The northern limit is Givat Hamivtar, where the 10th Brigade will operate. They will not cross south of the Mivtar. The objective is to connect with the Mount, but remember the Old City. You will have to bear right toward the Rockefeller Museum to be ready at any moment to burst through the walls and seize the Old City."

Until that moment nobody had so much as spoken the words "Old City," whose capture had been included in no early planning that I knew of. It was always said that the capture of the Old City would be by special order. What had made me think of it now, when we were fighting for the life of Jerusalem? What had prompted me to say to Motta, "Bear to the right so you'll be ready to seize the Old City"?

In an effort to reconstruct my thoughts of that time, I am tempted to attribute my words to yearning, the great longing that had been uppermost since 1948. To complete the task then unfinished, to bring to reality the semi-mystic belief, undispelled all those years, that the day would come when the job would be done. But that was not the whole answer. The longing existed, as did the belief, but when Motta Gur sat before me to receive his orders, cold, clear logic was added. When the battle for Jerusalem began, and when we captured Sheikh Jarrah and connected with Mt. Scopus, the next inevitable step would be a breakthrough into the Old City. I wanted to be prepared for that step. I added, "But be careful, the Sheikh Jarrah area is a fortress."

Gur replied quietly, "I know."

The discussion was brief. I told him about Uri Ben-Ari's brigade, which would be outflanking from the left in an attempt to reach the ridges before dawn. Motta wanted to move on; he was in a hurry to get to Jerusalem to reconnoiter the area in daylight with his battalion commanders. On June 3rd, when he had reconnoitered the Jerusalem Line prior to setting out for Mt. Scopus, his brigade had already been assigned the El-Arish objective. He had been sure the war would start before the convoy went up, and had not agreed to the request of his deputy, Lt. Colonel Moshe Peles (Stempel, who was killed pursuing a gang of Arab terrorists in the Jordan Valley in September 1968), to include the battalion commanders in his reconnoitering party. He had said that it would be unnecessary, because they couldn't be there on June 7th. Now he undoubtedly regretted that decision.

We agreed that he would give me his battle plan that evening in Jerusalem. Motta added that if he did not manage to reach Mt. Scopus during the night, he preferred stopping on the boundaries of the built-up area of Sheikh Jarrah to being trapped on the open slopes of Mt. Scopus in daylight.

Motta left and I got in touch with Zonik. "What's new?"

"Shooting."

"Any casualties?"

"Yes. A mortar shell fell at Nitzanei–Oz. Three members of the settlement killed. We're shooting back."

And to Moshik: "How are things at your end?"

"Nothing! Shooting, shelling, bombing. What's going on? Any chance of action? The boys are stamping their feet with impatience."

"We have to wait. Things'll work out."

And to the Commander of Gush Lachish: "Anything going on?"

"Kibbutz Lahav was shelled. No special problems."

"Keep your eyes open. The enemy might be planning something for Kiriat-Gat or Beersheba."

"Don't worry. We're watching."

Again I contacted the Jerusalem Brigade. There was still no communication with the C.O. or the forces attacking Government House.

Forward Command in Jerusalem

From the reports of the brigade commanders, I became more and more convinced that my place was in Jerusalem, where the command's main efforts were centered. The Jerusalem Brigade was already attacking from the south, at Government House, and the 10th Brigade would soon open a second front, north of the town. The buses carrying the paratroops were on their way and would soon arrive, requiring arms and equipment.

I called Arik Regev. "I'm off to Jerusalem and you're to remain here. Everything outside of Jerusalem is your responsibility. Watch out for Zunik's sector and especially Latrun. Go on pressing G.H.Q. till they confirm its capture. It's worthwhile concentrating a large force on Latrun. We've spilled plenty of blood there in the past."

The adjutant, Yoel Herzl, was outside organizing the forward command group. Central Command's wartime equipment was poor, without even an armored car for the command group, whose members travelled by jeep and command-car. In the jeep, driven by a regular army driver named Zabotaro, were Yoel, Koby Sharett and I, and in the command-car, the G-Branch sergeant, Intelligence sergeant and the clerk, Yehudith Yaari. Major Kimmel, Operations officer, his assistant Izik, and the deputy Intelligence officer were in the escort detail in an armored half-track. Lt. Col. Davidi, the Command artillery officer, accompanied the Command group with his H.Q. staff in the command-car and armored half-track. All these formed a sort of miniature divisional H.Q. which had been my intention. From the moment I left Command at Ramla, I considered myself not only the general officer of Central Command, but especially the commander of the three brigades to participate in the battle for Jerusalem.

At 15.15 the convoy moved off to the main road, passing the sentry at the entrance to the H.Q. camp. Until Ramla the going was heavy. We came across a 10th Brigade transport convoy, and it took a long time till we reached the level crossing east of Ramla, where Lt. Col. Menahem, Command quartermaster, reported to me. He was directing traffic on the main highway. In response to my questions he said that everything was under control and Uri had already gone by.

He saluted and had gone on before I realized that I had not asked him if he had closed the Jerusalem highway to civilian traffic. I later learned that he had forgotten and had remembered only after the 10th Brigade convoy had gone through Ramla. Since the posted duties of the guards were unclear, motorcars carrying VIP's (it was a Monday, the day the Knesset met, and dozens of M.K's were on their way to the capital) were allowed through by the military police, who feared reprimands. These and other vehicles which got through before barriers were erected delayed the 10th Brigade convoy and caused friction among the units.

At 15.30 we were still at the Ramla level crossing and I called Command to ask about Government House, where fighting, they told us, had started, but about which they had no news.

I imagined the overall picture: Uri's armor hurrying towards the assault lines to begin the attack; Motta's paratroops on their way to Jerusalem; in Jerusalem, Eliezer's Brigade already attacking Government House. Joy engulfed me. I knew that soon these three powerful streams would flood together into a tidal wave, to flow over and drown Jerusalem's bonds.

Attacking Government House

When the Jerusalem Brigade H.Q. was told to prepare for a counter-attack on Government House, the Brigade's G-Branch officer, Major Amos, began assembling the forces. Bombardment intensified and casualty reports abounded. The Brigade's medical officer recorded the reports and transmitted evacuation orders to ambulance units. Amos ordered the Brigade's mortar-unit commander to open fire on all the Legion's positions.

The Brigade commander, Colonel Eliezer Amitai, entered the war room and Amos told him of the preparations made for the counter-offensive, adding that he had ordered all units to meet Asher Dreizin at Allenby Barracks, and that he wanted to go there himself to coordinate the meeting and the attack.

The C.O., however, decided that Amos should stay where he was. "I'll go there and assume command," he said, and left. Outside the Evelina de Rothschild School he met the Brigade's A-Branch officer, Dov Bernstein, who had just returned from visiting a company commanded by Haim Guri, deployed opposite the police college. Dov reported heavily increased activity in that sector with the company under heavy bombardment, which had resulted in casualties, some of them fatal. He believed the enemy was preparing to attack there. The C.O. therefore changed his plans and decided to establish headquarters on top of the Histadrut building, where, he thought, he could devise strategy for a possible battle north of the city. He ordered the G-Branch officer to bring his field telephone, and together they climbed to the roof of the Histadrut Building.

Forces were meanwhile beginning to assemble south of the city. B Company of Asher Dreizin's battalion, the first in position, was given the task of seizing the agricultural school. It had arrived by bus around mid-day, shortly after the Jordanians had taken the palace at the height of heavy shelling of the school. The men had jumped out of the buses and raced between the trees of the farm, sinking deep into the mud left by the previous night's irrigation.

Lt. Col. Dreizin left for Allenby barracks as soon as he received the order and was caught en route by the heavy bombardment. His jeep and communications equipment were hit. Dreizin arrived at the barracks on foot, and ordered his mortar-battery to open fire on the ground of Government House and the area between it and the agricultural school fence. The force promised for the capture of the palace arrived late. The Brigade's reconnaissance company, commanded by Major Yossi, which travelled in armored half-tracks and jeeps, made its ponderous way under incessant shelling through the city's empty streets. Fallen trees and torn-down electric wires delayed them. Five of Aaron Kamra's tanks (a defective sixth was left in the Russian Compound) preceded them, but were halted at the entrance to the camp. Shells fell all around, the acrid smell of gunpowder filled the air, and weeds were burning sporadically. The tank's radio trans-receiver was released from camouflage interference and Kamra managed to make contact with Brigade H.Q., where Major Amos told him that the object was the capture of the palace. Now the reconnaissance unit and their vehicles arrived and halted near the tanks.

Asher Dreizin returned to his company in the agricultural school to await the promised reinforcements.

After a half-hour of radio coordination tests, all unsuccessful, the G-Branch officer instructed Aaron Kamra to move his tanks to the agricultural school and report to a lieutenant-colonel called Dreizin. Dreizin, angry and short-tempered, was waiting at the entrance to the school grounds, which were becoming less and less comfortable as the enemy barrage intensified. As the column of tanks drew near, bombarded by the Legion's guns, Dreizin ordered Kamra to take cover in the orchard and from there to open fire on the palace and on the Legion's positions in Abu-Tor. The tanks turned into the orchards – and began to sink in the soggy soil.

By that time the reconnaissance unit had also arrived and Dreizin had had time to plan a hasty attack. His B Company, already at the northern fence of the school, would cross the road, disperse into the thicket surrounding the palace and reach the building. At the same time the armored column would move on the palace in a frontal assault. He called Yossi: "Leave the jeep with the recoilless gun in the school grounds, follow the tanks with the half-tracks and capture the palace and whatever is behind it!"

Yossi asked for clarification, precise delimitation of the boundaries between his and the infantry's sectors, and the meaning of "whatever is behind the palace." Was it only Aerial Hill next to Government

House or also the "sausage position?" But Asher Dreizin was in a hurry. From his Command half-track he thundered: "Move at once! There's no time!"

At 15.10 the tanks revved up, but only three moved, the other two bogged deep in the mire. Kamra tried to help them extricate themselves, but a shell exploded near his tank, felling a cypress tree, which crashed down on his turret and his head. For a moment he was unconscious.

The three tanks lumbered out of the grove into a barred and locked gate. The lead tank burst through the gate and into the palace grounds, followed by the armored column.

The Legionnaires in the palace were thunderstruck. The earlier bombardment had wreaked havoc among them. Dead bodies sprawled on the ground and jeeps blazed. At the sight of the tanks, the enemy soldiers raced for their last three artillery-carrying jeeps. Lt. Colonel Dreizin spotted them from his half-track, grabbed his machine-gun, sprayed lead at the Legionnaires and set the three jeeps afire just as a burst of machine-gun bullets splattered against the side of the half-track. A bullet struck Dreizin's forearm. He managed to discover its source – a small bunker at the end of the square – and, despite paralysis in one arm, trained his machine-gun on it and silenced the bunker.

The armored column raced on and passed the palace, scattering the frightened Legionnaires into the thicket. Dreizin reached "Aerial Hill" and took it without a struggle. Here he halted his force and bandaged his arm, noticing that the blood from the wound had stained the half-track. He looked back.

At that moment the commander of the reconnaissance unit, Major Yossi, smashed through the palace gate and burst inside. Shots rang out on all sides and the mopping-up troops could not tell whether they came from inside the building or out. They began their operations, firing their Uzzis into the rooms and afterwards tossing in hand-grenades. In one room they were stopped at the last moment by a frightened shout in English: "Don't shoot!" About 30 people were there – U.N. observers, civilian employees of the Observer H.Q., women and children – who had locked themselves in when the Legionnaires occupied the building two hours earlier.

"We won't hurt you," Yossi assured them, "but don't leave this room."

He left one of his men to guard them and continued mopping up the

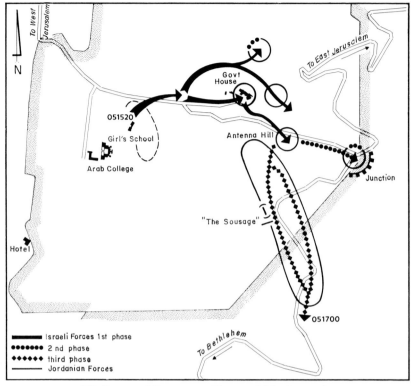

VI Capture of Government House and "the Sausage"

floors above. One of the U.N. observers called out, "Be careful. There are more of our people upstairs."

Yossi found them – about ten senior officers of U.N. Observer H.Q., headed by General Od Bull himself. These experienced military men threw themselves flat out on the floor as the shooting started. They jumped up when they saw Yossi, but he stopped them: "You're better off where you are. The battle isn't over."

When the Legionnaires realized that their men were being thrown out of the palace, they began to shell it. Yossi, reporting, was ordered to evacuate the U.N. personnel, who, with General Bull as spokesman, asked to be removed to East Jerusalem, where they lived. The Brigade adjutant supervising the evacuation said that the orders specified Jewish Jerusalem. The Norwegian general received the news equably, even accepting Yossi's suggestion that he lock his room and leave the key with a sentry. The latter, a member of the reconnaissance unit, found a lipstick left by one of the secretaries at Observer H.Q. and with it wrote on the door:

"This is the office of General Bull. Do not enter."

When the general was satisfied that his people were safe and well, he joined the evacuation convoy setting out for Jerusalem. Of the entire Observer H.Q. corps, only six Arabs remained at Government House. They were taken as P.o.W.'s. Yossi assured General Bull that no harm would befall them.

The "Private" Battle of Zerah Epstein

When the mopping-up operations in the palace had been completed, Yossi saw, through a window, the men of B Infantry Company, who had sallied forth from the agricultural school's orchard and were advancing, firing as they went, towards the thicket north of the palace. He was worried that they might attack the palace, and sent a runner, Corporal Zerah Epstein, to contact their C.O. and warn him that the palace had already been captured and occupied by an Israeli force. Zerah grabbed his rifle and tore across the palace grounds, discovered the company commander at the edge of the thicket, gave him the order and turned to run back to Government House.

In the thicket a weird battle was in progress between Jordanians scattered among the trees and Israelis dispersed in the thicket. The Jordanians were in complete disarray and trying to escape, but the Israelis happened to be in the way of their retreat. In the dim light among the trees, quick gun-fights flared up and as quickly died down, only to flare up again in another spot, and Epstein found himself in the middle of a shoot-out. "They shot at me from a dugout," he said when he was awarded a medal for bravery, "and I shot back. I tossed a hand-grenade into the trench and raced on ... suddenly I found myself all alone among the trees. From beneath one of them a Jordanian sprang out. I shot him and went on running. Somebody called out to me. I stopped and turned back. I saw it was a Jordanian soldier standing about two meters away from me. He saw me at the same time. We pressed the trigger at almost the same moment, but I was just a fraction quicker."

Zerah Epstein continued to carry out his "private" mopping-up operation in the thicket. He fired, was fired at: crawled, threw hand-grenades, continued crawling, finally reaching the fence at the edge of the thicket, where he found several men of B Company and joined them. When the battle ended it became clear that he had single-handedly mopped up a considerable part of the thicket area, and the route of his advance was marked by dead bodies of Jordanian soldiers.

The "Sausage" is Taken

I moved on with the convoy of the command group up the Jerusalem highway. At the Nachshon crossroads we met the end of the 10th Brigade convoy. Speed was out of the question, and traffic jams were all but continuous. In one of them, caused by an over-heated tank engine, I saw my brother-in-law, Haim Luz, a company commander of the 10th Brigade. The meeting was brief.

"What's new, Haim?" I asked.

"Nothing," he replied with a smile, "except that there's a war on, we're going to Jerusalem, and I am – here ..."

The traffic eased a little and we hurried on.

15.50. By radio to Arik Regev: "What's new at Government House?"

"We took it," he answered happily; "the Jordanians are on the run."

"Try and take whatever is behind the palace. Press Haim Bar-Lev to confirm it."

Behind the former Government House was the "sausage" redoubt. If we took it, the West Bank would be cut in two, because the single road connecting the Hebron Mountains with Jerusalem and Samaria passed through the "Sausage" fortifications.

G.H.Q. confirmed assault on the "sausage" and the order was transmitted to Asher Dreizin at about 4 o'clock. He was trying to ignore the pain of his wounded arm while assembling the remnants of his force, scattered around the battle area. Battle confusion prevailed everywhere and the men, for most of whom this was the first baptism by fire, seemed bewildered. Dreizin sent a soldier to meet and guide the reconnaissance unit's platoon or recoilless guns, which had been left at the agricultural school. With twenty-five men whom they had managed to assemble from B Company, the platoon was given the task of attacking the "Sausage." Dreizin continued to assemble and despatch men, as soon as they arrived, into the trenches of the "sausage" fortress. The position was well organized for defense. Its trenches were revetted and its bunkers covered. The battle was fierce. When it ended, the men of the reconnaissance unit, gasping for breath, staggered out at the end of the redoubt on the Bethlehem highway. They counted more than 30 dead Jordanian soldiers in the trenches and bunkers.

The "Sausage" was ours.

On the Jerusalem highway my convoy was brought to a virtual standstill because of a roadblock at the foot of "Finland Forest" near the Shimshon Junction. A Sherman tank blocked part of the road and a small *deux chevaux* car belonging to a Belgian tourist, who had tried to overtake the tank, was blocking the other half. Behind stretched a long line of armored half-tracks whose drivers were shouting and gesticulating. Finally a young officer took the initiative, walked up to the tourist, apologized politely, and asked her to get out of her car. A heavy-weight half-track drew near and unceremoniously pushed the *deux chevaux* into the ditch at the side of the road. Once again unimpeded the traffic began to move, and the armored half-tracks rolled by; their passengers, unshaven reserve troops, waved at the Belgian tourist and offered their sympathy.

At 16.00 I contacted Arik by radio: "The road is one big mess. Uri's tanks and transport vehicles are all mixed up with civilian cars and it's tough to move. The Jerusalem highway must be closed to civilian traffic. Station military police at the Shimshon Junction and don't let anyone through. Divert all civilian vehicles to the Beit Govrin road!"

I stopped crawling on the heels of the 10th Brigade by ordering the driver to turn toward Hartuv and go up to Jerusalem along the dirt track paralleling the railway line.

Again I contacted Arik: "What about the 60th Jordanian Brigade?"

"They haven't yet begun to move from where they were," he said, meaning that they were still in the Jordan Valley, so that my time-table, according to which they would not reach the hilltop till dawn tomorrow, was still accurate.

"Is Motta on the way?"

"On the way, and his flock with him" (meaning that his brigade was also en route for Jerusalem). "But he can't start before midnight" (meaning he cannot attack).

"That's quite all right. Go on pressing for Moshik's place" (Latrun).

Arik replied: "About the place, an alert has been given for tonight" (for possible action). "Meanwhile means are being assembled."

"Fine. Add the Command reconnaissance unit and the front'll crumble."

To Sur Baher

At 16.15 Arik announced: "Received confirmation to take Sur Baher!"

Such an announcement attested the dramatic change in the G.H.Q. attitude. This was the first agreed-upon conquest of any consequence; Government House had, after all, been taken only in response to Jordan's having occupied it. The deep flanking movement of the 10th Brigade as well as the impending paratroop attack on Sheikh Jarrah, although apparently aggressive, were actually defensive, for the purpose of protecting Mt. Scopus and Jerusalem from Jordanian attack.

It seemed to me that if they confirmed the capture of Sur Baher, they would confirm other attacks, such as Latrun. Time, therefore, was pressing and I urged my driver to hurry.

In a later conversation with H.Q., I asked Borka how things were going and he replied that, although the orders regarding the "bulge" (Latrun) were unchanged, we should be ready for night action, but not without specific confirmation. He added, "I doubt we can take the 'bulge' with the Command's forces."

I quickly weighed the pros and cons. My chief-of-staff was not the only one with misgivings about the Latrun fortress, and although I did not share his doubts, I could not ignore them. I therefore told Borka to add Ehud Shani (commander of the armored half-track unit) to those dealing with the bulge.

Borka then said something which caused me a moment's anxiety: "In Zunik's sector they've discovered a couple of dozen heavies [tanks]." I wondered if that meant a Jordanian attack on Natanya and if these were the tanks of the front-line armored battalion which had been bivouacked north of the Triangle, or if they belonged to the 60th Brigade, which had somehow crept in and got up on the ridges and continued west without our air force spotting them. Perhaps my entire calculations were wrong, and the Legion wouldn't attack in the Jerusalem sector at all, but in the Sharon, to try to cut Israel in two.

But to me it did not seem possible that an entire armored brigade had managed to escape the air force vigilance. If Borka was talking about a couple of dozen tanks, or, say, two platoons, it might be a local force deployed for a local operation, and I therefore told Borka that Yusuf (the commander of the armored force) could handle twenty tanks or so.

It turned out to be a false alarm. The Jordanian tanks in Zunik's sector withdrew without incident. I reverted to the matter of Latrun: "If everything is in order, you will advance on the bulge with Ehud's assistance."

He of course replied that they would be ready.

At 16.40 we left the dirt road and climbed to the asphalt leading from Bar-Giora to Tzuba. In minutes we were at the Tzuba Junction, about a dozen kilometers from Jerusalem and could see the roofs of the city. Not far from where we were stood Hadassah Hospital, with smoke rising from its chimneys, and the rays of the sinking sun reflected from its windows, shining like so many electric lights. At the edge of the road, I halted my Command group convoy. The Command artillery officer, Lt. Colonel Davidi, spread his map on the ground, ready to lay down fire to support the 10th Brigade assault, and began to check his radio communications system.

I telephoned H.Q. and asked Borka when Uri would start.

"I don't know," was the answer. "Not at the time decided upon."

For Borka's sake I said that our minefields were along Uri's route, in the center and to the left (they were near Mevaseret Yerushalayim and had been laid on my authorization two days ago, after the visit of Moshe Dayan), and would have to be removed before Uri went in. Then I asked him about the situation in Jerusalem.

"Everything is in our hands," he replied.

"See that they fly our flag from Government House and from the 'Bell.' Make sure the paratroops have flags with them."

The Inked-In Flag

There had been several flag-flying affairs. When we descended from Mt. Zion to the Old City in 1948, we had no flag with us, partly because in the Palmach we did not bother with such matters, so that when David Shaltiel asked me to fly the flag from the Dormition Church, I shrugged my shoulders. Where would I have found one? Nine months later, when the vanguard of the Negev Brigade reached Eilat, in Operation FACT, we still had no flag with us. The "inked-in" flag flown from the flagpole of the Um-Rashrash police station in March 1949 was a sheet, with the Star of David drawn in blue ink.

This time the Israeli flag, brought by one of the tank commanders, was raised above Government House in half an hour. After the observers had been evacuated and the U.N. flag lowered and removed, the tank commander whisked the Israeli flag from his pack and handing it to Yossi, commander of the reconnaissance unit, said: "Take it. The flagpole must not be without a flag."

Before the battle for the "sausage" position was over, Eliezer Amitai, who had been following its progress by radio from his observation-post atop the Histadrut building, decided to throw in Lt. Colonel Gideon's battalion. He ordered Gideon to leave the camp on Mt. Herzl and rush to Ramat Rahel, ready for action against the "Bell" position and Sur Baher village. At the conference of the Command's officers after the war, the Jerusalem Brigade commander explained that since the war of independence, a myth about the capabilities of the Jordanian army had persisted and he wanted to destroy it by capturing all the Legion's strongpoints in southern Jerusalem.

Gideon's battalion lacked transport facilities, as did all the others, and he began the long march from Mt. Herzl on foot.

Major Amos bombarded command H.Q. with requests to broaden the assault towards the "Bell" position until Arik Regev finally told him that the attack on Sur Baher had been authorized by Major-General Ezer Weizman. Ephraim Furan, chief-of-staff to General Weizman, was to say later that the Central Command chaps had squeezed the capture of the West Bank out of G.H.Q. drop by drop.

Amos radioed Dreizin, whose men were just taking the "Sausage" redoubt: "Can you carry on and take the 'Bell' and Sur Baher?"

Dreizin hesitated. His force, remnants of several units, was tired. Not only had there been casualties but, more important, they were short of ammunition. He was well acquainted with the "Bell" strong-point and its strong fortifications. But he hesitated only a moment, because the "Bell" fronted towards Ramat Rahel and his force could surprise it from the rear, from the direction of Sur Baher. Speed was therefore essential, he thought, before the soldiers in the fortified position had time to organize for peripheral defense.

"Ready to advance on the 'Bell'," he announced, "as long as we get ammunition."

Taking the "Bell"

He needed time to get ready. Soon an ancient armored vehicle, one of the two of the Mt. Scopus convoy, arrived from town loaded with ammunition, which was distributed among the tanks and armored half-tracks. Lt. Colonel Dreizin, biting his lip to deaden the pain of his injured arm, prepared for battle. At the head of the column he again placed the three tanks, and behind them the reconnaissance unit's half-tracks, some of which were empty. Dreizin intended to use them to pick up the men who had seized the "Sausage" position and were now reorganizing at the farthest end of the fortress. But when the column passed the "Sausage," the assault force was spread out along the entire position, tired and short of ammunition. They could not be quickly assembled and organized for battle, and time was of the essence.

Dreizin, therefore, carried on with his column of three tanks, four armored half-tracks and a jeep. They climbed the winding road to the "Sausage" fort, through Sur Baher village to Bethlehem. Here fierce mortar fire rained down upon the column, sending one of the tanks off the roadway into the wadi. The whole crew was wounded. The remaining tanks continued to lead the tiny convoy to the rear entrance to the "Bell" positon. Passing the shuttered and silent village, the column laid down a barrage of fire on Sur Baher's houses.

As they approached the "Bell," the tanks took up posts from which they could reduce the concrete bunkers to rubble with their guns. Dreizin's armored command car arrived just as some Legionnaires leaped from one of the damaged bunkers, to be cut down by the C.O. with his machine-gun. Completely exhausted, he urged his men off the vehicles and into the trenches. Yossi, commanding the reconnaissance unit, and the men in the half-track went on.

Mopping up was simple at first. The Legionnaires, surprised when the Israelis appeared at the rear, retreated to the flanks of the fortress on the lower part of the hill. Dreizin and his men rapidly reached the heart of the fortified position, the command bunker on top of the hill, attacked it with hand-grenades and took it. Then the force divided into two parts, one led by the battalion C.O. and the other by the C.O. of the reconnaissance unit. They invaded two communication trenches sloping down from the top of the hill, and from then on mopped up and captured position after position.

At this point, Asher Dreizin was wounded in the arm once again by hand-grenade fragments. Stopping briefly, he became aware that only a handful of fighting men were with him. The other two half-tracks had not arrived.

Climbing back to the top of the position on to the road, he passed the two tanks still pouring covering fire from their machine guns, and turned toward Sur Baher village. There he discovered the half-tracks, which had crashed into the wall of a building and stalled. The men, not knowing where to go, were waiting near their vehicles. Dreizin sent them on foot to the fortress and into the two trenches to continue mopping up.

It was so dark that the mopping-up teams had to advance with caution, but the enemy appeared to have fled. Positions were checked and reported empty by returning teams. During this period, Dreizin called the battalion commander: "Complete the capture of the position immediately. Gideon's men are advancing towards you from Ramat Rahel. Be sure not to open fire on them. When they arrive, turn the fortress over to them, leave your tanks, and return at once to Government House."

Asher Dreizin ordered the teams to enter the bunker at the top of the hill and under no circumstances to open fire. A soldier reported that a wounded fellow-teammate was lying in the lower trench and two men were sent with a stretcher to fetch him. A soldier with a flashlight was posted at the top of the bunker and directed to signal the relief force. The battle seemed to have ended and the tired men sank down at the entrance to the bunker and lit cigarettes.

Suddenly gunfire burst from the lower bunker. Dreizin thought his men were shooting at the relieving force, and as he sprang out of the bunker shouting, "I told you not to shoot!" his words strangled in his throat. Opposite, from the dugout, leaped seven Legionnaires, their guns spitting fire. These, the fort's last defenders, had hidden in one of the side trenches and were trying to escape under cover of darkness. They had come upon the two stretcher-bearers in the trench and killed them. Now that they had been discovered, they decided not to sell their lives cheaply. Surrounding the command bunker, they shot the battalion C.O.'s runner, an officer of Dreizin's crew, and a tank commander who happened to come around to ask what was new. The battalion C.O. was wounded again, this time in his other arm. Yossi and his men opened fire. Five Legionnaires fell; the remaining two vanished into the night.

The sudden battle had lasted only a minute and was followed by silence, punctured by shouts from the other men summoned by the shots to the bunker. There were fourteen of them, which meant that the "Bell" had been taken by not more than twenty men, six of whom were now casualties.

The relief force, after negotiating numerous barbed wire entanglements and minefields, arrived from Ramat Rahel. The dead and

10. Mobile command post at the Tzova Junction

wounded were collected, Dreizin's arm was bandaged, and he led his men back to Government House. There he organized the defenses of the palace in preparation for a possible counter-attack, and evacuated the wounded. Only after midnight, on specific order of Eliezer Amitai, did he evacuate himself to the hospital.

At the Junction

At 17.00 hours, I moved the command group to the junction opposite Givat Tzuba, where a few minutes later, Colonel Joseph Harpaz (Josh) joined me. Like many other senior officers, he was unemployed and wanted something to do. Having looked for me at Command H.Q. and at Jerusalem Brigade H.Q. he finally learned where I was. Now that he was there he was added to the command group.

As he had come from Jerusalem, I asked about things there.

"They're preparing to take the 'Sausage' and the 'Bell,' and capture Abu-Tor at the same time."

Our spot on the Jerusalem highway was in the middle of the war. In the dusk we could make out busloads of paratroopers snaking up the hills to Jerusalem. They passed us, and we could see the men, many somber, but some animated and talking. When they spotted us, a few of them waved.

I contacted the Jerusalem Brigade to inquire about preparations to support the paratroopers, and was told that the Jerusalem artillery was ready to close in on the police college and French Hill.

From beyond the hill opposite came the sound of explosions as the Legion continued to bombard Mevasseret Yerushalayim and Maoz-Zion. Every few moments an evacuation-tender carrying wounded arrived from there.

I contacted Arik to say that they were shelling Mevasseret and that I thought we should pay them back, but he said that there was no point at the moment, because the source of the shelling was still uncertain. (We learned later that these were the Jordanian batteries positioned at Hizma, northeast of Tel el-Ful.)

I suggested that Arik ask the air force to deal with the batteries shooting at Mevasseret, but he thought the idea was not feasible, because the 60th Brigade was moving and the air force was busy with them.

The information was both worrisome and helpful, because, though it solved the puzzle of the 60th Brigade, which was going, as I had expected, more or less according to my estimated timetable, the Pattons of the 60th would soon be in our sector and our armored force was still far from the field where I had chosen to do battle with them. I hoped the air force would strike at the Jordanian armor, delaying it and giving us extra time. And that is just what happened.

"Fougas" Over Jerusalem

At 17.13 I again contacted Arik to ask for news of Uri.

"He's been held up. He's in a low area and we have no contact with him, but he certainly won't be attacking by 17.30. By the way, in a quarter of an hour we shall have captured the "Bell.""

"You'd better do something about the shooting on Mevasseret!"

"Are they shooting from there?"

"Constantly. Has the air force attacked the 60th?"

"They will in another fifteen minutes."

A few minutes later Arik radioed to report that he had planes to deal with the Jordanians who were shelling Mevasseret. I wanted to be able to watch Uri's half-track crossing over the Green Line, but before leaving I told Yosh to join the Jerusalem Brigade H.Q. as my liaison officer and to tell Eliezer that he had authority to take Abu-Tor.

"He should also take Mount Zion," I said. "Tell him the air force will attack Jordan's 60th Brigade. Our 10th Brigade is trying to get to Tel el-Ful. At the same time the 55th will attack the police college. The Jerusalem Brigade is to keep five tanks near the palace and all the rest are to be transferred to the paratroopers. I'll be on the Castel when the 10th begins its attack."

Yosh climbed aboard his jeep and raced off to Jerusalem and we started towards Kibbutz Tzuba for the Castel. 10th Brigade trucks crowded the highway and vehicles evacuating wounded were speeding for Mevasseret Yerushalayim, greatly delaying our progress.

Suddenly the radio blackout of the 10th was lifted and Uri replied to my signal.

Impatiently I asked about the situation.

"Beginning to go in," was the reply. "Please wait."

"Along a number of axes?"

'Yes. Please wait," he repeated.

"Ahead of you is a narrow belt of our mines, in depth of threes. Better remove them." They were doing just that, he informed me.

The roar of guns beyond Mevasseret and Ma'alei Hahamisha, Uri's two breakthrough axes, grew fiercer. Just as I was thinking he was getting mauled, Uri broke in to say that he was being heavily shelled and needed air support. When Arik reported that it would be another few minutes before they captured the "Bell," I told him that anti-battery fire should go up against the Jordanians at Anata and Hizma, and that Uri was in urgent need of planes. Arik promised to ask, but said that the chances were slight.

The Command artillery officer reported that an artillery battalion was in position to cover the 10th Brigade.

At the moment that Arik contacted me again, I saw planes over Jerusalem: "Fougas! What are Fougas doing over Jerusalem?" I shouted into the microphone.

"They're attacking the 60th Brigade. Part of the supporting force for Uri."

Simultaneously Uri began his attack, for which, in accordance with the plan, he was given a couple of planes to attack the radar redoubt.

THE BREAKTHROUGH

Breakthrough – Police School Sector

When the 10th Brigade was ordered to climb up to the Jerusalem sector to break through to the ridges via the radar redoubt and Sheikh Abdul-Aziz, nobody was surprised. At the time of the alert, the 10th Brigade had been told to plan the capture of these objectives also and its officers had reconnoitered there a few days prior to the war. But the timing of the order was unexpected. At midday on June 5th, after the reconnaissance company returned from checking the approach roads, the brigade had been ready to advance on Latrun. Assignments had been distributed among the battalions and plans of action completed, which were presented to the commanders in the H.Q. tent. All were concerned with the problem of the mine-fields, several belts of which were purported to surround the Latrun fortress. The battalion commanders were discussing the matter when the telephone rang. The Brigade C.O. picked it up, listened and said, "Roger." Replacing the receiver, he said, "The Latrun assignment is cancelled. We're going up to Jerusalem."

The battalion commanders immediately sped off in their jeeps for their tank laagers. "Radio blackout ended. Open communications instruments, prepare to move." Seven minutes after receiving the order to go to Jerusalem, the Brigade C.O., Colonel Uri Ben-Ari, had his plans in the hands of the battalion commanders:

The brigade will break through at the Ma'aleh Hahamisha-Motza sector for Tel el-Ful to do battle with the enemy's armor.

A armored battalion will capture the three radar fortifications. The method: split bunkers with tank fire and capture the objective by armored infantry assault. The battalion will move along the main highway to its assembly point at Ma'aleh Hahamisha.

B armored battalion will take the fortified positions of Sheikh Abdul-Aziz and Khirbet e-Lauza in the same way. The battalion will move along the Ramat Raziel to its assembly point in Mevasseret Yerushalayim.

Both battalions have another objective – Biddu village and from there the capture of Tel el-Ful.

11. Artillery fire in the eastern part of the city

C armored company, which includes two companies of Sherman tanks of the 50th Brigade, a company of Centurions which joined the Brigade a day ago, a company of armored infantry, and the Brigade reconnaissance unit, will function as reserves.

The 120-mm mortar battalion and the command group will deploy near Castel, the main H.Q. at Ramat Raziel and the rear H.Q. at Eshta'ol.

At 13.25 hours the plan was radioed to the battalion commanders; five minutes later they were ordered to move off. Tank engines, half-tracks, trucks and jeeps roared, as the huge convoy in transit formation lumbered towards the Jerusalem highway. While the Brigade was leaving, the C.O. drove past to Central Command H.Q. From there, after he and I met, he radioed the commander of the tank battalions and the reconnaissance company to meet him at the Bilu Junction. Our discussion had underlined the absolute necessity for the Brigade to reach Tel el-Ful by morning, at all costs, before the Jordanian 60th. In assessing the strength of the two fortified enemy positions on his route and the topographical conditions impeding the movement of the armored vehicles, he decided to exploit not only the sole axis which would be available to him with the capture of the Sheikh Abdul-Aziz and Radar positions, but also to use all other possible axes.

When he met the commanders at the Bilu Junction at 14.15 hours, he changed the original plan by ordering the tank battalion to break through another movement axis at Tel el-Ful via Beit Kika and Beit Hanina and the reconnaissance company to capture Beit-Iksa, in preparation for a fourth alternative route. The tank battalion C.O., Lt. Colonel Zwicka, therefore sent his company commanders to Jerusalem to look over the route along which they were to effect a break-through.

The Brigade advanced slowly, delayed by the private cars on the Jerusalem highway, which had not been closed to civilian traffic as promised. Now and then tank engines overheated, had to stop, and blocked the road. "B" tank battalion, whose objectives were farther east, caused another delay when it passed "A" battalion, which had left its laager first. As the units neared the break-through area, the Jordanians spotted them from high on the ridges and bombarded them heavily, damaging a number of vehicles and wounding their occupants. Evacuation vehicles then joined the interminable convoy and maneuvered among the armor in their haste to get the wounded to Jerusalem. Some units split up. In the confusion of the bombardment, they missed the roads to their assembly areas and continued towards Jerusalem. Runners had to be sent to bring them back.

At 17.15, only four hours after the orders reached the laager in the Ben-Shemen Forest, the units began to cross the Green Line.

Crossing the Green Line

"A" battalion was the first into action, moving against the three radar positions, where the Harel warriors had spilled so much blood in 1948. There was no need to explain to the commanders the importance of the radar redoubts, the Brigade's westernmost objective. Not only were the Brigade's exploits in the War of Independence common knowledge, but everyone, except the "B" Company commander, Haim Kanon, had gone on the advance reconnaissance tour on the Sabbath and peered at the redoubts through their field-glasses.

With the battalion, when it left the Ben Shemen laager, were the tank company and the engineering platoon, which had received no assignments because of the hasty leave-taking. Taking advantage of his battalion's halt at the Nachshon Junction, to allow "B" battalion to pass, Lt. Col. Yigal asked for more directives from the Brigade C.O. and assembled his staff for a short briefing.

The convoy was bombarded so heavily as it neared its objective that the disposition of forces was disrupted. Only four tanks had thus far arrived at the assembly point designated by the C.O. Brigade, near the memorial to the Brigade's 1948 dead. Their communications equipment was so faulty that the platoon commander, Captain Uzi, had to try three tanks before finding one with equipment in working order. Heavy fire from the strongpoints greeted the four tanks hunching into position, three on the hill to the right of Ma'aleh Hahamisha and one inside the kibbutz itself. The operations officer scanned the highway for the other tanks, spotting two, then three more, all of which he directed to positions near the kibbutz cowsheds. Immediately the tanks opened fire.

The armored infantry were next into action. Haim Kanon, who could not find his objective, was told that it was the hill in front of him with a house on top of it. "B" Company had obviously reached the foot of the fortress by this time.

At 17.20, in spite of brutal bombardment on "C" Company and the tanks, precise shooting silenced one radar bunker after another and even the shelling stopped, because the Jordanian artillery observer officer had apparently been hit. Only a few 0.5 mm machine guns went on firing, and these the tanks were unable to detect.

At 18.00 hours the order was given to attack. "C" Company rushed to the edge of the minefield and was stopped and all the men were ordered off the half-tracks. The sappers opened a passage through the field and within ten minutes the company had penetrated Radar I. Opposition had been extremely slight – the tanks had shelled all the bunkers and those Legionnaires who had not taken to their heels were immobilized. By 18.30 "C" Company commander Avi Keren had radioed that the objective was taken.

The battle for Radar II was equally quick and decisive. "B" Company commander advanced over terrain that became too steep for the half-tracks and had to be covered on foot. Supporting fire from tanks and other armored half-tracks effectively silenced the enemy, but there was a slight delay at the barbed wire entanglement. The men had neither wire-cutters nor flame-throwers with them, but one of the officers managed to sever the wire with bullets from his Uzzi, and shattered four entanglements, through which the men forced their way.

Opposition was slight, and the stronghold was cleared in an hour, just before night fell. Haim Kanon removed his men from the trenches and deployed them on peripheral defense at one of the corners of the position, reinforcing their firing power with enemy weapons now cleaned and ready for action. Then he despatched his three prisoners-of-war and four wounded to the rear and reported that Radar II had been taken.

Although he had had faith in his plan, even the Brigade commander was surprised when Major Igal reported that the big radar had been taken. Very moved, a 1948 Harel veteran, he shouted into the microphone: "So fast? You're positive?" The C.O. of the battalion reassured him and was told: "On with all your might."

Even before taking the second fortified position, the battalion commander had begun preparing for the assault on the third. He summoned the tank of the deputy company commander, Amram, and advanced his armored half-track to the perimeter of the minefield. The sappers moved in and defused the anti-vehicle mines in their path, followed by Amram's tank, which exploded the liberally dispersed booby-traps, and finally by the battalion C.O.'s half-track edging carefully through the tracks made by the tank.

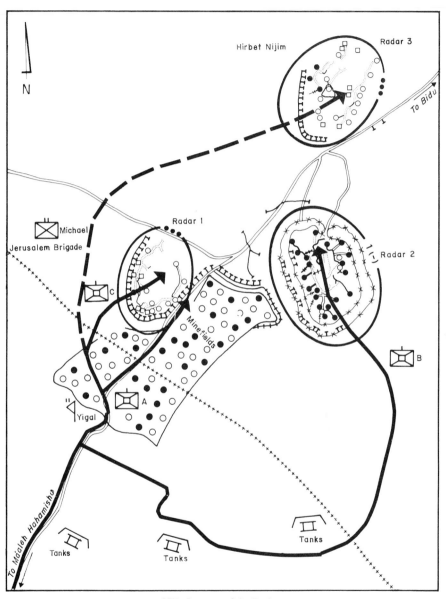

VII Capture of the Radar

...Travail...of the Sappers

At 19.45 hours the sappers were at the base of the already taken Radar
I. Despite their precautions, and the caterpillar tracks of the tank, the
half-track struck an anti-vehicle mine, and its driver was wounded.
From then on calamity followed calamity. Two of the sappers trod on
booby-traps and were evacuated to the rear, leaving the spearhead
without sappers and halting the advance. When the battalion C.O.
called for the tanks, the first to arrive was the company commander's,
which rammed into a heap of mines newly removed from the field.
They exploded; Captain Uzi was blown out of the tank and badly
wounded. One sapper stepped on an anti-personnel mine, and
immediately afterward the leg of another was blown off at the knee.
His screams troubled the air even after he had been taken away.

The column was bogged down in the middle of a minefield and the
sappers were numbered by their losses. To renew their courage, the
battalion O.C. summoned their platoon commander, Lt. Yaakov, and
told him to use flame-throwers, no matter where, just to give the men
a boost. The platoon's one flame-thrower, 9 meters long, was brought
in and blew up all the mines along its length, the battalion C.O.
walking in the lead, a prod in his hand. Behind him came the sappers'
platoon commander and after him two sappers, all walking to the end
of the minefield, where they were stopped by an anti-tank obstacle of
concrete dragons' teeth, behind which stretched an anti-tank ditch
three meters deep, and a bunker a meter thick. To the overwrought
battalion C.O. it seemed too powerful for his force to overcome, but
he persisted, and ordered the sappers' commander to blow up the
obstacle and the walls of the ditch, after which he and his men
dismantled the bunker and filled the ditch with stones, back-
breaking, hopeless labor. Slowly the ditch filled up, and after an hour
and a half, with the walls of the ditch blown in, the battalion C.O.
decided to cross it.

The tank revved up, lit its headlamps, and edged cautiously forward, all but turning over. Finally it slid into the ditch, righted itself,
and began to climb up the far side, seeming, before the breathless
men, to slip backwards. With a roar of its engine, its tracks gripped
the crumbling earth. One more heave, and it was across. The remaining tanks advanced in its tracks.

The battalion C.O. meanwhile contacted Lt. Colonel Michael
Paikes (killed while directing the capture of Abu-Tor), commander of

the Jerusalem Brigade battalion deployed to defend the Ma'aleh Hahamish area, who, though disappointed that an apparent outsider had been given an assignment which he thought belonged to his battalion, was amazed at how speedily the armored force had overcome so powerful a position. His battalion, he thought, could not have managed it with so few casualties, and, learning about the difficulty of getting through the minefields, offered to send his sappers' unit to help. As a result three Jerusalem Battalion sappers were wounded as well as eight of the armored battalion.

Neutralizing the minefields and crossing the anti-tank barrier were only two of Major Igal's problems. His battalion's time schedule had been disrupted by the holdup at the barrier and Radar III had not yet been taken. In spite of the lateness of the hour, it would take some time before his tanks and armored half-tracks could maneuver the minefields in the murky darkness and, advancing carefully and slowly, prepare to attack.

Aware of the problems, Paikes once again offered to help. His men had nothing to do and he would gladly take the position on behalf of the armored battalion.

When Igal radioed that a friendly force had turned up to help take Radar III, the Brigade Commander had no idea what he was talking about but gave permission nevertheless. Paikes was delighted. Igal fired mortars against Radar III and Paikes led his men in in a foot-slogging attack on the fortifications.

At 01.30 the "A" Battalion C.O. announced that all three Radar redoubts were theirs. They had maneuvered the mine-field, crossed the anti-tank barrier, and would go on to Biddu. But the Brigade Commander ordered them to wait, because "B" Battalion would advance on Biddu.

"B" Battalion to Abdul-Aziz

"B" Battalion had been on the go since leaving the laager in the Ben-Shemen Forest, halting for a moment to pick up a sapper platoon and a tank company, and to return to the tank battalion the company of Centurions which had been commandeered for the attack on Latrun. Then the battalion rushed down the road, stopping only at the approaches of the Castel, where it was bombed mercilessly by the Jordanians.

When the battalion was attacked, the C.O., Lt. Colonel Aaron, was in his half-track with the company commanders, driving to the Castel to meet the Brigade C.O., receive last orders, and take a final look at their objectives.

The nearest fortified position, right on the Green Line and considered the battalion's major obstacle, was the Sheikh Abdul-Aziz fortress, a Jordanian attempt to build a fortified settlement in imitation of the Israelis. It had failed, and the hill had once again been converted into a military position, which over the years had been dug into the ground – bunkers with deep, concrete-lined communication trenches – and surrounded by barbed-wire entanglements and minefields, an anti-vehicle mine next to an anti-personnel one. The original houses were used to bivouac soldiers. The second objective, Hirbet-a-Lauze, lay about 800 meters north of Sheikh Abdul-Aziz, a position that, after the battle, turned out to be the stronger, its communication trenches deeper and its automatic weapons more numerous.

The battalion convoy drew near to the Castel, where, in the fierce shelling, three men were killed and many more wounded. Once again the battalion C.O. and his company commanders went over the battle plan, which strongly resembled that of "A" Battalion.

At 16.45 the tanks maneuvered into position. The force which reached Mount Navar found that it had been previously occupied by Lt. Colonel Zwicka Ofer's Jerusalem Brigade battalion. The tanks had just started to over-ride it, since there was no other option, when an officer of the Jerusalem Battalion showed up to warn them about cases of ammunition in the tents. They were dismantled, and the company commander asked that the tanks be moved on in spite of Zwicka Ofer's warning that they were on the edge of a minefield laid the night before by Ofer's own forces.

The tanks, however, were moved cautiously. At 17.00 hours the shelling of the enemy positions began. The accurate marksmanship of the tankmen allowed "I" Company to draw near the objective. They rode on armored half-tracks led by four tanks, two of which struck mines. The others passed them and crossed over to the barbed-wire entanglement around the Jordanian minefield. A heavy barrage of shells behind them landed on the road, not touching the company. Since there was no Jordanian fire, the company commander, Asa Yagori, remarked to his deputy, 2nd Lt. Uzi Rosen, that the enemy had apparently run away, and he called on the sappers, who had been seconded to the company, to open a path through the minefield. Just as the sappers jumped out of their truck, a barrage of shells rained down, forcing them to take cover between the armored half-tracks.

The battalion commander, who was behind "I" Company, drove his half-track up to the platoon commander's, shouting "If we stay here we'll be bombed to hell and gone. Go it on foot!" Asa jumped down, placed a detachment from the nearest half-track in twos in front of the caterpillar tracks of the lead tank, and ordered them to go forward shoulder to shoulder into the minefield and open up a movement axis with the help of cleaning rods. He led them himself. The advance began, the tanks following, with the rest of the platoon on foot behind them, in the spoors made by the caterpillar tracks. Throughout, shells rained down. One soldier was hit, another struck by shrapnel from a booby-trap exploded by the tank tracks and the men, in their maddeningly slow advance, began to lose their nerve. Asa shouted to them to leap from rock to rock over the terrain and thus to get to the fence of the redoubt more quickly. One of the first arrivals threw himself onto the fence and the others climbed over his body and burst inside. Asa sent No. 1 platoon to the houses on top of the hill and No. 2 into the trench near the fence. Both advanced quickly and found the houses and the trench empty and the dead body of a Jordanian soldier in what was apparently the commander bunker. It seemed for a moment that the platoon C.O. had guessed correctly that the enemy had fled, and the men relaxed a little.

Suddenly a barrage of mortar shells peppered the redoubt, automatically directed from a maze of communication trenches and underground positions to which the redoubts defenders had fled. The labyrinth had gone unobserved.

The men were being hit. "Into the trenches!" shouted the platoon C.O. and himself led the assault. As he leaped into the bunker he was struck and killed at once. But his men followed, trapping the Legionnaires in a corner of the trench and wiping them out with hand grenades.

Lt. Colonel Aaron was with the men in the redoubt and organized the platoon for peripheral defense, appointing 2nd Lt. Uzi Rosen commander. Uzi, a young architect who had returned only a few weeks earlier from a lengthy post-graduate course in the U.S.A., warned Lt. Col. Aaron that he must be patient with someone so new at the job.

Hirbet e-Lauza Falls

When at 19.30 the battalion C.O. reported to the Brigade commander that objective I was taken, the breakthrough seemed imminent, but fighting was in fact protracted.

The Jordanians intensified their bombardment, aiming their shells with great accuracy on Sheikh Abdul-Aziz and the minefield in front. The sappers, ordered to widen the passage through the field, were hampered by the shelling and the battalion's remaining forces were stranded on the other side of the minefield.

Since Hirbet e-Lauza was peripherally defended, the battalion C.O. changed his plan and ordered "K" Company, scheduled to reach Hirbet e-Lauza in a wide flanking movement, to advance to the Sheikh Abdul-Aziz position and attack it frontally.

The tanks reached the edge of the minefield in Stygian darkness, broken only by explosions and tracer bullets, so that the drivers could make out only with utmost difficulty the white lines marking the path through the minefield and follow them with their tanks.

The breakthrough was just wide enough for the force to manage on foot, but not for 3-5 meter-wide tanks, whose tracks detonated booby-traps when they moved into the field. The men of "K" Company behind them, marching as close to them as possible for the cover they provided against bombardment and heavy machine-gun fire, began to be hit by shrapnel from the exploding mines, and the tanks themselves slipped their tracks one after another and were immobilized. Only four reached the battalion commander on the captured redoubt.

Gal reinforced "K" Company and ordered them to attack Hirbet e-Lauza. But the attempted direct assault along the road leading from Sheikh Abdul-Aziz to Hirbet e-Lauza failed and the battalion C.O. called off the attack, reverting to the original flanking plan, this time from the left.

In the dark and over difficult terrain, the force set out to reduce the gap between them and their objective. The terraces were as tall as a man, and the march was painfully slow. One platoon blundered into the beginning of a wadi, vanished, and was found only after considerable time. The men moved tortoise-like through what they thought was a minefield, but turned out to be soft earth mounded up by moles. Eventually, however, the force crept stealthily toward the enemy position from an unexpected direction, and at 22.00 hours crossed the fence and erupted into the trenches. There was fierce, close-range fighting, decided by hand-grenades and riflebutts. In half an hour it was all over, Hirbet e-Lauza fell.

But the battalion's hardships had not ended. In the assault 15 were killed and 42 wounded, and now, the objective taken, the battalion could not renew its advance, because its companies were split up between the two captured strongpoints and its vehicles and reserves were still on the far side of the minefield. Clearing the minefield and moving the battalion's units took all night and not until 4.00 o'clock on Tuesday morning could they advance once more. They took the village of Beit Surik without a struggle and were ordered to march via Biddu to Nabi Samuel.

Six Tanks at Hirbet Zahara

The tank battalion which was originally to have been kept in reserve but had been given an independent mission after the Brigade had set out, carried out the Brigade's assignment and reached Tel el-Ful on Tuesday morning, greatly reduced in size. After its breakthrough from Motza to Tel el-Ful via Beit Hanina, the battalion C.O. Lt. Colonel Zwicka and his company commanders hastened to Jerusalem to look at the axis through which he was to move his battalion. The unit consisted of two companies of Sherman M-50 tanks, commanded by Major Eitan Arieli and Major Uri Baraz, an armored infantry company under Captain David Cana'ani, and Major Aaron's Centurion tank platoon, which had been attacked 24 hours earlier. While the officers were in the Romema Quarter looking over their movement axis, the battalion and the Brigade convoy were slogging along the Jerusalem highway. The units lumbered toward their jumping-off position. Through heavy bombardment, which made for confusion, the armored infantry company almost joined "A" Battalion's assault at Ma'aleh Hahamisha and were extricated at the last moment by Lt. Colonel Eldad, the deputy Brigade commander, and sent toward Motza.

At 18.00 hours the battalion left the highway and began to negotiate the difficult route up from Cedars Valley (Emek Ha'arazim), where the tanks, especially the Centurions, immediately crashed into rocks and boulders, slipping their caterpillar tracks. A Jordanian artillery barrage, although it caused no casualties, took the drivers' minds off the route and more and more tanks were put out of action.

(During the night, the battalion C.O. was instructed to send a tank company to help "B" Battalion capture the Sheikh Abdul-Aziz fortified positions. The company selected managed with difficulty to crawl out of the battalion's forward movement axis, retrace its route, and

reach "B" Battalion as it was preparing to march from Hirbet e-Lauza
to Biddu.)

The battalion continued its difficult climb, the tanks smashing their
tracks against the rocks. The last Centurions held out only until Beit
Kika, where they foundered, leaving the battalion with only six
Shermans, about ten armored half-tracks and one mortar battery.
This was the force to arrive at dawn on Tuesday at Hirbet Zahara, the
hilltop opposite Tel el-Ful, to do battle with the 60th Jordanian
Brigade and prevent the capture of Mt. Scopus.

Breakthrough at Beit Iksa

The reconnaissance company was another unit fighting its way up the
stony route assigned by the Brigade commander. When it was given
its objective, somewhere near Ramla, it was minus six jeeps, taken by
the deputy Brigade commander to lead his units towards their jumping-off positions, as well as two jeeps and three armored half-tracks
marooned in the heavy traffic on the Jerusalem highway and not
recovered for several hours.

The company reached the bridge between Motza and Mevasseret
Yerushalayim at 16.00 hours and was led by C.O. Major Amnon
Eshcoli to a twisted bend in the valley, the route, he thought, to Beit
Iksa. The unit was under constant enemy observation throughout and
barraged by mortar shells. As the road became less and less negotiable
by vehicles, the men had virtually to carry the cars on their shoulders.
One of the armored half-tracks slipped a track and stopped, and
another crashed into an anti-tank barrier on the outskirts of Beit Iksa
and overturned. The remnants – the Command half-track, two mor-
tar-carrying half-tracks, and two jeeps – attacked the village, whose
defenders had only light weapons, and captured it. The enemy had
fled.

During the night the damaged half-track was repaired and brought
to the village and the two jeeps floundering on the highway rejoined
the company. At 2 o'clock in the morning the company was rewarded
for its back-breaking effort to open the route to Beit Iksa. The tank
battalion commander complained over the radio about his fuel shortage, making it necessary to find a way up with a tanker convoy
without having to run the gauntlet under enemy fire. The company's
C.O. interrupted and and told the tank commander about the tough
but safe route they had just negotiated. The commander of the Brigade engineers raced for it. On his way he "borrowed" a bulldozer

belonging to Keren Kayemet Le-Israel, the Jewish National Fund, to help him lay a truck route through the wadi. The fuel convoy made its way to Beit Hanina along the Beit Iksa axis.

At 3.30 a.m. the company handed Beit Iksa to a unit of the Jerusalem Brigade and then went on, this time along the more comfortable Beit Hanina-Nabi Samuel junction, where it was once again overtaken by the war.

13,505 Shells

At my command post near Tsuba, the minutes had become hours. Everywhere the war raged, the roaring guns and crackling mortar-fire in the breakthrough sector of the 10th Brigade loud in our ears and brutal to our senses. I didn't want to disturb Uri by asking for progress reports, but suggested to the Command artillery officer to add support to the 10th. At 18.00 Yosh returned to Jerusalem to say that Sur Baher and the "Bell" position were about to fall into our hands and that the battle would probably be over in half an hour.

At 18.23 I called Uri to get a report and was told by his deputy Eldad that Abdul-Aziz, the first objective, had been taken and the Radar was being attended to. At 18.30 Uri himself came on the line to say that the force at Aziz had withdrawn and that he was advancing cautiously.

Fifteen minutes later the Command artillery officer, Lt. Colonel Davidi, reported that they had finished supporting the 10th Brigade and were moving elsewhere. So meager was our stock of ammunition that the artillery on the Jerusalem front had to measure out its shells and ration each sector. When the war was over we learned that the shells fired by us on the Jerusalem front during the three days of the war totaled 13,505, in a battle using three brigades, an entire division. The American forces, in comparison, fired 200,000 shells during the same length of time on the Monte Cassino front in Italy in World War II.

At 18.55 I phoned Arik Regev at Ramla to hear the news about Eliezer, who, I was told, was climbing up to the "Bell." Arik said that there was fairly heavy shelling in town and that they were trying to get the Air Force to make a few bombing runs over the enemy's artillery batteries before dark.

"What's up with Uri?" I asked. Although only a few kilometers separated me from his Command group, the mountains between us and the proximity of telephone lines prevented direct contact with his headquarters.

"He's advancing on Radar II, is all I know."

Arik said that the other sectors were quiet, that Moshik was getting ready to attack Latrun, and that Motta had arrived in Jerusalem.

Paratroops in Jerusalem

The 66th Battalion was the first paratroop unit in the city. Like the entire Brigade, the men of the 66th travelled in buses, carrying their personal weapons and limited ammunition, because the bulk of their supplies, as will be recalled, had been packed in parachutes and left on the airfield. The battalion commander, Lt. Colonel Yossi, therefore wanted to get in early to equip his men more effectively. The Jerusalem Brigade had instructions to issue what he needed out of the quartermaster stores. Yossi left his men in the buses in the Beit Hakerem Quarter of Jerusalem and took a small Command group to Brigade headquarters. After a wild journey through streets strewn with cut telephone lines. electric cables, uprooted trees and rubble, dodging the unceasing shells, they arrived at their destination to find it deserted. The soldiers on guard told them that headquarters had been moved. "Where to?" Yossi asked. They shrugged their shoulders. The battalion C.O. happened to spot an officer he recognized, who told him that headquarters had been shifted to the Evelina de Rothschild School, but where that was the Command group officers, who were not Jerusalemites, had no idea. While they were wandering along the ripped-up streets, however, Yossi met the deputy Brigade C.O., Lt. Colonel Moshe Stempel, who had just come from the school and been told that Major Amos, chief of "C" Branch (Operations) of the Jerusalem Brigade, had returned to his old headquarters.

They all retraced their steps.

"At about 4 o'clock," Amos recalled, "a group of officers and sergeants of the reconnaissance and intelligence units of the 55th Brigade turned up and told me they had been given the job of taking Sheikh Jarrah, a surprise to me, because I understood that the Jerusalem and 10th Brigades were to make the attack. So when the 55th came asking for air-reconnaissance maps of the objective, I was at a loss. I told my operations sergeant to take down whatever was on the wall and give it to them."

The 66th Battalion commander collected what was offered: one map and one air photograph. (Additional copies were sent later but reached the paratroop units just before they set forth on their mission.) Yossi then went to the Histadrut building, on the invitation of the Brigade commander, to observe the breakthrough sector.

Meanwhile the deputy Brigade C.O. waited with Major Amos for the equipment and ammunition from the quartermaster stores, after which Amos returned to the Evelina de Rothschild School. There he met Motta Gur, who was looking for an officer acquainted with the Line to go with him to the observation post atop the Histadrut building. Amos suggested the so-called Fences' Commander (the C.O. of the company currently holding the municipal line), who accompanied Motta to the Histadrut building, on whose roof he met Eliezer Amitai.

Yossi and Motta inspected the Municipal Line carefully, especially the police school and Ammunition Hill (Givat Ha'Tachmoshet) nearby. Both strongholds were belching smoke and fire; the Jerusalem artillery had begun the softening-up process. Then Motta returned to the Evelina de Rothschild School, where Amos gave him a basement room, in fact the natural science classroom. Motta spread his maps and reconnaissance photographs on the floor, and began to plan his Brigade's assault.

At 7 o'clock that evening I was with the Command group near the Castel. Shells whined overhead, some, particularly the curved trajectories, exploding in the immediate neighborhood. The Chief-of-Staff contacted me from Command headquarters in Ramla to say that the C.O.G.S. had telephoned and received a full report and that my father-in-law was there and had also been given information. (My father-in-law, David Hacohen M.K., on his way to a meeting of the Knesset in Jerusalem with M.K.s Arieh Bahir and Dr. Rimalt, had been stopped by the military police near Ramla and decided to visit the Command. Borka welcomed them warmly, explained what was going on, and when asked how they could be of help, replied that they could help best by not interfering.) Borka suggested to me that all the forces move by night from the captured positions to avoid casualties from counter-bombardment.

It was the remark of a cautious man, working according to the book. Indeed, it is usual in war games not to leave the occupying force at the objective exactly because of possible bombardment. As it happened, I had no intention of leaving anyone in the positions and hoped that by morning they would all be far away.

The Radar is Ours

When I contacted Uri at 19.20 he had the great news that Sheikh

6*

Abdul-Aziz and the Radar were taken, although not the entire stronghold as yet, because of the mines, which had to be removed one at a
time. He said that Beit Iksa was taken, but problems existed along the
final axis of the tank battalion, a very difficult route. If the Radar axis
were opened, he said, the third route would be abandoned. He went
on to detail further difficuties, particularly those of the tanks impaled
on the rocky boulders.

I listened to most of what he said with only half an ear, because his
words about the Radar drowned out all else.

"The Radar is really ours?" It was hard to believe. We had fought
bitter battles there in the War of Independence and I knew its fearsome defenses.

In Zahal, when we wanted to practice taking an especially tough
objective, we used the Radar stronghold as an example, planning to
capture it with heavy artillery supported by numerous infantry, but
were never sure whether we'd thrown enough matériel into the operation. And now, in less than two hours, the Radar had been taken.
"The Radar is really ours?" I repeated.

Uri, in a voice hoarse with weariness, said simply, "It's ours."

Arik Regev radioed from Ramla to say that the defense minister was
in the Knesset, about to take his oath as a newly appointed cabinet
minister, and had asked that I present my report to him. Whereupon I
told Yosh to take over the command group, and to stay where we
were. "The 10th Brigade is to continue on to Nabi Samuel, and if it
succeeds – to A-Ram."

I set out for Jerusalem, past Hadassah Hospital, up the Ein Kerem
heights, and past Mount Herzl. Jerusalem lay ahead of us. To our left,
in the direction of the Tel Aviv highway, we could see the shells
flashing and hear the muffled thunder of the battle of the 10th Brigade
for the enemy positions. But even the lightning of the explosions
failed to penetrate the total darkness of Jerusalem. Its empty streets
only occasionally flickered with the shadows of air raid wardens, one
of whom shouted from the entrance of a building, "Turn out your
lights. There's a war on!"

Profoundly I admired the devotion of these people, all Jerusalem
veterans, uncomplaining survivors of 1948 who had endured the
endless years of life in a border town. They deserved peace and a
chance to rest, they whose hearts were heavy with fear for their sons
and grandsons in the thick of battle. But they waited not a moment to
respond when the call came. Of course they complained about their

tattered uniforms and the shortage of equipment, but they were stout-hearted and unflagging in performance of their job. They stood guard, oblivious to the shells, extricating casualties from stricken buildings, and fiercely adhering to the letter of blackout regulations. It occurred to me to suggest that they concentrate on more important objectives than us, since the blackout had little point when the Jordanians were indiscriminately shelling the whole town. But I was short of time.

We reached the completely blacked-out and apparently deserted Knesset. Segal, an orderly and an old acquaintance, was at the entrance.

"Where's Dayan?" I asked him.

"No idea. He was here and left."

"Has he taken the oath?"

"Who knows? All the ministers are gone. There's nobody in the building."

I walked away and contacted Command H.Q. in Ramla from the square in front of the building. "Where's Motta?"

"At Evelina de Rothschild."

Arik added that several minutes previously the Command base camp had been shelled, but that there had been neither casualties nor damage. The Command was beginning to feel the impact of the war, I thought. What Arik did not tell me was that Tel Aviv had been shelled, and that shells had whistled right over my own home in Zahala. Those in the Quarter, among them my wife and children, spent the night in the trench in the yard.

Never Forget the Old City

I was at the Evelina de Rothschild School at 20.25 hours. I knew the building well, having passed it every day when I was a child going back and forth to high school. It was an English-language school for girls and very popular with the daughters of the town's upper crust. I used to see an English girl of about 12 almost every morning, followed by an Indian servant holding an umbrella over her in winter and a parasol in summer, a perfect example of the white man's burden shouldered by the Empire.

On this night, June 5th, 1967, no air of romance distinguished the de Rothschild school. It was so dark that I groped around the courtyard to find the entrance and the basement stairs, where emergency headquarters of the Jerusalem Brigade had been set up. The courtyard, the building, the dimly-lit staircase, and the basement swarmed with soldiers – reservists – and hummed like a beehive. In a small cubbyhole downstairs lived the only two civilians on the premises, the caretaker and his wife, Mr. and Mrs. Matalov.

I passed their quarters and entered the temporary war room, with a telephone-choked table in the middle and male and female soldiers – clerks and signalmen – all around. In a room nearby Major Amos was shouting into a telephone. The battle for the "Bell" fortifications was just then in progress, and he briefed me tersely. Through a dim narrow corridor, lined wall-to-wall with paratroop officers in battle-dress, I managed to struggle into the big natural science room, shelved all along its walls with jars and bottles of lizards, grasshoppers, birds, chicken eggs, a goat foetus, and maybe a lamb, all swimming in formalin. On the floor, surround by this farmyard of preserved live-stock, sat Motta Gur with his officers, his eyes on an aerial photograph of the north Jerusalem sector.

"Attention!" someone called out as I sank down in their midst. Motta showed me his plan of action, just explained to his officers. It was simple in the extreme. The 66th Battalion would launch its assault on the police school and Ammunition Hill from the P.Ag.I. (Poalei Agudat Israel) houses, and would then bear right and advance through Sheikh Jarrah to the Ambassador Hotel. The 71st Battalion would attack from Nachlat Shimon, capture Wadi Joz and the Amer-ican Colony, and make its way to the Rockefeller Museum. Each battalion would be supported by Sherman tanks and command artil-lery units. The 28th Battalion would be the Brigade reserve. After the 71st broke through, the 28th would advance through the gap and move along Saladin Street towards the Rockefeller Museum and Herod's Gate, followed by the Brigade reconnaissance company, which would be prepared to enter the Old City.

He finished and looked at me. There was utter silence in the room. Everyone awaited my decision. As I weighed the pros and cons, I knew that Motta had fully understood me when I said to him in Ramla, "Pull to the right, and be ready to enter the Old City." He had assigned only one battalion to the so-called official mission of the Brigade, the breakthrough via Mt. Scopus, putting the bulk of its strength, two battalions and the reconnaissance company, into the objective of "pulling to the right, to the walls ..."

"Approved," I told them. "Take these objectives and let's await developments and, Motta, never forget the Old City!"

Crouching on the floor over the aerial photograph, trying to make it out in the dim light, we all felt that if everything went according to plan our final objective would be the Old City. I mentioned to Motta that half-tracks could not go through Herod's Gate, which I recalled vividly from childhood visits with my father. The stairs and the sharp turn would obstruct their passage. I warned him against damaging the Holy places, and against the possibility of involvement with the units of the 10th Brigade coming from the north.

"Okay," he said. "We'll stay inside the built-up area, south of Givat Hamivtar."

We decided that Givat Himivtar would be the boundary between the two brigades, and that "H" hour would be between 23.00 and 24.00 hours. I got up to leave, but before I went through the door, I looked back at him and said in a low voice, "Don't forget the Old City."

On the Roof of Histadrut House

Just before I left the school at 20.30 hours, I was told that we had taken Sur Baher. I contacted Arik Regev in Ramla from the jeep. "What's with the 10th?"

"They'll start again in half an hour," he replied, and I realized that if they started that soon, there was a good chance of their reaching the ridges before the Jordanians.

On our way to Histadrut House I noticed that the bombing was lessening somewhat. Shells no longer fell so near us, and even the far-off cannon seemed to roar less frequently. Because of the dark, Zabotaro, my driver, who came from the plains and was unfamiliar with Jerusalem, had trouble finding his way. But we arrived in ten minutes and took the elevator to the roof, where Eliezer Amitai, on the southern ledge, seemed to be trying to pierce the darkness with his eyes to see what was happening at Sur Baher and the "Bell" redoubt. Next to him were two signalmen, the brigade artillery officer, and several other officers. When I asked what was new, he described the capture of the "Bell" and the village and told me that, because Asher Dreizin had been wounded and evacuated to the hospital, the force was without a commanding officer. In Amitai's opinion, the Jordanians would counterattack during the night.

I looked around me. Among the officers, I recognized Colonel Yehoshua Nevo, an old acquaintance, who, like so many others without emergency postings, was looking for a job to do. Hesitantly I asked him if he would be ready to take over Asher's battalion. Ready? He jumped at the chance.

I told Eliezer that the paratroops would soon move towards their starting line and would attack before midnight. They would need support from the Jerusalem Brigade.

"From my point of view, everything's in order," he replied. "We're in constant touch with them and are giving them all we have."

The roof of Histadrut House looked out over the entire break-through sector of the 55th Brigade, allowing us, in the clear June night, to make out the large built-up block of Augusta Victoria, the skyline of Mt. Scopus and Givat Hamivtar, and even, in faint outline, *Hagiva Hatzorfatit* (French Hill). Almost at hand were the cupola of the Rockefeller Museum, the round Dome of the Rock, and the walls of the Old City. The huge searchlight on the roof beamed light on various artillery targets. The Arabs were now firing small arms only.

Paratroopers' "H" Hour

We returned to the jeep at 21.15 and after leaving Jerusalem's built-up area, I contacted Uri: "What's happening at your end?"

"We're clearing mines away."

"What are the chances for moving on?"

"Good, I think."

Five minutes later, by the time we reached lower Motza, Borka radioed that the Command camp had been bombed and suggested postponing the paratroop attack until the morning. "It will be easier with proper air support," he said.

Although my immediate reaction was to dismiss the suggestion, I began to reconsider and decided to go back to Jerusalem and talk it over with Motta. Back at the school, excitement had abated; the paratroops had left. In the war room I found Amos at the telephone. Gur had left Histadrut House for his Command group, which was in a private apartment on Zefania Street. I telephoned and asked what he thought about postponing the attack till morning, when air support was certain.

"I prefer to start at night," he said, "hold an area under cover of darkness, and then see how things develop ... there'll be more than enough for us to do tomorrow, and there'll also be use for air support ..."

I agreed, because fundamentally I believed that we should not wait. First of all, I had no idea of the whereabouts of the 10th Brigade and was no longer sure, after its enormous difficulties, that it could reach its objective by daybreak. The Jordanians might get to Tel el-Ful with their Patton tanks and attack Scopus without interference. Secondly, our experience in other wars with the Arabs, especially the Jerusalem experience, spoke clearly to the premise that what was not finished today might not be possible to finish tomorrow. Furthermore, international pressure for a cease-fire, as well as diverse complex, and no less compelling, internal matters, gave me grave cause for concern. And the paratroops, moreover, were trained night-fighters. They were at home with darkness, and knew how to exploit its advantages.

And I had still another consideration: our air force, which had performed magnificently at the beginning of the campaign, could not be utilized efficiently in that region. With zero distance between the paratroops' forming-up positions and the Jordanian defenses, the planes might hit the paratroopers or even Israeli civilians who lived in the P.Ag.I. Quarter and in the apartments nearby. They might even bomb one of the holy places with which Jerusalem was blessed. For all these reasons, I could say with Motta, "I prefer starting at night."

Later I contacted Arik and repeated that he must do everything possible to take Latrun – use Elisha's paratroopers, the unit from G.H.Q., Major Z's reconnaissance unit and Ehud Shani's half-tracks, and, if he could, get air support. "The main thing," I said, "is to take Latrun."

Arik was right on. "Will execute at zero three zero zero," adding, "If Latrun falls, the whole she-bang will collapse."

I ordered the Command group to proceed to Jerusalem.

A platoon of paratroopers, lost in blacked-out Jerusalem, found themselves in front of the Evelina de Rothschild School. Its commander, a lanky young lieutenant, told me, despairingly, that they were supposed to spearhead the attack and should by now have been in jumping-off position. But they had been sent off from Beit Hakerem without a guide, and had been walking in circles for half an hour. At my request, Amos gave them a scout to lead them to the Schneller Camp.

Tanks at Ma'aleh Ha'adumim

When a report came in from Mt. Scopus at 23.17 that there were tanks at Ma'aleh Ha'adumim, I contacted the High Command bunker and gave the information to the deputy Chief of the General Staff, Brigadier Haim Bar-Lev. "My guess is they're planning a counter-attack," I told him. "Request air strike with flares."

"Nothing doing," said Bar-Lev, cutting me short, and went on to ask about armor that could be sent to help Jerusalem.

"Only armored cars and a few light tanks," I replied. "Uri is stuck 6-7 kilometers from the Jerusalem highway. There are two or three tanks in the Government House area and at Sur Baher."

Bar-Lev said I would have to hold out with what I had till morning.

"O.K.," I answered, "but in the morning I'm hoping for serious air support. The air supervisor can direct the planes. Request also to plaster the Iraqis, if they've crossed over Allenby Bridge."

A minute or two later, General Bar-Lev radioed me to ask about developments. Nothing new, I told him and expounded upon my hesitations over "H" hour for the paratroops.

"It's still advisable for Motta to attack tonight," I said, "in order to hamstring the Jordanian counter-attack. My guess is the entire 60th Brigade is on its way up, which is what they're seeing from Mt. Scopus. If you can get the air force to attack the armor on the road to Ma'aleh Ha'adumim and Azaria, it might help the paratroop assault. If Motta starts tonight, we'll save daylight hours, and will also split up their effort. And if we get to Azaria quickly, they'll be forced to withdraw."

Haim Bar-Lev shared my concern about the appearance of the Jordanian armor, but repeated that there was no way of getting air support before morning. "The pilots are exhausted. They're sleeping." He did agree, however, that if conditions worsened he would try to get them out.

"How are things at Government House and Sur Baher?" I asked Amos.

"The force there has organized for defense," he said, and added, "I hardly think there'll be a counter-attack, but if there is one, it's more likely to be on Mount Scopus." He told me he had ordered the reconnaissance company back to town to serve as a Brigade reserve unit.

The Chief-of-Staff telephoned at 23.32 from Ramla to say that my request for a night air strike on Ma'aleh Ha'adumim had been refused. "It can't be done with flares. Only in the morning."

Amos had just spoken with G.H.Q. and reported that the chief of "G" Branch had telephoned to say that the paratroops were not to attack at night. He wanted to know when they would be ready to start their offensive and was told not before midnight and possibly an hour thereafter, giving them less than three hours' darkness. The "G" Branch chief therefore decided that, if this were the case, it would be better to wait until morning.

I did not agree, and said so to the Chief-of-Staff. "That's bad. Tell Haim Barlev that I think the paratroops must go into action tonight."

I also asked the Chief-of-Staff to send the armored cars up to Jerusalem – not the best answer to Patton tanks, but better than nothing. In response to my question about the 10th Brigade, Borka answered they were past the Radar and Abdul-Aziz fortifications.

I was amazed. "That means they've hardly moved. Are there mines along the Beit Iksa axis also? And what about the engineers unit I wanted? Has it moved off? I don't see how Uri will be able to stand up to the Pattons' counter-offensive in the morning ..."

The Air Force in Action

Bar-Lev was on the line again at 23.45 to say that there would be an air force night strike on Ma'aleh Ha'adumim. He had succeeded in getting the pilots, in spite of their exhaustion, to fly another mission. Clearly, it was impossible to remain indifferent in the face of a Jordanian armor advance on Jerusalem, with the 10th Brigade bogged down betwen the Radar and Abdul-Aziz and the paratroop offensive not yet launched.

I told Haim Barlev that Uri Was advancing with difficulty, but Arik reported at 23.50 that Uri had begun to move north from Beit Iksa.

In actual fact, only the 10th's reconnaissance unit, or its remaining two half-tracks and four jeeps, was moving, but I was not aware of that and informed Bar-Lev that since the 10th Brigade had begun to move, I was willing to wait another hour for a decision about the timing of the paratroop attack. If, in an hour, the Brigade's advance gave it a chance to be on the Ramallah highway by dawn, the paratroop attack could be postponed until the morning.

At 23.52 I told Eliezer Amitai that Motta would not attack before 1:00 o'clock and not without my orders. Amitai, who was in charge of the complex support for the paratroops' assault, would have to change his plans if the timetable were changed.

Afterwards I telephoned to Arik in Ramla to find out the whereabouts of the 10th Brigade. "I've promised to hold up the paratroops until I know. Check and report to Evelina de Rothschild."

Then I contacted Motta, who at that stage was not so keen about a night attack. His battalion commanders had been late with their plans of action and had not given them to the company commanders as soon as necessary. As a result, the men had not been properly briefed. Beyond this, several buses travelling without guides from Beit Hakerem in the Jerusalem blackout had lost their way. The spearhead platoon that I had found at the school was obviously not alone in going astray; some units had even been split up. Motta was now prepared to wait till morning.

I told him he'd have a reply at 00.45 hours.

"Promise You'll Take Me"

Into the basement of the Evelina de Rothschild building burst Rabbi Goren, covered with dust, his face black with soot. He had been in the south that morning with the armored infantry unit, which had attacked and vanquished the el-Kuba redoubt in the Gaza suburbs. Casualties were heavy and almost all the assault vehicles had been hit, including the Rabbi's half-track. For two hours he had lain on the ground, under heavy shellfire, clutching a *Sefer Torah*, the Scroll of the Law. When finally it was safe to move around, he helped to evacuate the wounded. At the Beersheba headquarters he heard for the first time about the battle raging in Jerusalem, and climbed into his car without wasting a moment and raced for the capital.

Streaking in like a whirlwind, he shouted from the doorway, "What's happening here?"

"What's happening down south?" I parried.

"Who cares about the south?" he cried. "Jerusalem and the Temple Mount, they are what count! You will make history now! Promise that when you go up to the Temple Mount, you'll take me too."

We had all thought of the words he was saying, but he gave them new meaning. His eyes burned, his dusty beard bristled, his whole person exuded faith and ardor.

"I promise," I told him. "When we go up to the Temple Mount, we won't forget you. Go get a *shofar* [ram's horn]!"

He went in the blackout to his father-in-law's house to look for a *shofar* to replace his own, lost in the advance on Gaza.

Paratroops Up and Away

Without our noticing, it was midnight; the next day, Tuesday, June 6th was upon us. Days were indistinguishable for all of us, but the clock was inexorable. At ten minutes after midnight I once again asked Arik Regev for news of the 10th. "I'll check and report," he said, adding that Moshe Yotvat had assembled his force and they were on the way to the jumping-off positions for the assault on Latrun.

I was delighted, and asked if there were any opposition ahead and where Moshe was at that moment. Arik said that he was just leaving and all was quiet.

A few minutes later Arik radioed:

"Uri reports he's beginning to move, and will reach the Ramallah highway by morning."

I decided that under such circumstances, the paratroops should start attacking towards dawn, to which General Bar-Lev assented, as did Motta when I told him. Motta's voice sounded weary, but a few minutes later he was back on the phone.

"Uzi," he said, "I've spoken to the battalion commanders and they refused to agree to a postponement." He explained that they had advanced their units to their jumping-off lines, where they were being heavily bombed and had suffered numerous casualties. If the attack were delayed, their options would be to stay where they were and risk further casualties, or withdraw. The latter would have to be done in broad daylight in full view of the enemy. "They want to begin at once," said Motta. "Please try to convince G.H.Q. to agree to a night-offensive."

What were the pros and cons? Postponement until morning was logical, given the promise of reasonable air support, but I doubted, as I've said, the efficacy of aerial bombardment in a built-up area, particularly in Jerusalem. Another reason for postponement was that Uri might not reach Tel el-Ful in time, in spite of his being on the move.

But most important, in my view, was the desire of the paratroop commanders to begin their offensive while it was dark. I knew those commanders, and respected their judgment. If they preferred a night-attack and had confidence in it, a night-attack it would be. Furthermore, there was the pressing factor of time: move quickly and do the job when it can be done. Only after the war did I discover how correct this instinct had been. That very night, June 5th–6th, the Jordanians realized that they would not be able to hold the West Bank. Early on Tuesday morning, say King Hussein's memoirs, General Riadh got Nasser's consent to try for a cease-fire order on the Jordanian front, to prevent the total collapse of the Arab forces.

We were unaware of the chance of an enforced cease-fire.

Upon reflection aided by hindsight, I know that had we not captured much of East Jerusalem that night, and had the Jordanians requested a cease-fire on the morning of the 6th, Israel might have consented.

Telling Motta that I would try, I contacted G.H.Q., and was told that, since General Bar-Lev was asleep, I should speak to General Zeevi.

"But didn't you agree with Haim to start in the morning?" he asked, when I had finished explaining.

I repeated my reasons for having second thoughts about a night-offensive.

He hesitated a bit. Finally he said, "Okay. The decision is yours. Does this mean you won't need the air force to soften up enemy positions in the morning?"

"Exactly. We start tonight."

The die was cast. I telephoned to Motta. "They've agreed to a night-offensive. 'H' hour – 02.00."

At 1:40 the Evelina de Rothschild school was heavy with silence, accentuated by the dull boom of explosions. H.Q. officers of the Jerusalem Brigade had fallen asleep on wooden benches or on the stone floors. The operations officer was trying unsuccessfully to locate a unit of the Brigade for the attack on Abu-Tor. From what I could make out, the unit had disappeared, but it turned out after the war to have been the Michael Paikes battalion, the mysterious "friendly force" which had surfaced suddenly to assist the armored battalion of the 10th Brigade and had volunteered to capture the Radar III fortifications for them. But when Major Amos sought to send the unit against Abu-Tor, Paikes was not only not in his headquarters, he was with the attackers of the Jordanian stronghold. He received the Abu-Tor order only the next morning, and had to look for a unit to guard the captured position before he set out. And since his battalion had no transport, they had to make the long journey from Ma'aleh Hahamisha to southern Jerusalem on foot, never arriving to start the attack on Abu-Tor until the afternoon.

All was quiet along the Jerusalem front. There were no signs of the anticipated Jordanian counter-attack on U.N. Headquarters, the former Government House, and there seemed nothing for me to do at the school. Now the action was in northern Jerusalem, where the paratroops would shortly launch their attack. That was where I belonged.

The night air was clean and soft after the smoke-filled basement of the school, but, outside, the sounds of bombardment fell heavily on our ears. I radioed Arik from the jeep and heard the latest reports from Uri. His spearhead unit had reached "Ballot" (the code name for Beit Hanina), which meant that things were proceeding as they should. We, my driver Zabotaro and I, started toward paratroop headquarters.

The Soup Kitchen Roof

We drove via Mahane Yehuda to Zefania Street in Geula. At the corner of Zefania and Nehemia Streets, we met the paratroops' forward command group on their way to the P.Ag.I. houses to watch the start of the offensive.

Tanks of the armored company attached to the Jerusalem Brigade were rolling down the slope with their engines switched off, bent on reaching their positions silently, without alerting the enemy. Long, silent columns of paratroopers marched beside the tanks, on their way to the front. Only the explosions from the adjoining sector punctured the quiet of the night. It was still and windless, not a leaf stirred, nor a stray branch. The sky was a deep blue canopy encrusted with stars, their radiance occasionally dimmed by streams of tracer bullets from the east, which quickly flared and as quickly vanished.

Our jeep followed the paratroop forward Command car. At 13 Joel Street, on whose roof the paratroops had their advance headquarters, a sign read, "Central Talmud Torah and Sanctified Yeshiva and Soup Kitchen Kiriat-Sefer."

The street was filled with paratroopers, waiting at the curb or in doorways. Among them was the young commander of the spearhead unit of the 71st Battalion, who had, earlier and erroneously, turned up at the Evelina de Rothschild School. As though at a signal, a salvo of shells greeted our arrival, exploding in the street, collapsing tiled roofs. There were calls for help, and stretcher-bearers came running, but the paratroopers never moved. They are engraved on my memory: in the din of explosion, the screaming of wounded, the scrambling of orderlies, the paratroopers stood firm at their posts in the doorways, on curbstones, patient, a tableau of unruffled courage, awaiting instructions.

Zabotaro sprang out of the jeep into a nearby house, Koby Sharett and I ran towards the Yeshiva, and Joel stayed to look after the jeep. We climbed to the flat parapeted roof. Its two huge water tanks,

12. The author on the roof of the paratroopers' command post

useless and empty, had been riddled by bullets and shrapnel. In a corner of the roof stood Motta's Command group: Stempel, his deputy, Amos, the Brigade's operations officer, "G" branch men, intelligence personnel, signalmen and runners, all in full battle dress, including steel-helmets. My peaked cap was out of place.

We looked down at our surroundings, trying to estimate by the firing in the various breakthrough sectors the severity of the battles. The sparse reports gave us little information, the unit commanders merely reporting, "Everything's under control...advancing according to plan..." The bombardment continued and the shells fell all around, a 25-liter cannonball crashing into the roof's parapet, covering us in dust, but hurting no one. A piece of shrapnel was later discovered to have sliced through a radio trans-receiver on the back of a signalman next to us. It was a miracle, one of a series of miracles. Had a curved-trajectory, instead of a flat-trajectory, mortar shell landed on that roof, everybody would have been seriously hurt. But when the shell hit, we hardly noticed, what with the fire that raged at the police school and the U.N.R.W.A. stores that blazed there, and the salvoes of bombs that fell near us.

We were still on the roof at 3:30, more than an hour after the paratroops had crossed the line, and we knew nothing. The police school blazed on, close by on Ammunition Hill. The fighting was fierce, to judge by the continued gunfire, but in the direction of the Mandelbaum Gate, where the 71st Battalion had broken through, all was quiet. We knew there had been casualties. Shells fell in the nearby streets, among the units waiting to go into battle. Over the radios on the roof came shouts indicating that the orderlies had been unable to locate the evacuation station, and Stempel, the Brigade's deputy C.O., went down to help with evacuation procedures. But of what was happening at the scene of the action we knew nothing.

For two hours I stayed with the forward Command group on the soup kitchen roof, leaning on the ledge of the parapet, willing my eyes or my field-glasses to see what the Brigade was doing, to make out the spot near the ridge of mountains where they were fighting. But I could only guess what was going on. Shells fell in salvoes or singly; tiles flew off the roofs and splintered on the sidewalks. Boughs of trees were pierced by shrieking bullets and fell with a sigh and a rustle; the moaning of wounded, the noise of explosion grew and mingled in the night, composing their own macabre symphony of war.

The Paratroop Battle Plans

Lt. Colonel Yossi, C.O. 66th Battalion, went with his company commanders to look over the battleground from the roof of the house on Zefania Street: by no means the best observation post, since they could see only the entrance to the police College, but neither the Line nor the break-through positions. An intelligence sergeant of the Jerusalem Brigade, seconded to the group to provide information on enemy dispositions, said a better place was the roof of a building in the Ma'abarot Evacuees Quarter, adjoining the P.Ag.I. They drove there under a heavy bombardment, found the roof locked, knocked on one of the apartment doors, and, by the light of a projector on the Histadrut Building, were able to see the Line through a window. On the basis of what he saw, and what the intelligence sergeant told him, Yossi began to devise a battle plan.

Meanwhile, the buses were arriving in Jerusalem with the men and were directed to Beit Hakerem, where the heavily-equipped soldiers had a chance to get out of the buses, stretch their legs and discuss their coming mission. Most were bitter that their parachuting mission had been cancelled and thought they were here to help defend Jerusalem. Very few were acquainted with the city or understood the significance of the roaring guns and the explosive flashes erupting mainly in the north.

Their spirits were lifted while they waited by the hospitality and Zahal-adoration of the Jerusalemites. Beth Hakerem opened its doors to the paratroopers, serving them hot drinks and fruit and sweets and, most important, urging them to telephone their families and best girls. Everywhere the telphones were busy, and when the long waiting period ended, and the soldiers were again in the buses en route to battle, they left behind lists of numbers to be called and messages to be transmitted for them. Beth Hakerem sat devotedly at the telephone, delivering messages through the night and all the next day, often after their authors had begun to fight in the alleys in the eastern part of the city or in communications trenches on Ammunition Hill.

Sometime after 10 p.m. Yossi completed his battle plan, which gave "D" Company, commanded by Giora, the task of pinning down the enemy and covering the breakthrough and made Dodik's "A" Company the spearhead. The attack was to start with a softening-up bombardment of the police school and Ammunition Hill. The 81-mm mortars were to pulverize the area between those two objectives. The tanks of two of the Brigade's armored platoons would advance under this covering fire, and would then take up positions in the P.Ag.I. Quarter and in the olive grove left of the breakthrough position. When the artillery had finished bombing, the tanks were to smash open the position of the police school, followed by another brief artillery bombardment, during which sappers with flame-throwers would break through the fence.

After they had breached the fences – one Israeli and two Jordanian – "A" Company was to enter and demolish the enemy position on the square in front of the police school. From there Dodik and his company would advance through the communication trench leading to Ammunition Hill, which they would attack from the rear. The supporting company, commanded by Gaby Geller, would take the police college building, and his deputy's company the Yellow Rag and the Tiled House positions between the college and Ammunition Hill.

"B" Company, led by Dadi, would wait to complete the occupation of Ammunition Hill, "D" Company, under Giora, would, with the supporting company in the police school, led by the battalion commander, attack the Sheikh Jarrah quarter, while the Jerusalem Engineers Company would widen the breakthrough so that the tanks under Captain Rafi Yeshayahu could go through to join the C.O.'s battalion.

Lt. Colonel Uzi, C.O. 71st Battalion, also prepared his plans, which were based on a quiet breakthrough of the earthwork fortifications on the Line in the Nahlat Shimon sector and rapid penetration into the American Colony and Wadi Joz. One tank platoon was provided as support.

The 28th Battalion, commanded by Lt. Colonel Yossi P., was the Brigade reserve during the break-through stage, and was scheduled to cross the line at the 71st Battalion's break-through point and bear right towards the Old City walls, the Rockefeller Museum and Herod's Gate.

The plans having been presented and confirmed by the Brigade C.O., the officers rushed off to Beth Hakerem to use the little time left to brief their men.

At midnight, deputy Brigade Commander Moshe Stempel informed me that he had not yet had the time to draw all the required ammunition and equipment from the Jerusalem Brigade. "H" hour was postponed first until 1:00 and then until 2 a.m.

The 66th Breaks Through

At 2 a.m. precisely the artillery barrage began. The huge searchlights on the Histadrut building shone like daylight on the police school, illuminating the 25-liter shells smashing its walls into rubble and shrouding the building in smoke. The C.O. 66th realized that the shell damage was minor and ordered that the bombardment plan be changed: the field-guns should be fired at Ammunition Hill and the 160mm mortars at the building, "for only the mortars are heavy enough to penetrate its walls."

He admitted after the war that at that point he considered the police school the enemy's chief stronghold and fortress. "We forgot the lessons of the reprisal raids, when again and again we realized that during a bombardment the Legionnaires came out of the buildings and were drawn up outside them. The destruction of the police building appeared to us a mission in itself..."

The tanks advanced at the same time. Although, according to their C.O., Captain Raffy Yeshayahu, they had been ordered to coast down the slope without starting the engines, to prevent the Legionnaires from hearing them approach, the tanks refused to move, and they were therefore told to switch the engines on. In any case, the bombardment muffled all other sound. Suddenly it stopped, and the tank guns roared, chiefly aiming at the positions around the college, because Ammunition Hill was hidden from the tankmen, just as the break-through point had been hidden from the Legionnaires on the Hill.

Now the Arab Legion retaliated in good earnest. A rain of mortar shells fell, near enough to destroy the tanks' exterior equipment, tearing out aerials, setting fire to camouflage nets, damaging telephones. Long bursts erupted from enemy machine-guns, aimed at the spaces between the houses, and extinguished the tanks' projectors one after another. The artillerymen were left with only the huge searchlight on the roof of the Histadrut building, which illuminated the upper section only of the police school.

Fifteen minutes later the constraining forces took up their positions. The sappers advanced. The battalion C.O. himself was near the fence. The Israeli fence was ripped and a flamethrower was tossed out to blast through the Jordanian fence, but to no avail. It simply attracted Jordanian attention and intensified the shooting. Men were hit, cries of "Medic!" and "Orderly!" were heard – cries as sharp as bullets in the ears of the paratroopers; cries that were to persist

13. French Hill under attack

throughout the twenty-four hour ordeal.

Three fences had been breached, and Dodik's men were streaming through the opening. But a fourth, not marked on our maps, blocked their way. A Jordanian machine-gun opened fire. Its crew was wiped out at once. The corpses of the Jordanian gunners fell into the communications trench. The paratroopers that leapt in stumbled over the Legion's dead.

The firing intensified. More and more men fell, but the advance continued. The men's back-packs scraped along the narrow sides of the steep communications trench, delaying, but not halting, progress.

On the edges of the trench were firing and observation positions, their apertures designed to face Jewish Jerusalem. They had to be cleared out with hand grenades. The trapped Legionnaires, unable to withdraw, fought like men at bay, shooting and tossing out hand grenades to mow down the oncoming force.

Dodik, at the head of his men, did not yet know how heavy their losses had been. When he reached the end of the communications trench he reported to the battalion commander that he had carried out his objective and was at the edge of the Ammunition Hill fortified position. When the C.O. asked if he could carry on and capture the Hill, he replied that everything had gone fairly well, and that he was ready to carry on. But when he called a halt to reassemble his company, the breathless fighters staggered in slowly, one or two at a time, shocked by the numbers of fallen who would have to be left behind while the rest went on attacking. Many were out of ammunition.

Dodik radioed his headquarters: "I have many casualties, and am very short of ammunition. I prefer that Dadi take the position, as originally planned..."

Neither he nor anyone in the battalion knew the nature of this fortified position, this Ammunition Hill of which they held one end.

Ammunition Hill

The fortified position known as Ammunition Hill lay some 300 meters from the police school. To protect the flanks of the school, the Jordanians began to strengthen it in 1949 and continued until, by 1967, it was an awesome fortress. From Jewish Jerusalem two elongated buildings could be seen on top of the hill, but a bird's-eye view showed that it was surrounded by a deep concrete communications trench with several internal cross-trenches.

Through our field-glasses we spotted fortified machine-gun nests on the slopes of the hill and along the periphery of the trench, positions usually so well camouflaged that they could not all be seen even with the most excellent glasses. There turned out to be 40 such positions in the fortress, some sided with concrete too thick for a single shell from a recoilless gun to penetrate. Not only did the emplacements cover all approaches, but protected each other as well. The positions at the center of the peak of the Hill dominated the communications trenches beneath, so that every inch of the fortress was covered. It contained, besides, an underground Command bunker with a large ammunition dump nearby. Each position was plentifully supplied with ammunition, which included hand-grenades, machine guns and recoilless guns. Further protection was afforded by Hamivtar Fortress, which was larger and higher than Ammunition Hill and about 800 meters north of it.

This was the fortress that Dadi, "B" Company commander, was now ordered to take. The company crossed the line after the support-ing unit and soon controlled the police college, mopped up the area with the help of Giora's "D" Company, and reorganized to assault the Sheikh Jarrah Quarter.

It was 2.45 a.m., an hour before dawn. Dadi's company moved towards Ammunition Hill. The lighter it became, the less could the paratroops exploit the darkness; dawn would be bloody indeed. Arab Legion snipers could easily and accurately shoot from inside their sheltered and fortified bunkers.

Dadi thought, upon setting out, that his mission would be easy: to take a not very sizable position manned by enemy troops already badly shaken by the heavy bombardment and the offensive action of "A" Company.

He reached a point on Ammunition Hill about 50 meters to the right of Dodik and his small force. As he advanced, Dodik signalled with a flashlight and radioed to ascertain whether Dadi had seen the flashes. Dadi had not, because, as they discovered in the morning, a pile of stones obscured them from each other. But although he did not find Dodik's tract position, Dadi did not lose his way, having been helped by the flares from the ammunition truck that was burning outside the police school. The blaze lit up the position directly in front of him and three small houses to his left, which a platoon under Yoram Eliashiv was dispatched to take.

Now came the first of many blows the company was to suffer. The machine-gun detail that Yoram sent into a trench on his left advanced a few meters and was ripped by Jordanian machine-gun fire from a higher bunker in the middle of the fortified position. All five men of the detail were killed.

Yoram and the remainder of his men captured and mopped up the three houses and continued along the central communications trench, which led to the barracks in the center, dodging Legionnaire fire all the way. After they had sprayed and captured the two barracks buildings only eight men were left. As they continued north, a shell from a recoilless gun exploded, fatally wounding Yoram. The leaderless men sank confusedly around him.

Meanwhile Dadi led the other two platoons along the eastern peripheral trench, where heavy firing in front and overhead cut down his men. Hand-grenades began to pepper the trench, thrown, it was soon discovered, from a house on the edge, on whose roof was a T.V. aerial.

The seriously depleted company pressed on. A mortar-bunker obstructed its route, forcing it into two sections, one of which moved into a flanking trench, where the heavy opposition decimated the platoon and its commander. Dadi, having wiped out the mortar-bunker, reached the spot below which, unknown to him, lay the underground headquarters bunker of the fortress. He counted his men and turned pale; only four remained. He radioed to Dodik and reported that there was nobody left that could fight.

The Battle of the Trench

While Dadi's "B" Company was in the trenches, Dodik was busy assembling the wounded and evacuating them under brutal, ceaseless fire. Suddenly shots from the rear were fired by Legionnaires who had managed to hide, had waited until most of the men had passed and then begun to shoot. Wounded men still lying along the trench answered their shots, and once the wounded were evacuated, the trench again had to be cleared of enemy snipers.

After Dadi's call for help, Dodik divided his company, one force to the central trench, where Yoram had routed out what nests of resistance remained; the other, led by Nir, Dodik's deputy, to the trench on the western periphery. The western trench, along the bottom of Ammunition Hill, was the most strongly fortified in the position, with numerous bunkers for the machine guns and recoilless guns. As Nir moved through it, the Legionnaires drew closer, crawling from higher up in the middle of the fortress to toss hand grenades into the trench.

The only means of protection for a machine-gunner was to leave the trench, creep along its rim, expose himself to enemy fire, and thrust back the grenade-throwers with machine-gun fire. Eytan Naveh, a young, strong moshavnik, volunteered, and not only drove the grenade-throwers away, but ran ahead of the force in the trench, shooting into it all the time. The Israeli soldiers found dozens of Legionnaires in their path, who had been hit by Eytan's bullets. Naveh, without protection or cover, visible to all, target for every bullet and grenade, gambled with his life – and lost, shot dead by machine-gun fire.

Another volunteer sprang to replace him, and the advance continued.

It was now daylight, and although most of the fortress had been taken, the battle was far from won. Daylight had forestalled the Jordanian defenders' last chance to escape, but they refused to part cheaply with their lives. Their shooting became precise and deadly. Even the firing from the Hamivtar strong-point took its toll. Men in the trenches were hit from inside the bunkers, and anyone who stood upright was hit by snipers on the Hamivtar.

Yossi, leading the remainder of his 66th battalion into the Sheikh Jarrah Quarter, followed by his deputy, Major Doron, had not given me an accurate report of the battle, but had radioed only the briefest information: "Advancing...soon completing... ." Once Dadi announced that he was on top of Ammunition Hill. When Doron realized, however, that the battle was not over and that Captain Yeshayahu's tanks were leaving to join the battalion commander at Sheikh Jarrah, he decided to send two of them to Ammunition Hill. They had little effect on the progress of battle there, because the Hill's slope did not allow them to traverse their weapons into the trenches. The paratroopers claimed, however, that the very appearance of the tanks broke the spirit of the defenders and gradually undermined their organized defense. When Doron saw that the Hamivtar shooting was taking its own toll of victims, he ordered two tanks to fire their cannon and machine-guns in that direction, to force the enemy soldiers to duck their heads.

The Big Bunker

At 5:00 a.m., when the tanks reached the Hill, only the big bunker was offering resistance. The paratroopers had not known about this bunker, whose protecting walls were 40 cms. thick, surrounding a

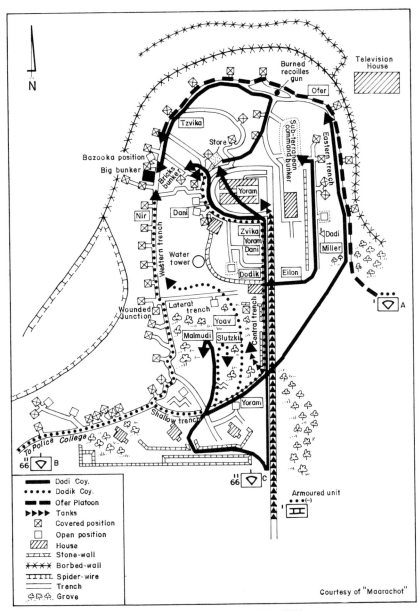

VIII The fight for Ammunition Hill

14. The Police College in flames

7

smaller well-camouflaged bunker dug into the slope of the Hill. It was invisible except when fire streamed through its apertures. Still inside it were at least one machine-gun and a bazooka, dominating all the western trench and the communications trench leading down from the center of the Hill.

The first to reach it was paratrooper Jackie Haimovitz, who had been in the central trench with Yoram. When their commander was killed, a second detachment arrived, under Lieutenant Zvi Magen, who took over the command and swept the whole lot forward with him. When he reached the next bend in the trench, however, a burst of Jordanian bullets from the big bunker killed him. Jackie, immediately behind him, continued to advance and entered a dead spot, from which the enemy could not see him. The other men held back and Jackie went alone.

Detachments of Nir's and Dodik's forces neared the bunker. Jackie shouted warnings to prevent their entering his "dead-man's gulch," into which a hand-grenade had been thrown, wiping out everyone in the bunker. But when the other paratroopers tried to move forward they were forced back by shooting from inside. A bazooka also failed to crack its walls, and the hand grenades that were tossed in failed to silence the defenders, who took cover in the inner bunker, of which the paratroopers were unaware.

Another soldier, Private David Shalom, managed to join Jackie near the bunker and together they subdued the men within. Jackie raced over to the men at the edge of the trench, grabbed their explosives, and in full view of the marksmen in the bunker, drew as near as he dared and relayed the explosives to David Shalom, now standing on the bunker's roof. David was no sapper. Haimovitz shouted instructions about how to lay and detonate the explosives. When they burst, the bunker burst with them.

Sniping continued. Here and there a Jordanian soldier was spotted trying to escape to the north, towards the Hamivtar. Now and then a hand-grenade was thrown, but the battle for Ammunition Hill was over. Battle-weary and stunned, shocked at the slaughter, the remnants of the two companies began to assemble their wounded in the police school.

While the battle for Ammunition Hill was in progress, the two other companies captured the Sheikh Jarrah Quarter, meeting with resistance even there, from well-fortified strongholds inside the houses.

The supporting tanks, however, helped to destroy them.

Just after dawn the forces reached the Ambassador Hotel; soon Israeli flags flew from the tall roofs of Sheikh Jarrah.

The 71st Battalion Breaks Through

The misfortunes which beset the 66th Battalion in the opening phase of the battle struck the other battalions as well. A shell fell on the 71st in their buses from Beit Hakerem to the breakthrough area in Nahlat Shimon, and in the ensuing confusion one bus left the convoy, turned down an alley, and promptly got lost. By an unlucky chance, this was the bus that carried the spearhead forces: five detachments of shock troops, each with a flame-throwing torpedo tube. After a hectic search in the breakthrough area for the mislaid bus, the battalion commander was on the point of postponing "H" hour until new spearhead forces could be organized and additional flame-throwers obtained, but at that moment the strays turned up.

The holding-down detail having grouped itself, the mortar unit attached to the battalion began to barrage the breakthrough area, firing hundreds of shells in a short time on a relatively small spot, with positive effect. More than one Arab Legion stronghold opposite the breakthrough point was abandoned. The companies took their places in the order of entry determined by the battalion commander: Uzi A's "B" Company, with three tanks and a detail of heavy machine-guns, were to cover Meirka's "C" Company, the spearhead force, which was to mop up the trench connecting the Jordanian positions opposite the breakthrough point. After them were the battalion commander and his group: "D" Company, under Moussa, was to quell resistance in the American Colony to the point where it met Wadi Joz; "E" Company, under Zamosh, was to pass through the "D" Company line and occupy the built-up area of Wadi Joz leading to Mt. Scopus.

Dan, the deputy battalion commander, was to supervise the various units until they had passed the entry point, after which "B" Company was to follow, having in the meantime completed its holding-down duties. After "B" Company were the three tanks and the jeeps with recoilless guns, which had been slightly in the rear.

In spite of the early confusion, the operation got off to a running start. Uzi A. and his flame-throwers approached the fence unseen by the enemy and stealthily slit it open. One meter of no-man's-land separated the fence from the nearest Jordanian obstacle. Dan, supervising the entry, was fearful of landmines and ordered a flame-thrower to be directed along the ground to explode the mines. The first weapon was a dud, but the second tore through the Jordanian fence. The break-through unit crashed across a second fence and a third, but the unexpected delay of the fences tied up the soldiers, already on the move, and they crowded through and in front of the entry point. The battalion commander, impatient in the rear, kept shouting, "Faster, faster!"

Finally the third fence was breached, and "C" Company swept into the communications trench, the enemy still apparently unaware of the attack building up from that direction. One of the Jordanian fortified positions, considered particularly tough by the battalion commander, was hit repeatedly until it caught fire. The "C" Company spearhead reached the next objective, a large building already earmarked as an assembly station for the wounded. There the Legionnaires awaited us and briefly gave battle.

This was the skirmish that apprised the Jordanian commander of the Israeli attack in his sector and that occasioned, in accordance with Jordanian standing battle procedures, an immediate bombardment upon the Beit Israel Quarter beyond the breakthrough point. The 71st Battalion, whose companies were now on both sides of the line, escaped the shells, which fell beyond them and landed instead on the assembly point of the 28th Battalion, waiting its turn to go through. Only at 22.30 hours had the commander of the 28th received his assignment to move through the two lines of the 71st Battalion, one branching toward Nablus Gate and the other toward Herod's Gate and the Rockefeller Museum. There he was to organize to break into the Old City, for which specific orders would be given him.

Yossi P. borrowed an aerial photograph from a 71st company commander and used it to work out his first plan of action, actually more than the company's order of entrance into battle. The plan called for Yossi Avidan's "A" Company to be in the lead, followed by battalion headquarters, "D" Company, "C" Company, and the supporting company.

He was still working this out when he received orders to leave Beit Hakerem. He briefed his men during their trip to the Beit Israel Quarter, but did not provide them with maps.

The men were relaxed and calm when they arrived. Since a break-through was not their job, even their personal equipment was far lighter than that of their comrades in other battalions. All their hand-grenades, explosives, and nearly all their water flasks had been given to a company charged with a special G.H.Q. assignment, and they were left with one hand grenade each and nothing else.

Shells on the 28th

The battalion commander was forward, near the breakthrough point, discussing the entry of his men with the deputy C.O. of the 71st, who wanted his jeeps to go through ahead of the 28th. The men of "A" Company waited impatiently against the walls of houses in Samuel the Prophet Street nearby. The other companies were in the rear, in the alleys of the Beit Israel Quarter. Ahead, beyond the breakthrough point, the sounds of shooting could already be heard as the spearheading 71st attacked the Legion's fortifications.

Suddenly high explosives began to burst non-stop. The Jordanians were shelling Beit Israel. We learned later that some twenty shells had fallen in one alley alone, where the battalion Command group and "D" Company were waiting, utterly decimating the Command group, including the battalion medical officer and his team. "D" Company was seriously harmed. More than sixty men lay in their own blood and their cries shattered the air.

In the confusion and bitter frustration of the moment, the men of "C" company, retreating from the bombs, stumbled into the ranks of the supporting unit and were ordered to send their medics to help the victims of the bombardment. The company therefore went into battle essentially without a medical team. When the battalion C.O. learned that his deputy had been hit, he replaced him with "Kache," commander of the supporting company, whom he summoned. But the entire supporting company, misinterpreting his order, advanced, all the heavy machine-gun crews still spread out in holding-down position. When the forces passed between the lines of the 71st Battalion, a "C" Company platoon was removed, added to Uzi's battalion, and with it reached the Rockefeller Museum.

In spite of the heavy bombing beforehand, the battalion never ceased fighting, never lost sight of its objectives.

'One Big Mess'

The march to the museum was not easy. Both battalions struggled forward through bloody battle raging in streets and alleyways, where, from within fortified houses and behind camouflaged positions, the enemy fired upon them relentlessly. Occasionally machine-gun and recoilless-gun fire burst from within the walls.

15. Embattled East Jerusalem

The war seemed one big mess to the soldiers, who moved aimlessly through bullet-sprayed streets, constantly forced to retrace their steps, running into fierce, sudden, shooting wars, watching comrades drop, immured in blood. But their objectives were clear; they slogged on; they accomplished their missions. While the 28th Battalion, stunned by its losses in the bombardment, was recovering, the 71st Battalion clashed with its first enemy obstacle, the so-called "big house." Only one in a row of houses fortified by the Jordanians and connected by concrete-walled communications trenches, the para-troopers had barely begun to attack it when they were fired upon from every direction. Soldier after soldier fell. A cement-block factory in the middle of the breakthrough area was commandeered as an assembly station for the wounded, and a sizable number of wounded and stretcher-bearers were soon gathered there, targets for enemy fire. It became apparent that the shots were coming from a nearby residence and a sortie detachment was organized, three of whose men were hit immediately. A second group stormed the house, peppered it with gunfire and grenades, but emerged into a blast of gunfire from a house nearby. Some of the men were hit, and the others had difficulty ascertaining which house the shooting came from so that a detail could be mustered to capture it.

While Meirka's company attacked the enemy's fortified positions around the breakthrough point, the two other companies advanced rapidly, literally sprinting between the bullets as far as a brick wall separating the cement-block factory from the back of Nablus Road. Somebody finally discovered an opening, and Moussa's "D" Company broke through, closely followed by Zamosh's "A" Company. They rushed headlong into Nablus Road, from which Wadi Joz Street branches to the American Colony and Wadi Joz. Left of Wadi Joz Street is the Sheikh Jarrah Quarter, where shots were being fired at the advancing column. The men who fell were carried to a protected yard and left there with guards while the rest continued to advance.

The deep narrow valley of Wadi Joz lies below the left side of the street, separating the American Colony from Sheikh Jarrah, passes through the Quarter that bears its name and then bears southwards, towards Jericho. Somewhere in that valley, Intelligence reported, an Arab Legion mortar battery was shelling Jewish Jerusalem.

Here Moussa's company left the column to wipe out and mop up the mortars in the valley. Advancing cautiously, they reached the mortar positions, which had already been abandoned. The enemy, however, had not gone far. From within the caves at the top of the wadi came the sound of voices, recognizably those of women and children. The paratroopers, about to toss hand-grenades, withheld their fire and shouted to the people inside to come out. The response was a long stream of bullets from the cave of Shimon Hazadik (Simon the Just), hitting one soldier. His comrades emptied their machine-guns into the mouth of the cave.

Gradually the paratroops overpowered both Quarters. Zamosh's Company marched in three columns on three parallel streets, spreading out on the border of the built-up area at the edge of Wadi Joz looking toward Mt. Scopus. The Jordanian soldiers fled towards the Augusta Victoria Hospital on the Mount, Zamosh's men at their heels. Shots from the hospital rained on the company positions, increasing so dramatically in intensity that Zamosh thought a Jordanian counter-attack was being prepared. His request that the Mount be bombed was granted with speed and accuracy. The shooting from there ceased.

The company stayed on the border of the Quarter all day, briefly and decisively fighting Legionnaires who, alone and in groups, sought to flee East Jerusalem and run for Mt. Scopus.

When the 71st Battalion had cleaned up the breakthrough area, the C.O. organized several units into a column, with himself at the head, and marched through the deserted streets of the American Colony to the back of the Rockefeller Museum. En route he collected the 28th Battalion's supporting force, which had been wandering around East Jerusalem for over an hour, lost and separated from the battalion, and searching now for the Rockefeller Museum.

Yossi P., commander of the 28th, radioed Uzi, C.O. of the 71st Battalion, for assistance in his assault on the Museum describing the losses his battalion had suffered while shelling the breakthrough area. All the men of his supporting company were casualties, he said. Uzi interrupted.

"No they aren't," he said. "Your supporting force is with me. I'll send them right along."

"D" Company Licks its Wounds

Yossi P. was understandably concerned when he heard that his Command group and "D" Company had been badly hit while waiting to enter the eastern part of town. He contacted the commanders of the other companies, who reported that they, too, had sustained casualties, but had not been put out of action. He decided, therefore, to carry on and gave instructions for medical teams to help evacuate the wounded, under the supervision of company commander Hagi. "When they're all evacuated," he told Hagi, "join me."

Hagi began to assemble his scattered forces, who managed to forget their fear and attend to the injured men sprawled on the road. The battalion casualty station had been bombed and was in shambles and Hagi had no idea of the whereabouts of the Brigade station. The surrounding darkness was punctuated by shots, exploding shells, and the heavy tread of the soldiers. There were not enough stretchers or stretcher-bearers to take care of all the casualties, and the men able to stand had to drag along by themselves.

...And Carries On

The convoy was lost until Hagi halted them some 300 meters west of the breakthrough and went to look for help. A group of soldiers in front of a house turned out to be the Brigade Headquarters group, whose deputy commander, Moshe Stempel, at once went to get ambulances to evacuate the wounded. By the time they arrived and finished taking the men to the hospital, it was morning. Hagi counted his men. Although only thirty were left, they were a fighting force. He divided them into three small platoons and set out to join his battalion. At Gan Abramov, not far from the breakthrough point, he found four more of his men, mainly heavy machine-gunners of the support group, assigned to holding positions during the bombardment and therefore unable to advance with their company. He added them to his force, along with a doctor and medical orderlies, reached the Rockefeller Museum through the sector captured by the 71st Battalion, and reported to his superior officer.

The 28th Battalion Advances

Yossi P. was ready to send his men through the 71st Battalion's breakthrough point, ordering Yossi Avidan to go first, but Dan, the 71st's deputy C.O., asked permission, as we have seen, to move the jeeps first. Yossi P. acquiesced, and the 28th advanced only after the jeeps had gone through.

"A" Company went first, while Meirka's company were still trying to take the Legion's fortified positions around the breakthrough point. Avidan's men passed them on the right, moving quickly towards Saladin Street. "We had no idea where we were supposed to fight," Avidan said later, "so we organized for classic warfare in a

7*

built-up area – two platoons forward, to clear out and mop up, and a platoon to the rear, to deal with road-crossings. But we did not know Jerusalem, and it never occurred to us that the buildings ahead were five stories high, with enclosed yards."

Because of the immediate sniper fire, buildings could not be cleared out and the original plan was scrapped. Avidan ordered his men to move forward quickly, and they did so, stopping occasionally to demolish a machine-gun nest in a back-yard. But despite the rapid advance, casualties mounted.

Yossi P., advancing at the head of "C" Company behind the spearhead group, saw that this was battle unlike any other he had ever fought in. Although his force was on an already cleared-out route, where the "A" Company wounded were lying unmolested in entry-ways and alongside the road, resistance continued. Legionnaires, who had retreated to the back-yards when "A" Company attacked, returned and blocked the road after the company had gone by and had once more to be driven back at the cost of new casualties.

Yossi P., fearing that "A" Company had been too weakened to continue at the head of the assault, ordered Alex, C.O. of "C" Company, to take the lead. Nearby, at a bend in Nablus Road, a gas station was converted by order of the battalion commander into a casualty station. A few meters away, the force was attacked opposite a cul-de-sac, delaying its advance and multiplying its casualties. The cul-de-sac later came to be known as Death Alley.

At about 4:00 a.m., after the sappers had widened the passage through the minefield in front of the police school, deputy company commander Raffy Yeshayahu assembled his two tank platoons (the other one was with the 71st Battalion in the Gan Abramov sector), which had previously been a firing base supporting the 66th Battalion. Captain Yeshayahu was in the lead tank, which a paratrooper directed through the mine-free passage. The tank nevertheless crushed and detonated dozens of booby-traps which had eluded the sappers, but the paratrooper, to Raffy's amazement, swung along cleanly, without stepping on a single one.

The passage beyond the mine-field was blocked by a low fence, knocked down by the tank, which managed at the last moment to avoid riding over it, while all around men shouted, "Don't move! watch out for our wounded!"

The police school was now cleared out and the C.O. of the 66th was preparing to march his men into the Sheikh Jarrah Quarter. The tanks joined him. At the Ambassador Hotel the force took its positions.

Raffy was told to return two of the tanks to Ammunition Hill and about an hour later to advance in support of the 28th Battalion, now in trouble on the streets of East Jerusalem.

Yossi therefore reorganized his forces. Alex, commanding "C" Company, was convinced that to move through streets thick with snipers meant heavy casualties, because he knew that the Legion's snipers retreated deep into the backyards as the Israelis approached and emerged when they passed by. So he altered the order of advance, sending his men through the backyards to rout out the snipers and force them into the street.

The change was effective, but the company erred by leaving the Nablus Road and returning to Saladin Street, followed by the Battalion H.Q. and "A" Company. The supporting company, however, was so far in the rear that it turned left instead of right and found itself in the American Colony, now being captured by the 71st Battalion. With the Battalion's command group they moved to the rear of the Rockefeller Museum.

To the Moslem Cemetery

In spite of the tanks, the fighting on Nablus Road was tough and protracted. Guns were fired at the Israelis from houses on both sides of the road and from the Old City walls at its western end, and although the tanks offered cover against the barrage and assistance in silencing some of it, cooperation between them and the paratroops was imperfect. The paratroopers, untrained in fighting with armor, tended to crowd the tanks because only a few knew that they could communicate by means of the rear telephones. After one tank commander had been killed and several crew-members wounded, the tankmen withdrew into the tanks and closed the turrets. To make contact with the tankmen, therefore, to guide them to positions opposite Jordanian strongholds, the paratroopers had to throw stones at the turret or bang on the sides with their Uzzis. On the whole, however, the tanks' presence was of great help.

The closer the column drew to the wall, the fiercer became the resistance. Yossi P. decided to get off Nablus Road and go to the Rockefeller Museum through the backyards of houses, protected from the terrible shooting from the walls. The tanks, whose commanders had not been apprised of Yossi's decision, suddenly found themselves without paratroopers. They lumbered to the end of the road, stopped, exchanged fire with the fortified positions on the wall until their ammunition ran out, turned around, and returned to the police college.

In the back-yards, the 28th Battalion split into three forces, one in the Rivoli Hotel on Saladin Street opposite the wall, where it was holed up until evening because it was in direct line of the wall's fire. A second force thrust towards the Schmidt Convent and Girls School, where they too remained shooting it out with the Arabs on top of the wall. The third force, and with it the battalion commander, pressed on through the back-yards and reached St. Stephen's Church and the Moslem Cemetery opposite Herod's Gate. There guns blazed at them and for the next two hours the men lay flat, taking cover behind the grave-stones in the cemetery, never showing their heads. From there, the C.O. radioed to Uzi of the 71st and asked for help in capturing the Rockefeller Museum, because of his battalion's losses and his present enforced immobility.

Within Grenade Range of the Old City

Uzi was in one of the Wadi Joz alleys a hundred meters or so behind the museum when Yossi P.'s appeal came. He said to Michael Adam, deputy commander of the 28th's supporting company, who was with him, "Your battalion's bogged down. You'll have to take the museum."

Michael at once began to plan.

The supporting company's paratroops swarmed over the museum under fire from the top of the Old City walls, and from a small olive grove to the north. The paratroopers raided and cleared the grove. They entered the museum through the unlocked northern door, captured it, and raised the Israeli flag. They cleared the route to the museum to make it accessible. Before noon the commander and men of the 28th were extricated from the Moslem cemetery and battalion headquarters set up in the museum. Only a few meters separated them from the walls of the Old City and Herod's Gate.

To Binyanei Ha'ooma

At 3:00 a.m. we were on the roof of the soup kitchen on Yoel Street, our eyes on the flames from the U.N.R.W.A. stores in the police school grounds. The battle for Ammunition Hill was not over. We tried unsuccessfully to reconstruct events from the radioed messages of the battalion and company commanders, but very few orders were given by radio. Only brief and non-committal news came from the brigade: "Advancing as per plan...everything's fine..." On the strength of these reports, we thought that the battle was ending and that if the paratroops were actually to take the police school and occupy the Sheikh Jarrah Quarter, the spotlight would focus again on the 10th Brigade.

From the Yoel Street roof I had no way of radioing Uri or my headquarters in Ramla. My equipment was in the jeep from which we had bolted, and I decided to go and get it, telling Motta that I would be back shortly. With Koby I went down the darkened staircase to the street.

It was deserted. The paratroopers who had been waiting had gone off to battle, but a salvo of shells greeted us nonetheless. We dashed across the alley into the sand-bagged shelter of the building opposite.

"Who's there?" came the frightened whisper from a ground-floor flat. The bombardment had been so long and so fierce that the tenants thought the Legionnaires had finally reached their quarter, but we assured them that we were Zahal soldiers and they relaxed.

When the shelling diminished, we went around the corner to the jeep, where Yoel, waiting impatiently nearby, had taken cover behind a wall. But Zabotaro had disappeared. We called him, searched frantically, and finally found him hiding in a shelter to escape the bombs.

When we tried to start the engine we discovered an unexploded 81-mm mortar shell between the rear wheels of the jeep. Very cautiously I maneuvered the jeep over the dud and out of trouble.

We drove towards the basement of Binyanei Ha'ooma, amidst the shambles left by the Jordanian bombs. Telephone and electric cables and wires were down. Water tanks on roofs were riddled with bullets and shrapnel, and water streamed into the streets, leaving gleaming pools everywhere. We passed shelled vehicles in front of bullet-ridden store shutters and uprooted tree-trunks blocking the roadway. The town had had it in a big way.

We had hardly reached Binyanei Ha'ooma when the radio began to crackle. "Report just received from the 55th Brigade: 'Police school taken'." At once I contacted Motta, who confirmed the news, adding that the battle for Ammunition Hill was still in progress. I did not at the moment consider this an objective of particular importance. From

the outset we had assessed the college as the primary obstacle, with
Ammunition Hill only a flanking strongpoint, used for covering-fire
and support purposes. Motta also said that after the college had been
occupied and cleared, some of the forces had gone into the Sheikh
Jarrah Quarter and taken the Eye Hospital and the Ambassador
Hotel. Everything was proceeding as planned.

Opposite Tel el-Ful

At 03.52 I contacted my Ramla headquarters to ask about Uri, who, I
was told, was struggling over the terrain and would soon need more
fuel for his tanks. I asked to be hooked into his internal radio network
and as soon as I heard his voice I asked for a report.

"I'm about one-and-a-half kilometers east of Beit Hanina, on a hill
about 400 meters long on a dirt-track." The map showed a hill marked
Hirbet Zahara (Tel Zahara), not far from the Ramallah-Jerusalem
highway. "Biddu is in our hands," he continued. "A second force is
east of it and in an hour-and-a-half most of us will be with the men at
Biddu."

"Do you intend to move on to the junction right away?" (the Beit
Hanina-Ramallah Junction).

"No. I need more men, but in the meantime, my unit is blocking
the junction with tank gunfire from a range of one-and-a-quarter
kilometers."

"Is there a force like yours opposite?" (I meant tanks).

"So far I've not seen one. Do you know anything about it?"

"I know there is one. From the highpoint [Mount Scopus] they saw
one climbing up from the Plains [of Jordan]. A large number. Air is
dealing with them."

"Do you want me to do anything?"

"The paratroops have done what they were supposed to. I want you
to turn right and liquidate their positions as soon as you reach the main
road."

These were the positions north of Jerusalem at Tel el-Ful, Shu'afat
and Givat Hamivtar. I figured that although they were strongly
defended from the south they were less well defended from the north,
at their rear, but it later transpired that they were defended peripherally all-round. Uri repeated my instructions.

"You mean that when I get away, I'm to take Tel el-Ful. Right?"

"Take it when you have the strength. Protect yourself towards the
north and east, and go full steam south."

The Capture of Nabi Samuel

At 01.30 hours Uri's "A" Battalion completed the capture of the three radar redoubts, and moved most of its force through the mine-field. "A" Battalion's C.O. reported to the commander of the 10th Brigade that they were ready to capture Biddu, but were told to wait, because "B" Battalion was going there.

Armored Battalion "B" was, however, still reorganizing after the hard battle for Hirbet e-Lauza. At 02.00 hours the Brigade C.O. ordered Armored Battalion "A" to begin an assault on Biddu, but an anti-tank obstacle on their route had to be blown up, delaying the attack until 02.30 hours. The force advanced under heavy fire from the fortified strongpoint of Jebel e-Sheikh where, behind a long stone wall, a Jordanian infantry company had taken up positions.

The C.O. wanted the lead tanks to stand in the field and demolish fortifications in the village itself, with the idea of softening up the village first and afterwards attacking the Jebel e-Sheikh position; "C" Company would meanwhile pass through the village to the fortifications. He reasoned that the position was defended to the south, towards Radar 3, but not towards Biddu village. His reasoning proved correct.

"C" Company, originally behind the tanks, pulled ahead while the tanks started the softening-up process. The men drove through the village, emerged from their half-tracks at the foot of the fortifications and spread out along the trenches. The battle that developed was so fierce that in the morning the bodies of 22 dead Jordanian soldiers were found in the trenches. Almost all the Uzzi ammunition and hand-grenades were dissipated in a battle whose outcome was decided only when the C.O. sent three tanks forward in direct support of the attackers. The retreating Jordanians opened fire upon the abandoned fortifications from an artillery battery positioned somewhere to the south. By order of the Brigade commander, the entire battalion reorganized in Biddu and its environs, which became the Brigade's firm base.

Armored Battalion "B" advanced and passed Beit Surik without a fight, waiting at the foot of Biddu until armored Battalion "A" had captured the village, and continuing thence on a good asphalt road. Because of that road, the Brigade commander thought that "B" Battalion should be the Brigade's spearhead and reinforced it. It was a considerable force, led by the four tanks from "E" Company after their battle for Sheikh Abdul-Aziz and Hirbet e-Lauza. Ehud Shani's armored cars came next, then three companies of armored infantry, with a tank company as rearguard. Because the road was narrow, the order of advance could not be changed and the battalion moved in identical order in all the battles fought that day. The armored infantry company, for instance, which had lost its commanding officer Assa Yaguri and many of its men at the Abdul-Aziz redoubt, continued to lead.

The men approached Nabi Samuel and prepared for battle, their faces grave and their minds burdened with the rumors they had heard of this fearsome village whose towering turret was plainly visible from the Jerusalem-Tel Aviv highway. Now everything was quiet. Not until the lead tanks had crossed through were light weapons fired. In instantaneous reaction, mortar fire was laid down upon the village, armored vehicles halted and traded shots, and the half-tracks waddled up the steep hill, their machine-guns spattering fire. The battle for Nabi Samuel was over in a matter of minutes. The half-tracks combed the village and reported that whatever snipers had hidden there were either dead or in full retreat.

The battalion's column renewed its advance. It was 6.30 on Tuesday morning, and the roar of guns could be heard from the east, where a tank battalion was fighting the vanguard of the 60th Armored Brigade, which had escaped the aerial bombardment at Ma'alei Ha'adumim and reached the mountain ridges.

Sherman Versus Patton

Of the entire battalion, only six Sherman tanks of Major Uri Braz's Company, some ten armored half-tracks commanded by Captain David Cana'ani, and one 81-mm. mortar battery reached Hirbet Zahara, covering the last stage of the journey in anxious anticipation of what awaited them. Were the Jordanian tanks already there? When the commander, Lt. Colonel Zwicka, looked up at the hill and the vehicles on the Ramallah-Jerusalem highway, he was profoundly relieved. No enemy tanks were in sight.

The tanks moved forward and opened fire on the highway. The marksmanship was good. An ammunition truck went up in flames, another overturned when its driver tried to avoid the truck ahead, and several drivers abandoned their vehicles and ducked along the edge of the road, which was soon empty of traffic.

A peaceful hour went by. Far to the rear, where "B" Armored Battalion had advanced, the shooting and mine explosions in the battle for Nabi Samuel could be heard. But here, on Hirbet Zahara, the war seemed to have ended. In the distance rose Tel el-Ful: above it on a ridge stood King Hussein's unfinished palace. At the foot of the Tel lay the houses of Shu'afat and Beit Hanina, shuttered and silent.

Suddenly a shell shrieked. The silhouette of a Patton tank loomed on the slope of Tel el-Ful. The Shermans opened fire, but the shells, which the marksmen were sure had hit the target, seemed to bounce off its armor, and the Patton withdrew and vanished. Six others immediately appeared on the ridge north of Tel el-Ful and an anti-tank gun on the Tel's slope opened fire.

Capt. Cana'ani was galvanized into action when he saw the Pattons. While the Shermans were practising marksmanship on the vehicles along the highway, his men had remained idle on the rear incline of Tel Zahara. Now he ordered them to leave their half-tracks, assemble their machine-guns and bazookas, and organize for ground defense. But to provide cover for the half-tracks was impossible, and because the steep and deeply pocked slope made mobility difficult, the vehicles could not be taken there, since Captain Cana'ani wanted to be ready to move as soon as the order came. So the half-tracks were exposed to Patton gunfire.

They were soon hit, one and then another smashed by shells and a third on fire. Two men of the armored infantry sprang towards it with fire extinguishers, but abandoned it to escape the bombing. The flames took hold again and the ammunition began to explode.

Captain Cana'ani took his men to the bottom of the slope, leaving the six Shermans and the Jordanian Pattons shooting it out on Tel Zahara.

"Can You Flatten the Guns?"

At 4.00 a.m. I spoke to Borka at Ramla headquarters. He complained about Moshik Yotvat's brigade, whose assault on Latrun was delayed, and suggested reinforcing it with half the armored vehicle company. I agreed but ordered that the armored vehicles be transferred to the 10th Brigade as soon as the Latrun action was finished.

Borka said that Zunik, commanding the Givati brigade, wanted permission to advance on Kalkilya.

"And what about Tulkarem?" I asked. "Of course he must have permission. Let him take the whole of Kalkilya. Put pressure on G.H.Q. to authorize it."

Then I reported to General Bar-Lev that Uri was assembling a force near the Beit Hanina junction and would attack Tel el-Ful within the hour and go south to Shu'afat. I also reported Motta's achievements: the police school, Sheikh Jarrah and the American Colony. I added: "Give the order and we'll proceed."

I was told to wait.

At 04.15, when I asked Eliezer Amitai about Sur Baher and whether he was supplying ammunition to Motta, I was given a message from Motta to the effect that the Jordanian artillery was heavily shelling his men.

Since the artillery was obviously from Hizma, something would have to be done at once. I therefore contacted Uri Ben-Ari:

"Opposite you, on the 'Courier' axis, about five kilometers to the east, three artillery batteries are sniping at the paratroopers. Can you flatten them?"

Uri had completely lost his voice after a night of screaming into communications equipment, and his intelligence officer answered for him that they would get word to me in five minutes.

While I waited I asked Dan, the intelligence officer seconded to the Command Group, for the exact location of the enemy battery. He said that, according to the map, there were Jordanian guns not only at Hizma, but at Hirbet Adassiya and al-Jib. I asked what he knew about enemy strength at Tel el-Ful.

Immediately afterwards I told General Zeevi in the Supreme Command redoubt that Hizma, Adassiya and el-Jib were bombarding the paratroops, and requested an aerial attack on them and on the entire route down to Jericho.

The other signals instrument began to squawk. 10th Brigade H.Q. wanted to speak to me. "We haven't enough fuel to carry out the attack," somebody reported, for the Brigade commander. "If you say so, though, we'll try it all the same,"

"It's not a question of my orders. You're on the spot and can see the situation for yourselves. If you can't do it, we'll look for another solution." I, naturally, believed that he was with his tanks on Tel Zahara and learned only later that this was not true.

At 04.40 I was told that the planes had taken off to attack the enemy artillery and contacted Lt. Colonel Davidi, heading the Command artillery:

"Land one burst of 155-mm. on Hizma, before the planes get there."

Immediately afterwards an observer in southern Jerusalem

reported that enemy armored half-tracks had been seen near Mar Elias, to which I replied that the C.O. Jerusalem Brigade should be informed. "He should fix 'em," I said.

Minutes later I told Uri that a kilometer ahead of him at Hirbet Adassiya was a 25-pounder artillery battery, and asked if he could get at them.

He could, but had hardly time to move his force before further information reached me, whether from the intelligence officer or the air force I cannot recall, which sent me scrambling for the microphone:

"Uri, a mistake. As you were. The artillery is not there, but at Hizma. The air force has just jumped them. If you have enough fuel, get up to Tel el-Ful."

"I need a helicopter. The movement axes are unclear."

Arik Regev, who had come on the line from Ramla H.Q., interrupted:

"Helicopter on its way to you at once."

"Where is Uri?" I asked, "and why does he need a helicopter?"

Someone replied on Uri's behalf: "I'm on the Castel. I can't reach my troops. The axes are blocked."

When Arik contacted me from Ramla and asked what to do about the villages near Latrun, I knew for the first time that Latrun had been taken.

Negotiating with Jordan

The authority to take Latrun had been given around midnight on Monday by G.H.Q., after much nagging from Arik Regev. Why permission had been delayed for so long was not clear. Even though G.H.Q. wanted to restrict the war on the Jordanian front and to remove Jordan from the war if it were remotely possible, it must have been obvious that from the moment the 10th Brigade began its attack on enemy positions north of the Jerusalem highway (at 17.30 hours), the extent of the war could not be limited. From then on the back of the Jordanian army had to be broken. Why, then, delay the assault on Latrun?

In seeking to answer this question, I have reckoned with the fact that even though the guns were allowed to speak, it was still not war, but a stage in the political struggle, managed in accordance with political considerations, which are not always brought to the attention of a general officer commanding a region. Taking these two reservations into account, therefore, the answer seemed to be that the declared aim of the political arm through Monday, June 5th, was to restrict the fighting on the Jordanian front and, if possible, to restore the cease-fire there. This goal was no less valid in the afternoon, after Brigades had been granted permission to launch an attack across the Green Line. The offensive action of the two Brigades had been defensive in purpose: to inhibit Jordanian armed attack on Mt. Scopus. The defense minister had abstained from authorizing any other offensive action on any other section of the Jordanian front.

All that day, furthermore, and until late at night, contact had been maintained with the Jordanians, via the United Nations, to effect a cease-fire. Late in the evening it was proposed that Israel would stop bombarding and encircling Jenin if the Jordanians stopped bombing Jewish settlements.

Then a message was received at G.H.Q. that Jordanian Long Toms were shelling Tel Aviv.

It is impossible to know whether that was the Jordanian reply to our proposal, or whether the timing of the bombardment was coincidental, but, in any event, it appeared to have ended the defense minister's hesitation. At 22.20 hours he said to the others in the Supreme Command's redoubt:

"We've stopped negotiating with the Jordanians."

Within ten minutes Northern Command was ordered to take Jenin. And at 22.50 hours the decision to take Latrun was reached and transmitted to Command about an hour later.

Latrun Police Station is Ours

The plans to capture Latrun, prepared promptly by Central Command, were carried out by Yotvat's Brigade. At midday, June 5th, Yotvat's reserve units, called up by radio, began to arrive and were ordered to replace the infantry units in the fortified positions. But since Jordanian bombing was becoming heavier, threatening the approaches to most of the redoubts along the line, the exchange of troops had to be postponed until dusk. Arik Regev began to reinforce Yotvat's Brigade with whatever came to hand: the Command reconnaissance unit; a company of light tanks; an armored vehicles unit, and a company of Shermans. When Lt. Colonel Elisha turned up with a paratroop force from another Brigade, looking for a job, he was also commandeered.

Finally permission to take Latrun was received. Although the Brigade's forces were still at the stage of leaving their positions and re-organizing, the commander had enough strength at his disposal for immediate operation. After the war, Moshe Yotvat's deputy, Lt. Colonel Naftali, said that one reason for attacking at once was that the 10th Brigade might finish its job in the Jerusalem area and ask to take Latrun itself.

In spite of the complete change in the composition of his forces, Yotvat decided to adhere to the original battle plan, a quick snatch of the Latrun enclave. The reconnaissance company was to put obstacles along the interior road to the enclave from Beit Likiya and Beit Nova, which were to be reinforced by the Command reconnaissance unit and armored vehicles. A second force, a company of Nahal troops with a tank platoon, was to feint an attack from the south, towards Latrun village, and was to be joined by members of Kibbutz Nachshon. Supported by these maneuvers, the main offensive by armor and infantry in half-tracks was to be launched straight down the road from Mishmar Ayalon to the Latrun police station.

Not everything went as planned, because the Sherman tanks for the main force and the armored vehicles for the reconnaissance unit never turned up. At 02.30 hours the reconnaissance unit left without waiting for the latecomers and a scout led them to the bed of the Ayalon River, supposedly easy to negotiate, from which they would surreptitiously reach Beit Nova. But the wadi bed was so muddy that their vehicles began to sink.

The infantry troops had a similar experience in their armored vehicles, which, with the tanks, were to attack the Latrun police station east of the artificial lake near Shaalbim. A scout was sent to lead the company through our minefield, on whose borders it was camped. Finding the clear lane was difficult, and the company commander dismissed the scout and decided to negotiate the passage himself. But when he sent his men on to the river-bed his command vehicles promptly overturned on the slope. Afterwards, they could not find a suitable place to leave the wadi and had to abandon two armored vehicles to the mud.

The forces nevertheless reached their objectives. The Command reconnaissance unit arrived at Beit Nova and the Brigade reconnaissance unit split up, one section moving towards Beit Likiya and the other to its position between Beit Nova and Beit Sira.

Latrun is Ours

By 4 a.m. all blockades had been set up and the diversionary force had opened fire on Latrun village. The infantry in its half-tracks had managed to struggle out of the Ayalon River, but was still on rough territory. The Brigade artillery, however, had been pounding at the Arab Legion's fortified positions for more than an hour.

Now the enemy was withdrawing. The reconnaissance men saw a stream of refugees, Arab Legionnaires among them, wrapped in blankets as though roughly plucked from sleep, moving towards Yailu and Beit Nova, and passing the blockading positions. At 04.40 hours, Lieutenant Gadi Gil, commanding the reconnaissance company, was authorized to attack Beit Likiya while the Command reconnaissance unit surrounded the fortified position near the village. Resistance at both points was slight.

The mobile infantry company was encircling the Latrun police fortress at the same time. "I knew that the area between the police station fences was mined," the company commander said later, "and I had no flame-throwers with me. But the tanks were nearby, and I climbed on the first one and asked its commander to smash down the fence and open a passage. He did so, and I entered the police station yard with the company right behind me. We got to a locked door, the tank battered it down, and we burst into the building and began mopping up."

The attackers thought at first that the building had been deserted long before, but the 20-odd beds in the dormitory were still warm. The entire Latrun enclave, which in 1948 had cost hundreds of Israeli lives without being captured, was now occupied in less than two hours without a serious fight.

Commander Moshe Yotvat, who had fought there during the War of Independence, attached his Command group to the force charging the police station, and at 5 o'clock that morning was able to report to Regional Command, "Latrun police fortress is in my hands!" The police station therefore became the target for all the units that had lost their way in the night, and one by one they turned up there.

Until now the conquests had been achieved by hard bargaining with Command Headquarters over every objective. Arik found it difficult to trust the minimal resistance in the enclave and, suspecting a trap, postponed permission to take Beit Likiya until he was assured that the tanks were fighting for the police fortress. He later delayed the attack on Beit Nova until he learned that the lost armored vehicles had returned and joined the reconnaissance company. When, shortly afterwards, the Brigade commander reported that the reconnaissance unit had driven through Beit Sira and found it calm and flying white flags, Arik decided that the enemy's defenses had utterly disintegrated.

"From now on," he instructed Colonel Yotvat, "go full speed along the highway. The whole axis is yours. You don't need authority for every objective. I hope you take upper Beit Horon by midday and from there move on to the Beitaniya junction."

Arik knew the region well and the pains the Jordanians had taken to fortify it; he never dreamed that the Brigade would get to the Beitaniya junction before the end of the day. "What shall we do about the four villages in the Latrun enclave? Take 'em?" Arik asked me.

"Sure," I said, "including Beit Nova." Even if a cease-fire were forced upon us, even if we were obliged to withdraw to the Green Line, I was determined that the Latrun enclave, that years-old thorn in our flesh, would never be returned.

June 6th, 1967

With the capture of Latrun, the Ramallah highway towards the mountain ridges was open for us, but I wondered whether enough 10th Brigade tanks would arrive at Tel el-Ful ready for battle. More than any other arm of the defense forces, the armored corps depended upon supply lines. Without fuel it was paralyzed. The 10th Brigade travelled emergency routes which, even under normal conditions, were uncertain, and now, jammed with dead tanks and out-of-action half-tracks, getting supplies through to Uri was problematic indeed. I thought of the road from Jerusalem north, through Sheikh Jarrah, and I contacted Motta:

"What's happening at your end?" He told me that the forces had been reorganized after the night-battle and that they had been heavily bombed. "We're about to shell their artillery at Hizma," I told him. (Lt. Colonel Davidi had informed me a few moments earlier that a mobile 155-mm. battery was ready to open fire.) "What about Rockefeller?" I asked, to which he repeated that the Jordanian bombardment was holding them up.

At 05.12 hours I asked Uri if he had taken Nabi Samuel and was told that the village was at that moment under attack.

"When will you be ready to attack Tel el-Ful?"

"Not right now. I've got to check the condition of the tanks there."

We were still talking when a violent explosion threatened to bring Binyanei Ha'ooma down on our heads. It turned out that the 10th Brigade, deployed in the square in front of the building, had fired a 120-mm. mortar battery at Nabi Samuel to support the attacking force. The mortars stopped. "Now the assault begins," I said to myself.

I returned to the basement, where there was a message from Arik: "The air force has detected a convoy of about one hundred vehicles coming up from Jericho."

I called him: "Air attention immediately on Jericho highway. And, since you've got the chance, on Hizma also. Has Uri taken off?"

"No. The air force say they cannot dispatch a helicopter because of air activity in the Jerusalem sector."

Uri reported the capture of Nabi Samuel, plus the fact that one of his battalion was tied down, forming a firm base in the captured village.

I contacted the C.O. Amitai to ask him to dispatch one of his Jerusalem Brigade units to take over Biddu and Beit Surik. He replied that his forces, the battalions of Zwicka Ofer and Michael Paikes, were in that sector, but he would send a guard unit, mobilized the previous day, to relieve them.

I suggested that he try to get a tractor for them to help open up a movement axis, and asked what was new in the south and in Sur Baher and Abu-Tor.

Amitai reported quiet at Sur Baher and no battle as yet at Abu-Tor, but at that moment received a message on a second instrument, which he passed on to me. It came from Mt. Scopus, where they could see air force planes swooping down on an enemy convoy coming from Jericho. The marksmanship was excellent. Vehicles were ablaze. When I was told that enemy vehicles had reached Shu'afat, I asked if they were tanks or soft vehicles, but they were apparently hard to identify. "Ask the air force to deal with them, too," I said.

At 05.45 Uri reported that he had given orders to capture Tel el-Ful and a minute later it was announced that opposite one of his tank units at Tel Zahara, Patton tanks had been spotted and armor was now battling armor. Several of our half-tracks were on fire. I contacted Borka at Ramla Headquarters to tell him that the first priority was a helicopter for Uri, and that the entire Brigade was being delayed. Since I couldn't get through to them, I wanted Borka to nag G.H.Q. "What about Latrun?" I asked. He replied that Yotvat was advancing along the Ramallah highway.

Signalmen at Binyanei Ha'ooma finally made contact with G.H.Q., where Eli Sarid, aide to C.O.G.S., answered. I asked that Uri be given a helicopter, preferably a Bell, and explained that each minute of delay was costly for north Jerusalem.

Immediately afterwards I said to Arik, "It's essential to move fuel to the 10th Brigade. He has fuel in his supply column and is opening up an axis for himself via Beit Iksa, but it would be better if the Command could give him engineering help." It was unfortunate that our engineering battalions had been sent to the southern front when we needed them so seriously.

At last I was informed that a helicopter had been earmarked for Uri, and at 06.30 hours, I contacted him to ask if he was attacking Tel el-Ful. He wasn't, and did not know when he would start, since there were fuel problems.

The fuel situation became more acute, and the deputy C.O., Lt. Col. Eldad, suggested that fuel be supplied, at least to the advance forces, by helicopter. When I instructed Borka to check out the possibility, he informed me that Moshik's brigade had taken lower Beit Horon. That was wonderfully welcome news, and Moshik's speedy advance surprised me, but my joy was not unmixed. The Brigade would now be near upper Beit Horon, whose winding road, snaking up the steep gradient, I could visualize, as well as the village, perched like an eagle's eyrie at the peak of the incline. It was a natural fortress on the Jerusalem highway, and an ancient historic battlefield, where Judah Maccabee had defeated the army of Nacanor. Now the roles were changed, and the Jewish army was struggling up the slopes against an enemy securely dug in at the mountain-top. When Borka suggested reinforcing Yotvat's brigade with the extra tank company the Command had placed at his disposal, I agreed. "Fine. And get them going fast."

At 06.50 hours the General Headquarters wanted news. I told them of Uri's fuel shortage, which I thought would be rectified within the hour, and said that he was opening up a route from Beit Iksa, but that it would be two hours before he joined the paratroop brigade in north Jerusalem. (I estimated 9:00 a.m., but Uri actually reached Hamivtar at 10 o'clock and captured it an hour later.) I told General Zeevi that there would probably be no enemy armor at Ma'aleh Ha'adumim.

Although the 10th Brigade continued to wait, I was no longer worried. The successful air force bombing of the convoy from Jericho and the rapid advance of Yotvat's Brigade cheered me considerably. It remained only for Uri to fuel up and begin to move. At 06.55 hours I asked to speak to him.

"After you take Tel el-Ful, continue to Shu'afat, French Hill and Hamivtar. Put a suitable force at the position towards the east and then go on to Ramallah."

THE OLD CITY STILL
"OUT OF BOUNDS"

Rockefeller Captured

At 7.00 a.m. Ramla informed me about futher reinforcement by a paratroop reconnaissance unit under Micha Kapusta, a veteran of the 101st unit, who had come looking for a job to do. He had always impressed me with his description of the upper Beit Horon fixed defenses, which, because they were dubbed unconquerable in our war games, we sought devious means of outflanking.

I considered including him in the attack on the stronghold. But by the time my suggestion reached Command Headquarters at Ramla his unit had left for Jerusalem, where it was eagerly adopted by the paratroop brigade. It would fulfill a glorious tragic role in Jerusalem in what came to be known as "The Battle on the Bridge."

At 07.47 hours Motta announced the capture of Rockefeller.

"Thank God. What about Herod's Gate?"

"We can see it from here. It's closed."

Beit Horon is Ours

Yotvat took upper Beit Horon at 8:00 a.m. His spearhead unit reached Beit Horon almost by accident. The Command reconnaissance unit finished cleaning up the Arab Legion's fortified position north of Beit Likiya village, and, according to the commander, "our momentum took us to the Beit Auer-Tachta junction [lower Beit Horon]."

The highway to Ramallah rises from lower Beit Horon in a steep, winding gradient, with upper Beit Horon at its peak. We knew that the Jordanians had fortified both villages as well as every terrace and bend along the road. About two kilometers south of upper Beit Horon, near Tira village, there was a large military camp with, we judged, a force of infantry battalion size. Whether or not the Jordanians ever studied *The Wars of the Maccabees*, their defense dispositions were nonetheless similar to those of Judah Maccabee against the army of Lysias: a strong restraining force atop the height, on upper

Beit Horon, and a second force to provide a flanking counter-blow on the army spread out in a long column along the narrow incline.

The commander of the reconnaissance unit had no time for such historical matters. "We attacked Beit Auer-Tachta," he said. "There was no serious resistance. Shots here and there, which didn't hold us up. We sallied in and whenever we saw anybody in khaki, we fired."

By the time the reconnaissance unit had finished mopping up in the village, the Brigade commander had organized the men he had assembled near the Latrun police station, taken his position in the lead, and rushed quickly ahead. The force climbed toward Beit Horon, the armored vehicles leading the column in case of a tank ambush, behind them the reconnaissance unit, and then the infantry in half-tracks, ready for an out-flanking movement against a road block. Now and then shots from light weapons were fired at the column and the Brigade commander urged his men to make better speed. He felt that the enemy defenses were crumbling and that the sooner he reached the ridges the less chance they would have to regroup.

Upper Beit Horon, astride the mountain, towered above the column, its stone houses tiered fortress-like on top of each other. To its right were the Jordanian fortifications, fronted by concrete walls serving as a tank obstacle, barbed-wire entanglements and machine-gun posts. The armored cars came to a halt and bombarded and smashed the bunkers from 400 meters away. The infantry dashed out of the half-tracks and burst into the fortified position from the flank, and the reconnaissance unit stormed through the village and swept toward the camp at Tira with the armored vehicles, which had ceased firing when the infantry jumped into the trenches. The camp appeared to be deserted, but when the first car had broken through the gate the unit commander, in a jeep directly behind, spotted several soldiers in mottled uniforms near one of the buldings.

"I thought they were ours," he said, "because the Legionnaires aren't usually camouflaged. I wondered where they'd come from."

Suddenly the mottled figures strafed them with machine-guns. They turned out to be part of an Egyptian commando batttalion, which had arrived on June 4th and set up headquarters at Tira. Two of its companies had been sent to the Latrun enclave early on June 5th, and the next night, a few hours before Yotvat assaulted the enclave, had begun to infiltrate Israeli territory, their main assignment Lod airport. They never reached their objective. Several, spotted in the Latrun fields on Tuesday morning, June 6th, when they attacked supply vehicles of the Brigade, were surrounded, and when the fields where they were hiding were set on fire, had to surrender. Some, who had managed to escape from the plains, retreated eastwards and ran into other Israeli units. Still more lost their way and wandered into Israeli territory. On the morning of the fourth day of the war, three of them were caught near Beit Dagon.

An accurate burst of fire from the machine-gun carrying jeeps ended the Egyptian action. From a heavily treed height east of the camp, shots whose source was impossible to pinpoint were fired at the column. The armored vehicles and jeeps continued toward the assault area, climbed the shoulder of the height and found themselves face-to-face with eight Jordanian recoilless-gun-carrying jeeps less than 300 meters away. The Jordanians fired first.

"They must have been scared out of their minds," the unit commander said. "There's no other reason why they didn't hit us. We were a perfect target."

Before the second round was fired, he managed to move his forces behind the shoulder of the slope. Mortar shells began to fall all around. The company commander called for full strength, and the armored vehicles kept the enemy busy. The Jordanians were well-trained. They pulled themselves together, changed positions after each round of shots and exploited the terrain to the full in order to find and take cover. But the Israeli column reduced their chances to zero. The tanks and armored vehicles spread out at the side of the road, and opened fire and set three Jordanian jeeps aflame. When our infantry began to outflank the enemy, the Jordanian commander gave the order to retreat. The road to Ramallah was now open.

The force regrouped. The Brigade reconnaissance unit set out with the Commander for Rafa'at village, east of the Bitunim junction, where they were to find and destroy the retreating Long Tom cannons. The remainder halted for refuelling. Everyone was tired and hungry – they had neither eaten nor slept since the previous night – but there was no food and there would be no rest. Elisha's paratroopers had brought rusks, which they divided with the soldiers of the armored infantry company, and they all sat on the vehicles for a little while and munched their dry biscuits.

The Option

The reports of the two Brigade commanders were electrifying. The paratroopers waited at the gates of the Old City, ready to attack when the order came. Yotvat's Brigade was celebrating victory on the heights of Beit Horon, and the armored corps, which had broken the Jordanian defenses west of Jerusalem, were ready to move on, to wipe out all the enemy strongholds in north Jerusalem.

If only these were not delayed. For beside the joy and satisfaction, suspicion was growing. That we were victorious was clear, and must have been equally obvious to the enemy, who, under the conditions, would surely try to crush my hopes and work on a cease-fire order. To Yosh Harpaz I said, "Now they [G.H.Q.] have to let us into the Old City! If not, a cease-fire will be declared."

My suspicions were not unfounded. King Hussein's memoirs record that he had at that moment concluded that the war on the West Bank was decided and that, with Egyptian General Riadh, commander of the eastern front, he had determined to present Nasser with the options which they thought were still open. Riadh sent a cable saying:

"The situation on the West Bank is worse than hopeless. The Israeli attack is moving forward on all sectors. We are being bombed from the air relentlessly and are not strong enough to stop them. The following options are open to us:

A political solution, to obtain an immediate cease-fire.

Evacuation of the entire West Bank tonight.

Holding out 24 hours more, in which event the destruction of the Jordanian Army will be unavoidable."

Twelve hours passed before Nasser's reply: "I believe our only option is total retreat from the West Bank and a cease-fire declared by the Security Council."

Uri was on the point of renewing his attack and breaking into Jerusalem from the north, from Givat Hamivtar. I was worried about a possible clash between his armored cars and our paratroop forces in Sheikh Jarrah. At any moment we might be permitted to enter the Old City.

I decided to return to the paratroopers. General Amos Horev, who had come into Binyanei Ha'ooma a few minutes earlier, and the Command signals officer left with me for the paratroop advance command group on the roof of the soup kitchen on Yoel Street. We arrived at 8:04 a.m. and went up to the roof, where things were exactly as they had been when we departed. The same group of Gur, Stempel, his deputy, several staff officers, some signalmen and runners were there, the fatigue on their faces etched deep by the morning light and their beards beginning to show. Somebody brought coffee, and we talked briefly. Motta was satisfied with the achievement of his brigade in the night battle, but he had no detailed reports and no word of how heavy his losses were. I looked north from the ledge of the roof. Dozens of buildings were burning and smoke lay like a cloud on the whole city, all the way to Mt. Scopus. The stutter of machine-guns and the explosion of shells persisted. The battle continued.

I contacted Eliezer Amitai, convinced that soon we would be given permission to enter the Old City. A discussion in which the defense minister participated was then going on in the redoubt of the Supreme Command, where it was decided that we would take the gates but not enter the Old City. I knew nothing of that and told the Jerusalem Brigade commander, "When the paratroopers begin, set off an explosion on your side of the wall, on Mount Zion, as a diversion."

Then I contacted Uri: "When do you start?"

"Not before 08.30," was the reply.

They Still Won't Let Me In

At 08.30 Yosh contacted me from Binyanei Ha'ooma and told me that Yotvat's brigade was continuing towards Bitonia. At 08.53 I asked, "Has Yotvat reached the Bitonia junction? Or will he attack it? Be sure that there's radio contact between him and Uri. Check what this flight is bombing. Over Tel el-Ful? Fine!"

A few minutes later Yosh transmitted Supreme Command's instructions about not entering the Old City and taking only the Jaffa and Damascus Gates.

"Are you sure?" I didn't want to believe him. "We'll try to take the gates." The order was a terrible blow.

The next few minutes were packed and tense. The 10th Brigade was about to begin an assault and we had to plan its next stages quickly. Yosh informed me that G.H.Q. considered it important to stop bombing West Jerusalem, and that the defense minister suggested that the 10th Brigade, after capturing Givat Hamivtar, carve a straight line to northeastern Jerusalem, thus controlling the deployment area of the Jordanian artillery.

I therefore worked out a plan:

1. The 10th Brigade would get to Hamivtar and French Hill and transfer a tank company to the paratroops; then it would bear north and east, destroy the enemy guns, absorb units of Yotvat's Brigade at the Bitonia junction and attack and capture Ramallah. Then they would continue north and

join the Northern Command, securing the roads leading to the Jordan Valley to prevent surprises from that direction.

2. The Jerusalem Brigade was to relieve the paratroops at the police school, take French Hill, Mt. Scopus, Hamivtar and Shu'afat, and then capture Augusta Victoria and A-Tur and block the approaches from Jericho.

3. The 55th Brigade was to assemble two of its battalions at Sheikh Jarrah, and be ready to move off with the 10th Brigade tank company. I did not specify where they were to move, hoping that the ban on our entrance into the Old City would be lifted, at which time the paratroopers would carry out the breakthrough.

The plan was soon changed, since it transpired that permission to enter the Old City would not be forthcoming. The Jerusalem Brigade, furthermore, was finding it difficult to assemble the force for its assigned objectives because two of its battalions were far from the Municipal Line. I therefore instructed Eliezer Amitai to take responsibility for the police school from the paratroops and to transfer to them the Brigade's assignment to capture Augusta Victoria and A-Tur.

The Air Force reported enemy armor on the movement axis to Hizma. They saw four Pattons on French Hill, which aircraft were dispatched to take out of action.

I was told that the defense minister would be in Jerusalem at midday and to meet him at the Schneller Camp. As I was leaving the Yoel Street roof, news came that Colonel Yotvat had been wounded in an exchange of fire with Jordanian soldiers in ambush near the Bitonia junction. His deputy, Lt. Colonel Naftali, had taken command, which I authorized.

Gur decided to leave Yoel Street and, since news from his battalion commanders was scanty, to establish headquarters at the Rockefeller Museum, closer to his troops and to the Old City, should the instructions be altered. I joined him.

The Hidden Scrolls

We set out in convoy. The paratroops' forward command group were first, in two armored half-tracks, with my group in two jeeps right behind them. With the command group were three civilians, the archeologist Abraham Biran and two of his professional colleagues, Joseph Aviram and Prof. Nahcan Avigad. Only after the war was I told the strange tale of the three archeologists and the 55th Brigade. Early Tuesday morning the door-bell rang at Yigal Yadin's house in Rehavia, Jerusalem. The professor's wife, Carmela, opened the door to find herself facing a tired and soot-covered paratrooper, one of those who had captured the Rockefeller Museum. He was a Jerusalemite whose wife had given birth the night before and who had been granted an hour's leave to visit her in the hospital. But the paratrooper had a more important task to perform first and hurried to the Yadin house to discharge it.

"Rockefeller is full of fantastic items," he told Carmela Yadin. "While we're there, we can take care of them, but we'll have to be moving on and it's important to have somebody around to keep an eye open."

He then rushed to the hospital and Carmela rushed to phone her husband at G.H.Q. Yadin, who hoped to find more sections of the hidden scrolls, immediately got in touch with the three archeologists and asked them to get to the Rockefeller Museum by any means available.

The alleys of Beit Israel and Sanhedria were empty of traffic. From windows and rooftops civilians waved to us, their faces full of confidence and faith in spite of their night of heavy shelling.

We stopped for a while at the P.Ag.I. houses to find out where the transit point was to the police school. Soldiers showed us a breach in the barbed-wire entanglement, where sappers of the Jerusalem Brigade were still clearing away landmines from both sides of the narrow passage which had been marked with white ribbons. We were warned not to step over the markers because the area was still heavily mined, but my jeep detonated an explosive that had apparently escaped the sappers. It was small, however, and caused no damage. We drove on, across the yard of the police school; to our right, the large U.M.R.W.A. stores were still burning; to our left, tired, soot-blackened paratroopers moved about their tasks. A stream of bullets from the flank bit the ground and sent swirls of dust around us. We accelerated through the camp gate, hanging by its hinges after its encounter with one of our tanks, and crossed an open field to the Jerusalem-Ramallah highway. Here we turned south into the Sheikh Jarrah Quarter, still and somber, its shutters closed over lifeless windows, and arrived at the Ambassador Hotel, from whose entrance paratroopers stared at us and waved in surprise at their commander. We went on towards the Wadi Joz junction, where the paratroopers had found time to set up a small, improvized memorial to their fallen comrades.

About fifty meters past the junction, one of the armored half-tracks of the paratroops' command group slipped a track, and its crew hurried into another half-track, which continued east. When shooting started and bullets shrieked above us, Amos Horev, who was in my jeep, urged me to go back. "This is no place for people in jeeps." I agreed perfectly and told Motta I was returning. At the Wadi Joz junction, instead of going to the Ambassador we continued south on the Nablus Road to find out how far the paratroopers had advanced. Near the American Colony Hotel, we were again surrounded by the sight and sound of war. The house of Anwar Nusseib, one of the richest and most important men in Arab Jerusalem, was burning; from behind it guns could be heard; on the road was a Jordanian recoilless-gun-carrying jeep with the bodies of two Jordanian soldiers on the front seat.

A paratrooper, crouching behind a stone wall, gestured to us. "Don't go any farther, there's fighting going on."

The Spanish Consul

As we swung back towards the Ambassador, we noticed a huge flag fluttering from the Spanish Consulate on our left.

After the war, the Consul told me that "when the shooting started on June 5th, the Arabs in Jerusalem were filled with optimism. They boasted about how soon they would be in Tel Aviv. But during the night everything went berserk – instead of an Arab advance, your bombs fell all around, so near that the house shook. Glasses fell off the shelves; nothing was steady. I sent the staff down to the basement because the explosions and the bullets were coming closer and closer.

"Suddenly there was a burst of gunfire and the front door was smashed open. I went to meet the intruders. They were your men, their faces flushed with battle, their machine-guns gripped tight. I was quite sure they would start shooting. 'I am the Spanish Consul,' I called to them in English. 'Are there any Arab Legionnaires here?' asked one of the men. When I said no, he persisted. 'On your honor?' When I gave him my word he said something to his men and they left. If you ever find out who it was, thank him for me. People don't usually act like that in the midst of battle."

We reached the Ambassador, which bore no signs of the previous night's uproar. The only visible evidence of war were the Israeli soldiers standing, sitting, lying exhausted near its entrance. Some rested against the gift-shop window adjoining the hotel, but nobody touched the expensive cameras on display.

Doron, deputy commander of the 66th Battalion, came towards me, said that everything was fine, and that the C.O. was up ahead. He came with me to reconnoiter the hotel, whose dining-room had clearly been evacuated in a hurry. Breakfasts lay uneaten on the tables: pots of coffee and jugs of milk, rolls and fruit, and even limp and colorless omelettes. The hotel guests had fled without tasting their hearty East Jerusalem breakfast. On the sparkling clear bar counter was the barman's duster, and on a shelf an array of very good whiskey, to which the paratroopers wandering in the dining-room paid no heed. Coca-Cola and fruit juice served them well enough. The sun shone through the wide east window, dappling the walls and the glass and suffusing the pictures and ornaments with its own gold. If not for the war, this would have been a delightful hour of the morning.

Assault on the Mivtar

As I was taking leave of Doron on the hotel steps, he called my attention to Givat Hamivtar, where a tank was blazing. I knew then that Uri was there. We rushed into the jeeps and out to the open space past Sheikh Jarrah, where I contacted Uri.

"What's happening on the Mivtar?"

"The first assault failed," Uri rasped, "and we're organizing for the second."

Tel el-Ful Falls

Around 5 a.m., roughly twelve hours after it had crossed the Green Line, the 10th Brigade reached its objective on Givat Zahara, ready to do battle with the Jordanian armored forces and prevent their attacking Mt. Scopus.

But what a pitiful bunch it was. There was, as we know, only Major Uri Braz' tank company, really a company in name only. Of its original fourteen tanks, seven were in the minefields of Sheikh Abdul Aziz and Hirbet e-Lauza, and on the rocky, winding road they had travelled. An eighth had overturned in the dark near Beit Hanina, leaving six at Givat Zahara. There were, besides, ten half-tracks of Captain David Cana'ani's armored infantry company and the battalion's mortar battery.

Somewhat later, the Brigade reconnaissance company arrived from Beit Iksa and placed itself under the command of Battalion Commander Zwicka. It was only a token force of four armored half-tracks and three jeeps, the rest of the vehicles, including twelve Centurion tanks, having been bogged down by rocks and almost impassable road hazards.

This was the force scheduled to stop the 60th Jordanian Armored Brigade, with its one hundred brand new Pattons. For the moment, however, no Jordanian tanks were to be seen and the battalion commander deployed his half-tracks at the top of the hill, the tanks and mortar battery behind them. The reconnaissance unit took up blockading positions towards the north. Machine gunners of the armored infantry fired on traffic along the highway and on the concentration of recoilless-gun-carrying jeeps and other anti-tank weapons in the Jordanian army camp on the ruins of the Neve Yaakov settlement. The battle between the Shermans and the Pattons referred to earlier had been fought here, after which our force remained on Hirbet Zahara awaiting reinforcements, ammunition and fuel.

An hour passed.

Armored battalion "B", which had captured the fortified heights of Sheikh Abdul-Aziz, what remained of two tank companies, and half the armored vehicle company under Ehud Shani advanced along the chaotic movement axis. It captured the village of Nabi Samuel and joined the leaders of the column of Natan Piram's tanks, and the others as Hirbet Zahara. A few minutes later a helicopter carrying Brigade Commander Uri Ben-Ari landed at the foot of the hill. After hours of pleading for a helicopter to take him to his advancing troops, because the movement axes were blocked by brigade units, he had finally, thanks to a brief cessation in Israeli Air Force bombing, been accommodated. The helicopter made a second flight with the Brigade's intelligence officer, and at 8.30 Ben-Ari met with the force's commanders at the foot of the hill. He was quick and matter-of-fact, as usual. "'B' Battalion will attack Tel el-Ful immediately; 'C' Battalion will marshal an aggressive reconnaissance toward Hizma, east of the highway, where the Jordanian guns that bombed Jerusalem are deployed. They are to be knocked out."

Zwicka assembled his men and Aaron left to take a look at the objective, Tel el-Ful, a steep, exposed slope, at its foot a built-up area among whose houses, he had been told, Patton tanks were hidden. Aaron quickly completed his battle-plan: the armored vehicles would try to outflank the Tel and blockade its eastern slope with fire-power. The next force to move out to Hizma would act as a fire-base, and under its covering fire the tanks would charge, with the armored infantry behind them.

No sooner said than done. The tanks opened fire, the armored vehicles began their flanking movement and the strength began to sweep across the top of the Tel. The armored vehicles met the enemy first. They passed between the outer group of houses of Shu'afat, climbed the high Ras a-Tawill hill, and at the bottom saw the Jordanian force of recoilless-gun-carrying jeeps and dozens of soldiers. The vehicles fired and the Jordanians raced for cover among the houses. Just as Ehud Shani radioed his two platoons to attack, fire from the flank opened on the armored vehicles, one of which was hit before the men could discover that the shooting came from three Patton tanks. The gunner of the company commander's car managed to fire a shell at a Patton at the moment that the Patton was aiming at him. But the car was hit by another tank, and Shani and the gunner were both killed. The tank, however, was destroyed by another armored vehicle and the third tank disappeared. The armored cars carried the wounded to the highway.

Tel el-Ful was taken, almost without resistance, despite the forecasts. The assaulting tanks were fired on from a house at the foot of the hill, but two well-placed shells put it out of commission. The force swept through the area. Following them were "I" Company's armored half-tracks. The commander, Uzi Rosen, occupied the skeleton of King Hussein's palace with two of his platoons, the third having been stuck somewhere near Nabi Samuel. The huge structure was completely empty. Uzi Rosen was a young architect, and he marvelled at the building.

"I'd like to stay here awhile," he told Aaron, his superior officer, who had just arrived. "It's pretty exciting architecturally." "There's no time, Uzi," Aaron replied. "I promise you a trip round the palace when the war's over."

At that moment the tanks' guns began to roar at three Pattons about 1200 meters to the north. The tank-penetrating shells were efficient: two Pattons caught fire and the third fled.

That, apparently, was the end of the advance force of the 60th Brigade, which had succeeded in climbing to the ridges despite the air force bombardment on its movement axis.

The Mivtar and French Hill

When Lt. Colonel Aaron reported that Tel el-Ful was taken, Uri Ben-Ari came to the hilltop and ordered him to attack the Mivtar and get to Jerusalem after the air force stopped bombing. Ben-Ari cancelled "C" Battalion's reconnaissance assignment on Hizma and ordered it to set out for Ramallah instead.

"B" Battalion was deployed for attack; a tank company was left as cover on Tel el-Ful; an armored infantry company reinforced with tanks was to lead, and "I" Company to follow with the battalion headquarters; two tanks, a platoon of armored infantry and the armored vehicles were to go east towards French Hill. The remaining strength was concentrated on the Mivtar.

As the last of the planes vanished, Lt. Colonel Aaron ordered the men to move off. Major Piram's four tanks climbed quickly to Givat Hamivtar, hardly taking time to spot the barbed wire, bunkers and trenches of that powerfully reinforced position to the left and right of the road, at which they had to fire when they had passed by. Thanks to their speed, only the whip-end of the steel meant for them landed, and, in spite of machine-guns, recoilless guns and hand-grenades, not a tank stopped, although all four tanks were hit. Anti-tank shells perforated the armor of the company commander's tank, but did not blow it up. The external equipment of the others was damaged and they were smoke-filled, but there were no casualties. Soon they were beyond the range of enemy fire and raced southwards, climbing the hill beyond which lay Jerusalem. The commander called a halt, but the lead tank had reached the peak, where, with Jerusalem before it, it was hit. The marksman was one of our tanks at the Ambassador Hotel, stationed there to watch for developments beyond.

The crew boarded the next tank, and Natan Piram began to lead his now shrunken force back into the hail of fire from the Mivtar. "I" Company's three half-tracks, with the battalion C.O. following, were some distance away and, because they were slower, they got the full brunt of the fire from the fortification.

"Swing right! Charge!" the battalion commander thundered at Uzi Rosen, and the words gagged him as the barrel of a recoilless gun behind a barbed-wire entanglement was aimed at him. Instinctively he tried to swing the half-track's machine-gun towards the enemy, but Uzi's half-track was first, and smashed into the position and crushed the barrel of the recoilless gun.

Zeev Merenstein's half-track, behind the company commander's, pulverized the barbed-wire and burst into the enemy position, where immediately before him was a destroyed bunker with an abandoned recoilless gun, an 0.5 mm. machine-gun and a wounded machine-gunner. Fierce fire peppered at him from bunkers farther away, the nearer ones having been hastily abandoned by Legionnaires who fled doubled-up through the trenches. Merenstein pointed his machine-gun at the trench and fired a long burst.

The other half-track waited on the road. Lieutenant Mordechai Goldstein, young, moustached and smiling, commander of the battalion's sapper platoon, who was in the battalion commander's half-track, noticed the driver's hesitation, jumped on to the bullet-swept roadway and ran towards the waiting half-track. "Get going. Move on to the bunker!" he yelled. The driver moved.

From a bunker close to the stone gateway of the fortified position, machine-guns spat bullets against the sides of the half-track. "Hand-grenade," Goldstein yelled at the closest soldier and, clutching the grenade, the young commander sprang from the half-track into the trench to the bunker. Two steps forward, and a Legionnaire aimed his rifle. "He was more confused than I," Goldstein recalls. He grabbed the rifle, yanked it away and became the aggressor. Threatening the Legionnaire with his own rifle, Goldstein forced him out of the trench while he walked the length of it, reached the bunker entrance and cried, "Hands up!" Ten Legionnaires walked out with their hands up.

The company commander's half-track penetrated the fortified position, firing machine-guns and tossing hand-grenades into every corner in a barrage that sent the Legionnaires packing. One stopped for a moment, drew the pin from a grenade and threw it into the half-track, killing, among others, Uzi Rosen, company commander for a day.

The driver took his bloody vehicle back to the road and north to Shu'afat; when Lieutenant Merenstein saw him leave, he, too, withdrew. Lieutenant Mordechai Goldstein, marshalling ten P.o.W.'s, was the last to go.

While the three half-tracks were fighting for the position, the Brigade commander was coming with reinforcements: the remnants of the Brigade reconnaissance company in jeeps and one half-track, which would, the commander hoped, deal the subduing blow. But powerful enfilading fire from a plane sweeping to the roadway, guns blazing, put the whole force out of action. The two jeeps caught fire, the half-track was hit, the communications equipment in the C.O.'s half-track was destroyed and the C.O. was slightly wounded. He retreated to the plain between the Mivtar and Tel el-Ful, about 400 meters away. Aaron joined him there and the two reassembled the force. The wounded were evacuated to the assembly station at Beit Hanina junction, and helicopters summoned to fly them to hospital. Contriving a fighting unit out of the men and machines remaining was a heartbreaking job. Major Piram's three tanks, with two shells apiece and very little fuel, were sent with half-tracks to Slaughter Hill to fire on French Hill.

The Brigade C.O. brought the rest of the strength from Beit Hanina: a tank company which had refuelled and rearmed while waiting, thanks to that part of the supply convoy which had reached the Beit Hanina crossroads after an exhausting struggle up the Beit Iksa movement axis, and an armored infantry company. They were placed under the command of the Battalion C.O., who was ordered to return at once to the attack.

Had Lieutenant Merenstein, on Slaughter Hill, had a radio transmitter, he could have told Aaron that the attack was superfluous. He could see the stream of Arab Legionnaires who had abandoned their positions on the Mivtar and on French Hill and were now slipping into houses at Shu'afat, to reappear in civilian clothes and depart eastwards. This first attack by Israeli armor, made with a tiny force and in fact repulsed, was enough for the men of the Jordanian garrison. But Merenstein's half-track had no radio contact with the battalion C.O., nor did Piram's tanks with anyone at all, and they were therefore hit by a brief, wild barrage from the Mivtar. So the onlookers at Slaughter Hill watched the column reform – tanks leading the armored infantry – for another try.

The last of the Jordanian defenders saw it, however, as well, and, when the columns started to advance, leapt up and fled, taking the French Hill defenders with them.

At 11 o'clock Colonel Uri Ben-Ari was able to report: "The Mivtar and French Hill have been captured."

Delay at Abu-Tor

We left the Ambassador Hotel for Binyanei Ha'ooma on the route to the police school, now clogged with supply units trying to reach the school to rearm and refuel the tanks in tandem with the paratroops. A random Jordanian shell set fire to an ammunition truck, which not only blocked the road but became a furnace of exploding shells. I considered turning back and looking for another route, but time was short and I decided to risk it. The drivers gave the jeeps full pedal and we dashed through the gap in the minefield, past the burning ammunition truck and made it. We arrived at Binyanei Ha'ooma at 10.55, and at 11.30 Haim Bar-Lev radioed for news. I told him that we had taken the lot and that a supply axis via Jerusalem had to be opened for Uri, which I was attending to. A few minutes later, Uri, in reply to my question, said that his men were south of French Hill in Shu'afat, on the Mivtar.

"There are similar forces at Hizma," I told him. "Make a fighting reconnaissance in the same direction and then move to Ramallah."

Uri asked if fuel could be sent him, making it clear that his fuel and ammunition problems had not been solved. I told Kimmel to arrange with the Jerusalem Brigade the opening of an axis to the 10th via the police school, and Amitai to open a main axis [i.e. the highway] to the north. I asked him about the situation in other sectors of his brigade, to which he replied that Mt. Scopus was quiet, but that a Patton on the Mount of Olives was pounding us at Government House and Sur Baher.

"And at Abu-Tor?"

"Getting ready."

The Abu-Tor Quarter, rather a secondary position with no significance for the battle for Jerusalem, was on my mind. I was worried about a cease-fire and I knew that if Abu-Tor were captured the Old City could be encircled from the south, facilitating our taking it if permission were given.

There were many complications. In the morning, after Lt. Colonel Paikes' "mislaid" battalion had been traced to the Radar 3 redoubt and replaced by a battalion of guards, the men made a long trek, first to Ein Kerem and then to the German Colony. Abu-Tor was originally to be attacked at 11.30 a.m., a time when some of Paikes' battalion was still on the march. The supporting tanks had not yet reached Government House and "H" Hour was therefore postponed until 2.00 p.m.

"Cutting the Ribbon"

At 11.55 the helicopter carrying the Minister of Defense landed on the square in front of Binyanei Ha'ooma. He was out before the blades of the helicopter had stopped spinning; after him came the chief of "C" Branch, General Ezer Weizman, and his assistant, General Rahbam Zeevi. The minister was in an aggressive mood, for reasons unknown to me, and had hardly set foot on the ground before he looked around for the car. "Why aren't we moving?" he said querulously. He was chafing at the brief wait while the car turned around to become part of the convoy.

"I knew you were coming," I said, in an attempt to dispel the tension, "so I left the cutting of the ribbon on the way to Mt. Scopus for you." He did not so much as smile and when I asked if he preferred travelling by command-car or half-track, he said only:

"What difference does it make? Let's move."

We moved off, Dayan next to me on the front seat of the command-car, the others in the rear. As usual on such journeys, he removed his black patch and put on a pair of dark glasses. Behind our car came a jeep which should have been followed by a security detail in an armored half-track. But its engine stalled, and rather than anger the minister, we went without it. We drove quickly, past the P.Ag.I. houses and between the white strips on the minefield in front of the police school. Sniping had ceased, and the building and environs were deserted, except for a holding unit of the Jerusalem Brigade.

We entered the Ambassador Hotel, and looked through its windows towards Wadi Joz. Silent, red-stone houses covered the slope opposite, the Mount of Olives rising to the east. The minister's face gradually grew calmer, but he was still impatient.

"Come on. Let's get to Mt. Scopus," he urged.

Doron, the deputy battalion commander, was still there. I asked him for a security detail. He provided us with two recoilless-gun-carrying jeeps and we set out, past the Mt. Scopus Hotel and the British Consulate. The streets were empty, the houses were shuttered and apparently deserted. Climbing to Mt. Scopus, the built-up area behind us, we could see to the north, ahead of us, the bleached, so-called Lime Position on a chalk hill left of the road. Two figures were standing there. "Arab Legionnaires," I said to Dayan, but he shrugged. "Not so terrible."

We travelled in silence past the Lime Position and the orderly, cared-for rows of gravestones in the British Cemetery. We had reached Mt. Scopus.

The garrison on the Mount knew of our arrival and as we went through the gate the men cheered and shouted. We waved but did not stop, hurrying by. That was the extent of the ceremony marking the appearance of the first unescorted Jewish convoy to Mt. Scopus after nineteen years of siege.

On the Roof of the National Library

"Where's the best observation point?" Dayan asked, as we passed the neglected and rundown University buildings, a sorry sight for all of us.

"The National Library," I replied. From the library roof, with its convex dome, the Old City and its ancient walls, the Temple Mount and its gold and silver mosques, lay glistening before us. In the valley of Jehoshaphat the grave of Zacharia, Yad-Avshalom, and the Bridge of Gethsemane rose from the enchanting sea of silvery, ancient olive trees. We gazed at Jewish Jerusalem: the Y.M.C.A. tower, the square, sturdy King David Hotel, the Mount of Olives and the Augusta Victoria Hospital to the east, a canopy of pine trees, and the Judean Desert, bare and rocky all the way to the misty blue of the Jordan Valley and the Dead Sea.

About 2,000 years ago, Titus had stood on Mt. Scopus to look at a view described by Josephus Flavius:

And at night after joining the Legion which came from Ama'us to his army, the Caesar left Givat Shaul [Saul] towards morning and reached the place called Scopus, whence the City can be seen and the Temple appears in all its greatness...And when anyone ventured to look towards the Temple, the brightness made him turn his eyes away from it, as though the rays of the sun blinded him. And to strangers who go up to Jerusalem it looks from the distance like a snow-covered mountain, for those places not coated with gold are of pure white, and upon the tip of its cupola shine special gold pegs, put there so that the birds of the sky will not come down and make the place dirty. (*The Jewish War*: Book E.)

When Moshe Dayan breathed, "What a view," I understood his feeling. This day, this sixth day of the sixth month, one thousand nine hundred and sixty seven, had made it all worthwhile.

That was the one moment when Dayan gave way to his emotions. With the breathtaking view before us, I thought I could exploit his mood and I said softly:

"Moshe, we must go into the Old City."

"Under no circumstances." he rejoined.

Later it became known that at a cabinet session, Ministers Allon and Begin urged permission to take the Old City, but Dayan insisted that encircling it and controlling its gates was enough. "It will fall like a ripe fruit, in any case, and the Arabs will wave white flags in surrender," he said.

16. With Dayan on Mount Scopus

17. Dayan at a command post

On the roof of the National Library, my question seemed to have brought him back to the business in hand.

"How were things in Latrun?" he asked.

"Excellent. They all fled. And we've taken Beit Horon also."

"Good thing they ran in the right direction and not towards Tel Aviv."

That was his single concession to small-talk, after which he immediately returned to the pursuit of the war. He spoke in that staccato style of his which Koby found difficult to keep pace with. His words reflected his present attitude towards the West Bank:

"Now we have to occupy the Jericho Road; that will be the main blockade [confronting the Legion, if they tried to counter-attack], because our first order of business is to remove Jerusalem from the war arena [which meant taking all the ridges east of Jerusalem from Mt. Scopus to the junction of the Mount of Olives], and push the enemy's guns away from the city. The question is, can the Jerusalem Brigade do it alone? Because I would prefer Uri to come up north."

Here he inserted what was for me a completely new idea: "Uri should go to Dado instead of to Ramallah." In other words, Uri was to extricate himself from the complicated struggle for the city and hurry to join the Northern Command. At that moment bitter battle raged between an Israeli and the 40th Jordanian Armored Brigades in the Dotan Valley. Dayan may have been worried about its outcome and wanted to create a diversion, by which part of the Jordanian Brigade would be forced away to meet the threat to its flanks from Uri Ben-Ari's men.

"If possible," he continued, "Uri should be relieved today [of a task force of tanks with which to take the eastern ridge], and we should seal it off, mine it, and widen and thicken it [the blockade], load it with anti-tank guns, and thus deflect Jordanian armor from Jerusalem … but without all this Vatican business [meaning without entering the Old City]. The area must be cleared of snipers, tanks must be deployed in direct fire-laying positions, and every shot of theirs must get a responding shot from us. We must move around conspicuously [thus demonstrating our presence there] so that they know it is not a temporary situation. Above all, we must seal it off securely."

At this point I asked what was to be done about Hebron.

"The south is an entirely different matter," he said. "Nablus must be taken in any case. But Bethlehem and the neighborhood around it is something else again."

Summing up, Dayan repeated, this time as an order, his instructions to transfer the entire 10th Brigade to the eastern ridge, which they would proceed to take.

"I prefer that Uri move northwards," I said. In other words, to Ramallah. I argued that the whole of the 10th Brigade was not needed for the capture of the eastern ridge, that one tank company to reinforce the paratroopers was sufficient. But he would not hear of it. Later, during luncheon in the "Mountain King's" dining-room, I asked Weizman and Zeevi to intervene for me; they promised to do their best to persuade him. The decision was not definite, because in the midst of a discussion with somebody else Dayan said to us, "The important thing is to reach the Azaria junction quickly," which I interpreted as implied agreement with my plan.

The atmosphere improved, and after lunch we visited the defense position on the mountain. Menahem Scharfman, the "Mountain King," seized this chance to note the good work the mountain garrison had done, even during the fighting.

As we were about to drive back to town, Dayan, in a much better mood, declared that the journey had been "a short one, but impressive." We got to Binyanei Ha'ooma at 13.15 and Dayan and his retinue boarded a helicopter. I picked up my equipment and signalled for Motta and Uri.

Attacking Abu-Tor

Moshe Dayan had made it clear to me that the political echelon had given the green light to taking the whole mountain range and linking up with Northern Command, removing Jerusalem from the war zone by capturing the ridges dominating it to the north and east. On that understanding, I could plan the next moves. At this moment, the situation in the Central Command theater was that the 10th Brigade had captured the enemy defenses north of the city and had rendezvoused with the paratroop brigade. The armored brigade was worried about supplies and about its tank force, which had shrunk because of technical mishaps caused by difficult terrain. They were, nonetheless, ready to undertake the next assignment.

The paratroops had occupied the whole of the built-up area betweeen Ammunition Hill, Sheikh Jarrah, the Rockefeller Museum and Mandelbaum Gate, had handed over the police school defenses to the Jerusalem Brigade, and were also ready for the next task.

The Jerusalem Brigade had taken over from the 10th the holding of the Sheikh Abdul Aziz-Radar sector, and from the 55th, the police school. One of the Brigade's battalions was deployed for assault on Abu-Tor, to be carried out within a few hours, after which they too would be free to do another job.

Yotvat's Brigade had reached the Jerusalem-Ramallah highway and occupied the Atarot Airport. The C.O. had been wounded, his deputy had taken command and the force was ready for further employment.

Since the main campaign had moved north of Jerusalem, there was no point in keeping the main headquarters in Ramla, far from the battlefield. Directing tactics with the aid of so limited a command group as mine was difficult. I needed assistance and proper headquarters. While the C.O.'s of the 10th and 55th Brigades were being called to their radios, I contacted the chief of staff at Ramla and said:

"Forward H.Q. with Arik Regev, to come up to Jerusalem at once. The rear headquarters will stay in Ramla and you with it."

Borka asked what background material the intelligence officer was to bring with him. "Have him clarify it with G.H.Q.," I replied, "but, meanwhile, information about the mountain range and ridges, and perhaps about the Jordan Valley too."

At 13.40 I got in touch with Eliezer, still on the roof of the Histadrut building, and told him to take advantage of the general Arab withdrawal by moving down along the Abu-Tor and Mount Zion axis, thus circumscribing the walls of the Old City from the south. "If there's no resistance," I told him, "use the *nahal hashiloah* [the Siloam River] and Ras el-Amood axes as well." If the Jerusalem Brigade captured Ras el-Amood, half the job of dominating the eastern ridges would have been achieved.

Amitai asked about Bethlehem and Hebron, and I said that he would get separate instructions for Bethlehem.

When he added that he had no contact with the paratroops and could not coordinate his actions with them, I said,

"They've already started, and you don't need radio contact at the beginning. Give the order to attack Abu-Tor."

When I told him that the Arabs were making a general withdrawal, I did so because I had just received that information from the Supreme Command.

Hussein to Nasser

At 12.30, having long awaited a reply from Gamal Abd el-Nasser to his urgent 6 a.m. telephone message, Hussein sent another message:

"The situation rapidly worsens. In Jerusalem it is hopeless. Besides our heavy losses in the air, our armor is being destroyed at the rate of one tank every ten minutes. As General Riadh reported in his cable this morning, enemy strength is chiefly concentrated against the Jordanian army. I trust you will let us have your opinion as soon as possible."

King Hussein's memoirs paint a more plastic picture of the situation, viewed from reports from the various fronts:

I shall never forget that Tuesday morning, June 6th, the second day of the war. Our forces held on to the West Bank as though possessed. Everywhere – in Jerusalem, in Ramallah, in Hebron and around Nablus – we fought hand-to-hand, from trench-to-trench, from house-to-house, on roofs and balconies; we fought for every fence and pit! The ferocity of the battles is confirmed by the Israelis themselves, who said that the fighting on the Jordanian front was the bitterest of the whole war. Thus are we able to explain the extent of our losses in three days of war – 6,094 dead and missing.

King Hussein exaggerated. There was no fighting at all in Hebron: resistance in Ramallah was slight. The greatest over-statement, however, was the estimate of Legion casualties, which, in fact, did not exceed 500 dead. Hussein's number was correct only temporarily, because thousands of Jordanian soldiers, recognizing that the war was lost, stripped off their uniforms, mingled with the civilians and crossed to the east bank of the Jordan. It is nevertheless true that where battle was joined, particularly in Jerusalem, the Jordanian soldiers fought valiantly and the war was bitter and ruthless.

"The Israeli confirmation" of the Jordanians' bravery, as quoted by Hussein, was what I had said at the first press conference after the war.

Nasser did not answer Hussein's cable until almost midnight, whereas Field Marshal Abd el-Hakim Amar answered General Riadh's morning cable several minutes after it had been sent: "Agreeable to withdrawal from West Bank and arming of civilian population."

This did not in fact happen. General Riadh indeed instructed that an order be issued for complete withdrawal from the West Bank at noon on Tuesday; according to Hussein's version, the order was issued. When it was discovered, however, that the Security Council had been summoned to vote on an immediate cease-fire, the Jordanians decided to try to hold out, on the chance that the cease-fire would salvage at least a measure of the destruction, and cancelled the general withdrawal order.

Silence at Abu-Tor

Immediately after my conversation with Eliezer Amitai, Uri came on the line and I asked him where he was.

"I've just come from the mountain. All of French Hill is ours. Empty and deserted."

"Where's the rest of the force?" I asked.

"On the northern objectives, some of them reorganizing."

"The Arabs are making a general withdrawal," I told him. "You must hurry. I need ten tanks from you, which should stay on the Mivtar and move south at my command. Some of the others should go to Hizma and the rest to Ramallah."

When he said that the ten tanks were ready to move south, I replied that the Hizma assignment was simple. "Drive away the Jordanian artillery. Everything else, by all possible routes, to Ramallah. Yotvat's force is also at your disposal. In half an hour, a liaison officer will be on the Mivtar to receive the ten tanks. Please attend immediately to the fighting reconnaissance of Hizma. When will you be able to begin moving north?"

"I'll let you know at once," he answered, and I said that I would be waiting impatiently.

By the time that conversation was over, Motta was on the line and I asked him if he could take the Intercontinental Hotel on the Mount of Olives without too much trouble, if he got the help of "heavies" from Uri. "There's no further resistance, right?" I added.

"Wrong," he said. "There's shooting from the Old City walls and from inside the built-up area. The casualties will be brutal."

"If you have 'heavies', can you climb up from Rockefeller, via Wadi Joz, straight to Augusta Victoria?" I wanted to know. That seemed to me a better route than going via the University to Augusta Victoria, which was heavily mined, and would be a long slow passage through a minefield that would have to be neutralized.

"There's a large force there," said Motta.

"The Jordanian Army has retreated to the East Bank. My assessment is that the whole thing there will collapse. Bring Uri's 'heavies' to you at Rockefeller and send them up to A-Tor, the hotel and Augusta."

"So far it's all clear, but it will take time. The 'heavies' are on the Mivtar. I'll send for them."

"These instructions must be executed promptly," I said. "Can you finish within three hours?"

"Hopefully," he answered.

"The 10th Brigade will get to Azaria from the rear. Let me know the exact time the 'heavies' reach you, so that I can organize the movements of the other forces. Pick up the ten tanks and you'll take the whole of that eastern ridge. You agree it can be done?"

"Of course," was Motta's reply.

My plan was a sort of compromise between my desire to pit the 10th Brigade against Ramallah and Moshe Dayan's proposal to take the ridges commanding Jerusalem and setting up a powerful blockade eastwards. I expected to use those forces of Uri's attacking Hizma on another assignment, a deep flanking movement towards the eastern ridge, which would bring them to Azaria from the east. Once Motta took the Mount of Olives and reached Ras el-Amood, opposite the Mount of Olives junction, two blockading positions would be established east of Jerusalem, one at Azaria and the other at Ras el-Amood, leaving the rest of the 10th Brigade, reinforced by Yotvat's men, free to attack Ramallah.

Uri contacted me to ask me to give up the fighting reconnaissance on Hizma. "I want to move north," he said.

"Why?"

"If we carry out the reconnaissance, we won't be able to move north for at least two hours."

"Right," I said, after a moment's thought. "Set up a firm base at Tel el-Ful to avoid surprises from the east, and start moving north."

Again I contacted Eliezer Amitai: "Have they started at Abu-Tor?" When he said that they hadn't I was furious. "When are they going to move? Open an axis to Ramallah at once, via the Mandelbaum passage, for Uri's fuel."

Eliezer said that Jordanian "dragons' teeth" were still blocking the road. "Send the engineers down to blow 'em up," I replied. "Let it be one city. And once the road is open, send the military police to keep order."

Tank Trouble

The 10th Brigade tanks took so long to arrive at their rendezvous with the paratroopers that I decided to go and find out the reason for the delay. Teddy Kollek arrived as I was leaving, and I invited him to join me. We drove to the police school, and from there, for Teddy's benefit, to Mt. Scopus, where he stood, his eyes on the Old City and his voice low with emotion. "I'm terribly excited, but I'm trying not to show it. I always believed that the city would be reunited, which is why I opposed building new municipal offices and vacating the ones where Arab and English mayors traditionally sat. The old building stands in the heart of the united city...but not one of us ever dreamed that Jerusalem would be unified so quickly."

We turned back towards Givat Hamivtar, still a shambles from the battle some hours earlier. A damaged Sherman tank sat silently at the roadside, the nose of a destroyed armored half-track sniffed the air above the communications trench of the fortified position. In that half-track, Uzi Rosen, C.O. of the attacking company, had died. Bunkers torn open by tank shells gaped obscenely, army blankets, ammunition cases, abandoned equipments, weapons, bomb bandoliers, war materials without number were visible through the openings. Black gunpowder stained the hillside, and fence staves coiled with barbed wire stood at crazy angles where the armored force had broken through.

A company of tanks stood there idly, since there were no fuel pumps, while their crews dragged jerrycans and poured their contents into the fuel containers, a long and arduous task. The C.O., Major Eitan Arieli, informed me that his company was to reinforce the paratroop brigade.

"We had to wait for the fuel. We'll finish refuelling and get to town."

I made it clear that he had to get to the Rockefeller Museum and that speed was essential, and left for Binyanei Ha'ooma. I was sure that the paratroops could attack very soon, but still the tanks failed to turn up. Refuelling took longer than anticipated and, when that job was over, two of the twelve tanks were unable to move and there were communication flaws in several others. The signals technical detail of the battalion had been wounded the previous night when the command half-track in which they were riding struck a mine on the outskirts of Biddu.

Major Arieli decided, however, to move off with the ten mobile tanks, regardless of their condition, but he did not know the way to the Rockefeller Museum. He knew only that he was to follow a jeep with a couple of scouts from the paratroop brigade. But the column got tied up with the supply convoy of the 10th Brigade, which was headed north, and took forty-five minutes to find its way to the road at the bottom of the Old City walls. It was fired upon from the walls, and although the thick armor repelled the shots, the tank commanders had to duck inside the turret. When the first three tanks turned down the path to the Rockefeller Museum, the driver of the fourth, oblivious, continued towards the Nablus Gate with the rest of the column behind him. Major Arieli called them by radio, but his signals equipment was out of order and there was no response. He continued to follow the paratrooper navigators all the way to the Rockefeller Museum and then reported to Motta. A jeep was dispatched to search for the lost tanks, but returned without them, because when the tanks discovered that they had lost their commander they halted opposite the Nablus Gate and were stung with fire from the walls. Nobody came to rescue them, and they perforce returned to the one place they knew, Givat Hamivtar, where they were found the following morning in time to join the paratroop battalion on its way to Mt. Scopus.

I knew nothing of all this, when I returned to Binyanei Ha'ooma, confident that the tanks would soon reach Motta and enable him to begin his assault. At the police school, on the way back, we stopped to ask three civilians what they were doing there. They turned out to be well-known journalists from the London *Times*, the Los Angeles *Times* and *Time-Life* magazine, assigned to cover the war from an East Jerusalem hotel. Battle and bombardment had sent them rushing for shelter, and they emerged from their hideout when shooting abated to discover that Zahal had captured the area. They ran to the post-office to dispatch the news, but that building was closed. Faithful to the press slogan that the news shall get through, they decided to walk to the western city to send their dispatches. Now they were en route, telegrams in hand, but were lost in the maze of alleys, had been entangled in barbed wire, caught in the snipers' cross-fire and had almost plunged into a minefield. I asked them about their experiences and about the atmosphere in the city when war broke out, and then showed them how to get through the minefield. When I met them again, at a press conference a few days later at Beit Sokolow in Tel Aviv, I was glad to hear that, although they had not been accredited to Israel, they had been well treated by the Israeli postal services and their cables transmitted.

I returned to Binyanei Ha'ooma where, at about 5 o'clock in the afternoon, General Haim Herzog, Military Governor (Reserves) of the West Bank, was waiting impatiently to discuss operation of the military government. He had assembled a group of experts in various fields who were working on plans, but had not yet organized his head-quarters. He intended to conduct operations through the Arabs themselves: with the personnel of the Jordanian government and municipalities. He raised the matter of control by the military forces in the area and suggested attaching the border police guards to his administration, but when he asked that other forces be placed under his command, I said that I would need authority from the defense minister.

General Herzog remained undaunted, however, and for fifteen minutes discussed ways of setting up screens between Jewish Jerusalem and its eastern sector to prevent plundering of homes and desecration of holy places. He was silenced only by the sudden entry of Major Kimmel and his dramatic announcement:

"The Jerusalem Brigade has taken Abu-Tor."

The Capture of Abu-Tor

The authority to take the Abu-Tor Quarter had been given on Monday night, but was not carried out because of complications, mainly concerned with lack of reserves. The Brigade's one reserve unit in southern Jerusalem had been assigned to the battle against Government House, which spread to the "Bell" Position and Sur Baher, thus inducing the Brigade commander to add the battalion camped at Ramat Rahel to his force. Two Brigade battalions – Lt. Colonel Zvi Ofer's and Lt. Colonel Michael Paikes' – were defending north Jerusalem, Zvi Ofer having relieved Lt. Colonel Aaron's battalion of its duties as a holding force at Biddu, with one of his companies on the Mivtar and French Hill. Paikes, as we have seen, had volunteered to capture the Radar 3 stronghold.

When Paikes was ordered to go to southern Jerusalem and take the Abu-Tor Quarter, he was at Radar 3, far from his headquarters. By the time he received the order it was early morning, and he had to find a unit to hold the position for him, after which he was able to reassemble his men and set out on foot, since he was without transport. He went to the Evelina de Rothschild School for his orders, and on Tuesday morning took his company commanders to observe the objective and decide how best to capture it.

The Abu-Tor Quarter was one of the few sections of town where Zahal had a topographical advantage over the Jordanians, who were disposed in four fortified positions, opposite each of which an Israeli position had been set up at a distance of not more than a few meters.

Paikes therefore decided to place a company opposite each of the fortified positions and to fight as though each was a separate objective. Only the supporting fire from the battalion's mortars and machine-guns would be directed at all the objectives collectively. Later he was told he would be supported additionally by three tanks from the force at Government House. Because the terrain made it impossible for them to operate close to the attacking force, Paikes decided to use them as a firing base for "A" Company, which was opposite the southernmost objective, nicknamed the *lulav* (branch of the palm tree).

The Jordanian *lulav* position was in a two-story building on the southern slope, whose second-floor windows facing Arab Abu-Tor were gun apertures, and whose sole entrance was on the other side, facing the slope. Captain Moshe, commanding "A" Company, had therefore to make a flanking approach across the exposed slope, which is why Paikes wanted tank support for "A" Company. The tanks were to deploy themselves on a branch of the Hill of Evil Counsel, overlooking the valley between Government House and Abu-Tor, where they could provide fire-cover for the company's attack. About a hundred meters north of the *lulav* was the fortified house of the *mukhtar* (headman), which also fell to the lot of "A" Company.

"B" Company, commanded by Captain Eli, was to attack the *arieh* (lion) fortification in the center of the Quarter, on the boundary line. Also in a two-story building, it could be distinguished only with difficulty from the surrounding houses. The Israel *arieh* position was fifty meters opposite and had been exchanging shots with Jordan for twelve hours.

"C" Company's objective was Beit Hampachlecha (Platoon House), "D" Company's under Captain Uzi, the "House with the Yellow Shutters." Both were in the northwestern section of the Quarter, the "House with the Yellow Shutters" on the slope facing Mount Zion, about forty meters from the Abu-Tor observation post overlooking the Old City.

While the Battalion C.O. and the company commanders completed their plans, the soldiers from the western Jerusalem positions got to the highway and were bused to the Baka'a Quarter, briefed and told to advance towards the line of battle. It was 3 o'clock in the afternoon, at the height of the softening-up bombardment.

Lulav and Arieh

Whether the bombardment had alerted the Jordanians to what was happening or the scouts on the ridges overlooking the Quarter had spotted the approaching columns, the Jordanians mightily stepped up their shelling, and a barrage fell on "D" Company as it crossed Hebron Way, near the railway station. The street was littered with wounded and the company withdrew to Baka'a. The commanders of the other companies had not been hurt, and realized that the place safest from Jordanian shells was the one closest to the Jordanian positions. They hurried their men along.

An explosive charge on the *arieh* position began the assault and shattered the upper floor of the Jordanian fortified house. Inside, the Israelis found the bodies of six Legionnaires. At the sound of the detonation, two tanks at Government House fired on the Jordanians' *lulav* position and the supporting company's mortar shells ripped the slope with smoke bombs. Under cover of the smoke, one of the platoons swooped towards the slope to the entrance to the building and quickly cleared it out. The company commander dispatched a four-man machine-gun detail across the road for the assault on the *mukhtar's* house. All four were hit crossing the roadway, crumpling against each other one by one, struck by an unseen sniper. Moshe sent a bazooka expert to the roof to rout out the sniper, but he was hit in the act of aiming and fatally wounded.

Five dead in two minutes, and the sniper still at large. Benny, Moshe's deputy, inching along with the company, by chance detected a fortified position ten meters away from the machine-gunners lying dead on the road. Instantly he tossed in a hand-grenade and silenced the sniper, whose body was found later, witness to his having stayed behind to cover the retreat of his comrades.

With the sniper disposed of, no further obstacle blocked the assault route to the *mukhtar's* house, which was quickly put out of action. Then, in conformity with British war doctrine, the Legion's guns on the Azaria ridge opened fire on the positions they had so hurriedly vacated, hitting "A" Company men, who had not yet dug in to the newly captured positions.

Beit Hamachlacha was extremely hard to capture. The leading platoon of "C" Company quietly approached the boundary fence, blazed it open with a flame-thrower shell, and leapt through, to be stopped by another fence. Again the flame-thrower, but this time the Jordanians were alive to the attack. Heavy Jordanian machine-gun fire burst forth from the cemetery on Mount Zion. Under cover of the Jordanian shooting, the Israelis were able to blow up the fence. But five men had been wounded and the others were loath to continue the attack. Kuty, the platoon commander, took the initiative by throwing grenades between the fences so that the wounded could be removed. The advance proceeded, blocked by more barbed-wire. No flame-throwing shells remained, but a soldier of the spearhead troop threw himself on the entanglement and crushed it with his own weight. The men climbed over him into Platoon House.

Opposite the "House of the Yellow Shutters," into which the retreating Legionnaires from *arieh* and Platoon House had fled, "D" Company had retreated from the heavy shelling and only a holding force remained to secure the position, which had been reinforced in the meantime. The firing from the "House of the Yellow Shutters" forced the men holding the position to take cover. They could not understand why their company had not attacked, and were about to withdraw, a dangerous action under that raking fire.

Finally, the assault was launched. Uzi evacuated the wounded to the rear and reorganized his force, really only an enlarged platoon of exhausted men. But at the sight of their wounded comrades they were overcome with fury and stormed the "House of the Yellow Shutters" and made it theirs.

The Death of Battalion Commander Paikes

After the battle the men began to comb the houses in the Quarter for Jordanian soldiers hiding among the civilians. They were not easily distinguishable in civilian clothes, sometimes, even, in pajamas, but they were usually given away by their army boots, which they had forgotten to change. In the course of the search came the word that among the battalion's casualties was the C.O., Lt. Colonel Michael Paikes.

At the beginning of the attack, he had been behind "C" Company with a limited command group, the intelligence officer, Johnny Heiman, two signalmen and a reconnaissance sergeant. When the "A" Company commander radioed about hidden snipers, the C.O. sent Johnny Heiman to order the commander of the supporting company to bombard "A" Company's front. When Johnny returned, the C.O.'s group had advanced through the opening in the fence to Arab Abu-Tor and were in a Jordanian communications-trench halfway down the slope by the time he caught up with them. "B" Company was then searching the houses in the Quarter.

Suddenly a Legionnaire with a rifle dropped beside them in the trench. He was as astonished as they were and had hardly recovered from shock before Johnny pounced, and snatched the rifle from his hand. Three more Legionnaires, who had evaded the house-searching troops, followed him into the trench. Two sprang out immediately and raced down the slope, but the third fired a shot from the end of the trench before escaping. Michael Paikes sank to the ground with a back wound. The bullet punctured his lungs and when Johnny bent over him, he had begun to choke.

"I'm finished. Nothing to do," he whispered.

At that moment, one of the escaped Legionnaires returned and attacked Johnny, who managed to knock the rifle out of his hands and to fall with him to the ground, where they lay locked together. The Legionnaire tried to slip his bayonet out of his belt; Johnny's Uzzi was around his neck, digging into the other man's chest. They gave up struggling for their weapons and Johnny's fingers crept toward the Legionnaire's throat and the Legionnaire's teeth grazed Johnny's jugular. Slowly Johnny's grip tightened and all at once he swung his Uzzi free and fired point-blank at the Legionnaire, who fell dead.

By the time the battalion medical officer arrived in answer to the radioed call, he could do nothing except confirm the death of Michael Paikes. Major Johnny Heiman was to meet his own death on the Golan Heights in the Yom Kippur War of October, 1973.

The Order-of-the-Day

"Eliezer has taken Abu-Tor and Uri can proceed to Ramallah," Major Kimmel informed me.

The 10th Brigade had apparently succeeded in rearming and re-fuelling and was on its way to Ramallah. The Jerusalem Brigade's capture of Abu-Tor meant that the Municipal Line had been destroyed everywhere except in the Old City. I asked Kimmel to contact the paratroops and find out when they would start.

I was in high spirits. I composed an Order-of-the-Day:

Today Jerusalem is to be liberated.
In the south and in the north the city of our ancestors
is in our hands.
Our army is still poised.
Men of this Regional Command, be resolute.
Do not waver.

(signed) Major-General Uzi Narkiss
G.O.C. Central Command

Later I asked Kimmel about Yotvat's Brigade, which, it will be recalled, had been ordered to wait at the Bitonia junction to join the 10th Brigade, when, its job in northern Jerusalem taken care of, it attacked Ramallah. I emphasized this instruction repeatedly because of the possibility that the two units might encounter but not recognize each other. Moving tanks, enveloped in dust, are not easily recognizable. At the time that the 10th's move northwards was uncertain, Arik Regev ordered Lt. Colonel Naftali, who had assumed command of the Yotvat Brigade, to get his force close to the main road and put a blockade northwards.

The 10th Brigade did go north, but was unaware that one of our own forces was parked on the highway. There was therefore serious danger of a collision, but although Arik Regev was no tankman and knew nothing of the communications system of the corps, he managed to arrange contact between the two. This took so long, however, that anxiety mounted, relieved only when Major Amnon, the commander of the Brigade's reconnaissance unit, finally got to Yotvat's tanks. Amnon recognized one of the tank commanders, a kibbutznik from Ma'abarot. The 10th was able to continue its advance, with the Yotvat Brigade at the rear.

General Haim Herzog, who was with me when the report about Abu-Tor and the advance on Ramallah came through, decided that it was time to do something with the military administration.

"My headquarters are in Ramla," he grumbled, "and my men have yet to receive an order."

"If you come back at 8 o'clock tonight, I'll have talked to Haim Bar-Lev," I answered.

"Shall we settle ourselves here at Binyanei Ha'ooma," he asked, "or in the eastern part of the city?"

"I suggest the Ambassador Hotel in Sheikh Jarrah."

"I think it would be better if we were close to the Jerusalem Brigade," he argued.

"Let's decide this evening."

Itzik, the deputy operations officer, was sent to the 55th Brigade to check their activity. The paratroops had had a hard day. After the break-through battle, with its tragic casualties, after taking the entire built-up area of northern Jerusalem, including the American Colony and the Wadi Joz Quarter – all since the morning – the men were now cleaning out the last nests of resistance and reorganizing, bringing supplies and ammunition and evacuating their wounded. Their new assignment, which I hoped would be the last in Jerusalem outside the walls, could not be executed for several hours for the technical reasons of refuelling and the traffic jam at the police school, which prevented my placing a few tanks at their disposal.

At 17.58 I told the quartermaster officer who had arrived at the police school that a major priority was to open a route for the Shermans of the 55th.

When Haim Bar-Lev contacted me, I was able to tell him that Uri had taken Kalandia, that Motta was waiting for the Shermans, that the Jerusalem Brigade was using military police to close the line, so that nobody could enter the area. I asked his opinion and that of the defense minister and whether General Herzog should set up his military administration. If affirmative, a statement should be issued throughout the West Bank. "We're awaiting orders," I said.

Ramallah Falls

At 18.10 Kimmel announced contact between the 10th and Yotvat's Brigade, and two minutes later the command artillery officer, Lt. Colonel Davidi, reported that the Brigade commanders were quarreling. "Yosh says range in on Ramallah. Uri says don't."

The dispute arose out of the differing viewpoints of an armored corps and an infantry man. Yosh Harpaz could not imagine launching an assault on a town before softening it up by bombing, whereas Uri, chafing over the time already lost, refused to wait. He ended the discussion by ordering the Brigade units from the plains to wait on the outskirts of Ramallah, while his Brigade, under cover of its own armor, broke into the town without a softening-up bombardment.

At 19.27 I asked Uri to report his position and ordered him to avoid hitting the radio station and equipment. But he was in the throes of battle and his deputy replied that he had gone into Ramallah on his own.

Only a few units participated in the Brigade's assault on Ramallah – a reconnaissance company, a tank company under Major Uri Braz, two armored infantry companies and a mortar battery. The reconnaissance company led the column, which halted when shots were fired from the hills south of the town. The reconnaissance company went to the rear, behind the tanks, which moved into position to return the fire. The C.O. ordered the tank battalion commander to advance and break into the town, and then formed his men into two columns, with orders to move quickly, firing all the time. The armored vehicles rolled ahead, bulldozing down everything before them.

The Brigade commander had correctly assessed the absence of serious enemy resistance in Ramallah, so that, after the peripheral shooting had been silenced, only snipers' guns popped occasionally in the streets of the town and heavier shooting came from one of the houses in the center. When the infantrymen went in to clean up, they found several dead Legionnaires inside. But the major fighting went on while they were driving, with no mopping up afterwards. Machine-gunners fired through the windows and cannons shattered obstacles on the roadway. It was all over in twenty minutes. The men halted north of Ramallah, near the radio station, from which about a dozen Legionnaires escaped. Ramallah itself was silent.

"Ramallah is in my hands," came the C.O.'s report, after which he put the small force with him into a night laager and regrouped his remaining men.

At 19.45 the C.O.G.S., whom I had not talked to for some time, telephoned. I reported the closure of the municipal boundary and my use of the military police. "What's the policy now?" I asked. "Do we go south? Uri's in Ramallah and in a couple of hours will meet the Northern Command armor. I can also go east with a force commanded by Yosh, who can go straight to Jericho instead of to the north. Another alternative is for Uri to go to Sartaba."

Indeed, all the alternatives were open – Hebron, Jericho, the Jordan Valley – but the C.O.G.S. gave me no unequivocal reply.

At 19.55 the Command artillery officer, Davidi, informed me that the paratroops were ready to attack Augusta Victoria. Some of the tanks had arrived, but were short of ammunition. Even so, the Brigade commander, under the impression that the Arabs had withdrawn from the ridge, suggested exploiting it and not waiting for support from the Command artillery, believing his own mortar batteries would be enough. I agreed.

Arik Regev arrived from Ramla and took control at Binyanei Ha'ooma. We decided that if the Brigade had no other assignment from the Plains, they could mop up the West Bank the next morning, from the ridges west. The 10th Brigade would move east to Jericho and the Jordan crossings.

Meanwhile, the attack by the Givati Brigade was gathering momentum in Natania, one of the most sensitive sectors of the Central Command.

Kalkiliya is Captured

During the afternoon of Monday June 5th, we got news of Jordanian armor near Hirbet Azun, a diversionary tactic, we were to discover, when we interrogated prisoners after the war. The Arab Legion commander in that sector was afraid of an attack, particularly when he learned that the war had spread to Jerusalem and Jenin and that he was therefore without hope of reinforcement. So he moved his tiny force back and forth, and thus made it appear to our observers that thirty tanks were threatening Natanya.

Zunik Shaham, C.O. of the Givati Brigade, was unequivocally ordered to dig in and not to retreat an inch, no matter what. He and his men resolutely carried out their assignment, coming under heavy bombardment for twenty-four hours and sustaining numerous casualties without abandoning a single portion. On Tuesday morning, Zunik felt that the enemy had spent its resources and urged Ramla H.Q. to let him attack. He received permission only at midday, however, for the limited action of driving a wedge between the enemy's lines and taking the fortified position at Suppin, behind Kalkiliya. This position had been attacked by paratroops, who had infiltrated into Kalkiliya on the eve of the 1956 Sinai campaign and had suffered heavy losses. The position had since been considerably reinforced and was manned by a force larger than a company and supported by artillery. All its approaches were artillery-ranged.

Two Command tanks hit the bunkers directly, the artillery bombarded them, and the assault was launched. The position was captured handily, even without the air bombardment that had been part of the original plan, but was so late in arriving that Zunik decided to proceed without it. He ordered his force out of the position as soon as it had been captured and to withdraw several hundred meters away. Our planes appeared by chance after the position had been emptied and dumped their bombs, uprooting concrete bunkers. When the infantry returned to the position and saw the destruction, they congratulated themselves on their luck.

With the capture of Suppin, the residents of Kalkiliya began to flee and Zunik begged to continue his advance, sure he could reach Nablus. But we were worried about a possible encounter between the Central and Northern Command forces, who were also on their way to Nablus, and therefore gave Zunik permission to advance only to Azun, some seven kilometers eastwards.

An International State

As I promised Herzog, we began to discuss the establishment of the military administration at 8:00 p.m., with Teddy Kollek in attendance. I opened the discussion by saying, "That which we feared has come about. We've established an international state and only God knows what will happen. The Arabs are fleeing. There's trouble in Musrara. I've ordered the area closed and have asked the defense minister to appoint a military governor, which is a political act, in the ministerial sphere."

I was talking about the confusion and lack of design, for which all of us were to blame. To our surprise, we had captured, or were about to capture, the entire West Bank, which, two days earlier, nobody would have thought possible. It had been a military action which the political leadership was uncertain how to handle, or indeed if it wanted to handle it at all; we had no blueprint for dealing with the Arabs. The discussion ended with instructions to close the Jerusalem border and a warning against looting and robbery. I hoped for upper-echelon instructions about the establishment and policy of the military administration.

The Battle for Gethsemane

Micha Kapusta's reconnaissance unit had been busy all day, having reached Jerusalem the night before, although when Kapusta finally found the Brigade commander it was after midnight and he was told that there was nothing for him to do. In the morning, however, he was ordered to go via the police school to the eastern part of the city, there to assist the 28th Battalion in its action at the Rockefeller Museum.

Unlike the 55th Brigade, most of whose equipment was still on the landing strip, Kapusta's reconnaissance company had everything it needed, including ten reconnoitering jeeps, five recoilless-gun-carrying jeeps and four command-cars, organized into five platoons. The men were experienced fighters, who smashed Legionnaire resistance in the eastern side of the city, and made short work of the snipers on the Old City walls. They bivouacked in three buildings opposite the Rockefeller Museum and gave a hand to whoever needed one, chiefly small detachments of the 28th Battalion bogged down in the fire-raked alleys. In the afternoon the unit was in a joint action with a tank force and the 71st Battalion, assigned to take the Augusta Victoria ridges and A-Tur.

In a briefing at the museum, Gur decided that the tanks would lead and that the force would divide into two at the ridge; some of the tanks and the reconnaissance unit would take A-Tur and set up a blockade facing Azaria; the remaining tanks and the 71st battalion would capture Augusta Victoria.

The Brigade commander and his deputy advanced with the three unit commanders – Lt. Colonel Uzi of the 71st Battalion; Micha Kapusta, of the reconnaissance company, and Captain Raffi Yeshayahu, deputy commander of the armored company – to the stone wall at the edge of the American Colony, where Motta pointed out the direction: for a short distance they would follow the road leading to Gethsemane, turn left at the first bend, go into the wadi, and continue on the road up to Mount Scopus. The attack was set to begin at 5 p.m. in broad daylight, and seemed error-proof. But difficulties nonetheless arose, particularly in moving the tanks and coordinating the forces, an apparently endless task, during the course of which afternoon gave way to dusk and dusk to dark.

Only at 7:30 p.m. did action begin. Four 10th Brigade tanks positioned themselves at the boundary of the American Colony and began shelling enemy positions on the A-Tur ridge opposite, hitting several and setting fire to a Jordanian recoilless-gun-carrying jeep.

At 22.00 hours the main force moved, led by Raffi Yeshayahu's tanks. They left the shelter of the American Colony fence, moved down the road, without lights, to prevent being spotted, missed the left turn leading to the A-Tur ridge and continued down towards Gethsemane. From A-Tur, Augusta Victoria and the olive grove surrounding the Russian church at Gethsemane, bullets and shells pounded them, but the heaviest shooting came from the right, from the walls of the Old City. Road flares allowed the Jordanians to train their weapons accurately.

Raffi Yeshayahu peered out of the turret of the lead tank and was immediately hit above the eye by shrapnel. His face was so bloody that he could hardly see, nor could he find the fork on the left which would have taken him to his objective. He ordered the commander of No. 2 platoon, behind him, to lead in his place. Soon he found himself on a bridge, about which no mention had ever been made at the briefing. He called a halt, reported his error, and asked to be led to his objective.

The Brigade commander ordered one of the tanks on the firing base to beam its projector on the fork in the road, but Raffi radioed that the beams were not strong enough. Motta therefore told him to switch on his own projector so that his position could be traced, but bomb flashes, tracer bullets and exploding flares so confused matters that Raffi's light could not be distinguished. Micha Kapusta, still waiting at the American Colony, was ordered to find the tanks, bring them back and show them where to turn. Micha transferred the order to Yishai, commander of the reconnaissance platoon. The four reconnaissance jeeps started off, but in a few minutes Yishai's jeep returned alone. One of the men was dead, two, including Yishai, were wounded, and only Benny, the driver, was unhurt. Before the jeep stopped, Yishai shouted, "Quick! A doctor and orderlies! The platoon is being cut to pieces!"

That was Micha's first intimation that the tanks were at the Gethsemane Bridge, where they were under constant fire, which was trained on the jeeps when they came within range. The casualties were so heavy that Yishai ordered his men out of the jeeps and deployed them for defense, while he ran for help, having never made contact with the tanks.

Before that, Raffi decided that he had gone too far, and ordered the tanks back to the American Colony, while he covered the withdrawal. The shooting intensified and the explosions lit up the whole area, so that Raffi saw the last tank receive a direct hit and burst into flames. On the bridge he saw a burning jeep. When he discovered that he was alone, he ordered the driver to withdraw, in the course of which the tank careered into the bridge parapet and plunged down the abyss. The entire crew lost consciousness when the tank crashed to the bed of the wadi. How long they lay there nobody knows, but they awoke one by one and crawled out of the tank, gradually recognizing each other in the darkness. They huddled under the bridge, trying to clear their heads, aware from the noise of battle above them that the area still belonged to the enemy. They stayed where they were. Hours later, or so it seemed, the battle noises died. They could see movement and hear voices farther down the wadi, possibly Legionnaires looking for them. When the voices faded, Raffi ordered one of the men to get the maps and personal weapons out of the tank; equipped with machine-guns, the men felt more secure.

Because of the persistent silence, Raffi assumed that the attempt to take the ridge had failed and that he must get out of the wadi before dawn. He and his men began to crawl westward up the wadi, reaching the paratroops' farthest position on the outskirts of Wadi Joz as dawn was breaking. He heard with relief, before he was rushed to the casualty assembly station, that the No. 2 Platoon's tank crew had also returned safely from the bridge.

But the drama of the bridge did not end with the escape of two tank crews. When Yishai informed his C.O. that the platoon was trapped on the bridge, Micha ordered Yamo of the 2nd Jeep Platoon to get his men out of the jeeps and on to the ground to fire on the positions at the corner of the Old City walls opposite. He ordered Dubbi of the 3rd Jeep Platoon to rescue Yishai's men, and he himself drove to the Rockefeller Museum to ask Motta for tanks to come to the rescue.

Lieutenant Jacob Ilam's detachment started forward. Beyond the defense-wall, the area was raked with bullets from the position at the corner of the walls, and the men had to leap across, crouching, covered by Yami's platoon. They reached the bridge, where a tank and two jeeps were burning, with their wounded alongside. As Corporal Jacob Shindler, the platoon medical orderly, ran to the nearest jeep, a flare burst, illuminating the whole bridge, followed by a hail of bullets. A man next to him dropped. Shindler reached the jeep, lifted up one of the wounded men and ran back. Again he returned to the bridge and bent over a soldier whose clothes had caught fire, and tried to tear them off. But the man's screams were so agonizing that Shindler beat out the flames with his bare hands and bent to pick the man up. At that same instant he heard a noise like a bullet striking flesh, and the man died in his arms.

Shindler looked around. Twenty meters away, in the middle of the bridge, Lieutenant Ilam was bending over three wounded men. As Shindler moved closer, a flame shot up from one of the jeeps and exposed him completely. A long burst of machine-gun fire bored a line of holes in the asphalt, each one a little nearer to Shindler, who sprang, without thought or hesitation, into the abyss. He landed heavily, dislocating his foot. His face and the palms of his hands were scorched. For a few moments he lay quietly and then began to crawl up.

When Raffi's three tanks managed to get off the bridge, they returned to the outskirts of the American Colony and were directed by Amos, the G-Branch officer of the Paratroop Brigade, to the turning to Mt. Scopus, where they were joined by 10th Brigade tanks. Major Arieli assumed command and the 71st Battalion followed them. They had not gone far when a message from the Brigade commander brought them back:

"Warning from Mt. Scopus that Jordanian armor, possibly 40

9

tanks, is coming from Ma'aleh Ha'adumim toward Jerusalem. Since it may counter-attack, the G.O.C. Central Command has ordered the attack on Augusta Victoria stopped and defense organized against armored offensive."

Hearing this, Micha commandeered two tanks and ordered them to the bridge to cover the movement of the men withdrawing on foot. One of the tanks was hit immediately and began to burn, and the second, its turret struck by an anti-tank shell, retreated. The flames from the jeeps on the bridge were dying down and even the shooting was petering out, encouraging Micha to make one last attempt to get to his men. With Yami's men as cover, he, together with the men from the command-car and Meir Har-Zion, the battalion's first C.O., who had joined as a volunteer, scrambled into the wadi, where they could move unimpeded until they reached the supports of the bridge. While the men searched for wounded soldiers under the bridge, Micha and Meir climbed a pipe onto the bridge above.

"The tank on the bridge was burning and its ammunition began to explode," Micha said later, "so that I could see three of our men motionless in the middle of the bridge. Because of the exploding ammunition and the shots of the enemy, I could not get to them. I crawled as close as I could and called out the names of my men. Not one responded."

At two o'clock in the morning, Micha moved all his men to the safety of the wall of the American Colony and counted them. Yishai's platoon was the most severely cut down and Raffi Yeshayahu's tank crew were still missing. Micha told the Brigade commander that despite their losses his company was ready for the next assignment, but he was ordered inside the Colony to deploy his men to meet the Jordanian armor.

The Enemy Armor in the Valley

At 22.14 Menahem Sharfman reported from Mt. Scopus that an enemy force had entered Augusta Victoria and that heavy vehicular movement was coming up through Ma'aleh Ha'adumim, adding, minutes later, that tanks had also been spotted.

"Can you see them?"

"With difficulty. But I can hear them!"

"How many are there?"

"At least forty!"

Perhaps this was the Jordanian counter-attack. I told Lt. Colonel

Davidi that they must be bombed and Arik Regev that planes must be ordered at once. I contacted the C.O. of the 10th Brigade: "Enemy armor coming up from the valley. Secure your positions towards the east!" And I informed Amitai, telling him to organize for defense at Government House and Baher. I cancelled the assault on Augusta Victoria and ordered the paratroops to the edge of the built-up area of East Jerusalem, there to deploy for defense.

Around midnight I contacted Haim Bar-Lev and explained that the paratroops' assault had been stopped because of the Jordanian armor and the necessity to be prepared for a counter-offensive. Bar-Lev concurred and I urged an air strike on Ma'aleh Ha'adumim; the Command artillery had begun to shell the incline half an hour ago. He promised to do his best, and he did.

Aircraft roared overhead. I went up to the roof of Binyanei Ha'ooma, where I could hear the explosions in the east, and could see clouds of dust above and to the north of Ma'aleh Ha'adumim. In seconds the horizon was alight with a flash that turned the cloud a scabrous mauve, the color of foreboding.

The air strike broke the back of the Jordanian counter-attack before it had time to develop, trapping the Jordanian armor in a narrow pass, from which it could neither escape nor spread out. Several tanks went off the road, some overturned, some continued for a few meters, stopped and were hit. A few succeeded in turning around in an effort to save themselves by retreating, but they, too, were hit. The blaze of the tanks provided an excellent target.

The roar of the aircraft diminished, but I stayed on the roof. With the bombardment over, the city's silence seemed strange and profound, disturbed only by brief bursts of gunfire. The headquarters' staff slept for the first time in two days, and in the laagers north of Ramallah and Tel el-Ful, the armored troops, after hours of refuelling and rearming, wrapped themselves in blankets and lay next to their tanks. At Wadi Joz, the American Colony and the Rockefeller Museum, the paratroops mourned their casualties, and their dead, but used the few night-time hours to rest. The men of the Jerusalem Brigade reorganized after gruelling hours of battle and awaited orders.

Everyone was waiting for tomorrow.

Lifting the Embargo

Just as dawn was beginning to lighten the skies on Wednesday, June 7th, I left the roof of Binyanei Ha'ooma and went downstairs to rest.

Except for the clerks manning the telephones, headquarters was asleep. It was as though the whole world were holding its breath and waiting.

I could not sleep. I waited. I knew that the day would bring Central Command's final plans, that the paratroops would capture Mount Zion, the tank corps go down to the Jordan Valley, the Jerusalemites get through to Bethlehem and the Hebron mountains. As to the Old City, I contemplated it with pain. I had, after all, been given a definite order: "Do not enter." But nonetheless something whispered, "Today the embargo on the Old City will be lifted."

There was a pale light in the war room, illuminating the duty officer between two telephones, the signals clerk, next to him, her eyes red with tiredness, and opposite her the clerk who kept the operations register. I glanced at the register. Very little had happened during the past few hours, neither the armored brigade nor the paratroops had anything to report, but the Jerusalem Brigade needed 0.5 ammunition at Sur Baher and the Yotvat Brigade reported two half-tracks in need of repair and requested a workshop detachment.

The Intelligence sergeant, whose job was to mark enemy movement on the large map, returned the Jordanian armored brigade to Jericho, using colored pencil. Even here nothing had changed.

I went outside to watch the dawn break and to let the breeze cool my skin. In the pervading quiet, the occasional shell or rifle-bullet exploded with shocking force. I went back to my room.

But, at that moment, the quietest since the war began, grave political decisions were being made. Decision-making had begun the previous evening at 8 o'clock, at a meeting in Tel Aviv of the Ministerial Committee on Matters of Defense. At the request of the defense minister, "the subject of the Old City was examined."

When Moshe Dayan left the meeting and returned to G.H.Q., he repeated his earlier order to surround the Old City, but to enter only under specific orders. But about an hour later, when he heard about the movements of the Jordanian army, he said, "We must finish taking Jerusalem tonight and tomorrow."

I, however, received no operational order.

Later that night, after the air force had routed the Jordanians, their army was in full retreat, but I still had no orders.

Early Wednesday morning, Minister Menahem Begin heard a B.B.C. broadcast, reporting a Security Council declaration of a cease-fire, effective at noon. He had been willing to accept the defense minister's arguments that it was worth waiting for the Old City to surrender without a fight, but now he feared that the cease-fire would be implemented before the Old City surrendered. He telephoned the Prime Minister, insisted that he be awakened, and demanded an immediate meeting of the Ministerial Committee on Matters of Defense. The Prime Minister consulted the Foreign Minister who was cognizant of the political events, and thought that the decision to enter the Old City must be taken quickly. Interior Minister Moshe Shapira agreed, and it was decided not to wait for surrender, but to take the Old City without delay and to transmit suitable orders to the army.

The Threat of a Cease-Fire

At 05.30, when Yoel Herzl burst into my room to say that the deputy C.O.G.S. wanted to speak to me, I guessed that it was about the threat of a cease-fire. "We must surround Jerusalem and enter the Old City," he said. I was more than ready to act at once, and contacted Motta to tell him about the cease-fire and that he must capture the Augusta Victoria ridge and smash into the Old City. "When can you begin?" I asked.

"I'll check." Since his forces had been moved back the night before to defense positions for the anticipated counter-attack, time was needed to return them to the point of attack.

The war room was completely awake and tense with excitement. I told Arik that we had to organize support for the paratroopers. "Warn the Command artillery officer and we'll hold our own planning session." Immediately after Arik left, Motta phoned to say that they would be ready to start at 8.30 to which I suggested that they stop at Augusta Victoria and let Eliezer Armitai come up from his side towards Ras el-Amood, but Motta objected for fear of an accidental encounter. "It'll be best if we take the whole lot alone," he said.

"But hurry," I told him.

Haim Bar-Lev phoned to say that he was coming to Jerusalem in an hour, and at 6.00 a.m. Uri's scouts above the Hebron axes, Jericho and the Nablus-Ramallah highway reported that no enemy was to be seen. In fact, reports were shooting in like bullets: the armored brigade of Northern Command was on its way to the Damiya Bridge, having destroyed the 40th Jordanian armor, and an augmented Iraqi brigade with artillery and tanks was in the Jiflik region.

When I had a chance, I contacted Uri to ask if he was ready to go from the Ramallah-Jericho road to the Jerusalem ridges, and he, terribly eager to get to Nablus ahead of Northern Command, asked if he could also go north, to which I consented.

"Yesterday we were told to give eleven tanks to the paratroops, but they weren't taken," he said. "May we use them? They're on the Mivtar." Actually, only the seven tanks lost on the way to the Rockefeller Museum were there. Out of contact with their company commander, they had asked the Brigade for instructions.

I told Uri that he couldn't have them and then told Motta, the paratroop C.O., to take them. "What's new?" I asked.

"I've moved tanks opposite the corner of the Old City wall," he said, "and I need artillery support. I've sent to the Mivtar for the tanks," he added.

Again Uri came on to ask if he could also move down along the Hizma axis. "Do I have to get into Azaria?"

"I'll check," I said, and a bit later informed him that almost no enemy was left and that the 60th Brigade had retreated to Jericho, where he might meet them. "But I don't really think you will. Move along the Ramallah axis until you can cross to the Jericho-Jerusalem highway, maybe via Hizma. And on your way to Jerusalem, don't let the twists and turns at Azaria confuse you. Incidentally, Motta may be there too."

At the same time, Lolik, the air-support officer, was receiving reports from the pilots, who had just stopped bombing the objective, saying that the enemy seemed to have withdrawn completely from northeast Jerusalem. When I discussed this with Arik, I pointed out that there was no point in continuing to bomb the ridge if the enemy had left. But Arik did not believe that they had and we decided to go on supporting the paratroops from the air. We sent Lolik to the Histadrut roof, the best place to direct the planes to Augusta Victoria. I ordered the 55th and the Jerusalem Brigade to pay attention to events on the ridge and report on the presence of the enemy.

Uri Ben-Ari, who had moved his men towards Nablus on the way to the valley, reported that he was at the Atarot Airport and needed a helicopter in order to join the Brigade.

By 07.15 our artillery was shelling Augusta Victoria, and five minutes later Eliezer Amitai called in. "The Arabs want to return to their villages."

"Which villages?"

"Silwan, Sur Baher, Abu Tor..."

"Wait," I told him.

At 07.35, while I was on the telephone with the C.O.G.S., Haim

Bar-Lev arrived and listened to my report to the chief.

"We cancelled the night attack on Augusta Victoria because Jordanian armor was coming to Jerusalem through Ma'aleh Ha'adumim. Motta is on his way to the Mount of Olives via Mt. Scopus, and Uri is coming in from the Jericho side."

Haim Bar-Lev smiled with delight and said:

"The order is to enter the Old City, but with prudence. No unnecessary casualties and no destruction of holy places. They're pressing for a cease-fire. We've reached the Suez Canal and have cut off the Egyptians who are still there."

This meant that the war was coming to an end. "It's essential that the paratroops carry out their operation." Bar-Lev went on, "but the Old City must not remain an Arab enclave, like Mt. Scopus. The question is how, when and with what can you take the Old City, so that there's a minimum of shooting and no shelling?"

There it was; that was precisely my own question. On Monday night, I had confirmed the plan calling for Motta to assign the breakthrough task to one of the two battalions which had pulled right towards the Old City. This plan stood. Now Motta ordered the 66th Battalion to go on via Sheikh Jarrah to Mt. Scopus, from which they could capture Augusta Victoria, and the 71st Battalion to attack it from Wadi Joz and Gethsemane, leaving the 28th Battalion free, ready to break into the Old City after Augusta Victoria had been taken. Now, because of the possible cease-fire, I weighed the advantages of attacking the Old City without waiting for the fall of Augusta Victoria.

I glanced around at the small group in the war room, augmented a few moments earlier by Colonel Shlomo Lahat ("Chich"), a veteran tankman. When the war started he was on a mission in South America, but although he hurried home, he had arrived as the war was concluding. I was his last hope for a crack at the action.

"Chich," I said, "would you like to run up to the Mivtar, collect some of Uri's tanks and one of his armored infantry units and move them to the Rockefeller and contact Motta? And then, with the force at your disposal, you will break into the Old City."

"No shelling," Bar-Lev repeated, "and as little shooting as possible."

I had to contact Motta to find out the whereabouts of Uri's tanks. 'I need them for another job. Are they still on the Mivtar?"

"No," Motta replied, "they're here with me, to support the capture of Augusta Victoria." Apparently the 66th Battalion had picked up the tanks on the way to Mt. Scopus.

We had no option, therefore, but to wait, until the Mount of Olives ridge had been captured. "Never mind," I said, "Chich will join Motta and after the ridge is taken he'll command the force going into the Old City."

As Chich was leaving, Dayan telephoned, and after Bar-Lev had reported our decision, asked if he thought Chich was up to giving the order to open fire on Jews who might be looters.

Haim covered the mouthpiece, and repeated Dayan's question to Chich. Into the instrument he said, "Absolutely. No doubt about it."

Chich went on his way.

The sense of the war's ending dissipated for a moment with the news of the Jordanian armored force near Jericho. They were the remnants of the 60th Brigade, whose confusion of movement reflected the disorder at the Jordanian headquarters. The twice-ordered general withdrawal from the West Bank had now been cancelled for the second time. "On the night of June 6/7th," say Hussein's memoirs, "feverish efforts were made to obtain a cease-fire...several units began to withdraw...but towards morning, orders were given to the Imam Ali [60th] Brigade and to the King Talal [3rd] Infantry Brigade, to hold on to Jerusalem to the last man..."

I told Uri about it. He agreed. And I told Bar-Lev that Uri wanted permission to capture Nablus.

"Absolutely not," he answered. "He can go only as far as Hevara (the border between the Central and Northern Commands)."

Augusta Victoria Through the Smoke

When Lolik reported that the Air Force was ready to bomb Augusta Victoria, I asked for a strike on the newly appeared Jordanian armor.

"O.K.," he replied. "When the first flight hits the mountain, we'll send the rest to take Jericho."

At 08.30 we all went out to the square in front of the building to watch the first flight in action. The planes dived, dropped their bombs, climbed, dived again to fire their rockets. Augusta Victoria was a column of smoke. They made their last climb eight minutes later and Lolik radioed to Davidi, the artillery officer, to tell him that the planes had finished and he could begin. In a moment, mortar and cannon were on their way, and Motta telephoned: "We're off..."

Augusta Victoria Captured

As the 66th Battalion started, Deputy Battalion Commander Doron broke ranks and rushed to Givat Hamivtar to collect the 10th Brigade's missing tanks, which set off at once, although their commander knew nothing of the assignment.

The 77th Battalion, on the march to attack Augusta Victoria from the slopes of Wadi Joz, came under heavy sniping from Arab Legionnaires on top of the Old City walls. The casualties forced the men to retreat to the built-up area, from which snipers and machine-gunners exchanged shots with the fighters on the walls, which persisted. Uzi, the battalion C.O., asked for an artillery bombardment, and, as soon as the shooting stopped, the tanks advanced and Uzi could organize his forces. The tanks were first, followed by jeeps, with anti-tank guns and the two paratroop companies on their left. The second wave was made up of two more companies and half-tracks.

At 08.30 the air force, followed by artillery, began the softening-up process. The men moved from their positions, the tanks firing as they went forward, bombarding the petrified enemy inside Augusta Victoria. Yossi, C.O. of the 66th, already on Mt. Scopus and deployed in fortified positions, looked down at the slope and caught his breath. Every man was exposed, a live target, virtually like figures on a target-range. "Had there been any kind of force in Augusta Victoria," he said, shaken, "we would have been cut down like toy soldiers."

Only sporadic shooting came from the fortress hospital, there was no artillery at all. Kapusta's reconnaissance company had been added to the assault force, and the moment the first soldiers broke through the barbed wire around the hospital, Motta ordered the tanks and the reconnaissance unit to outflank the building and head for the A-Tur ridge and the Ras el-Amood junction.

Augusta Victoria was ours; its surrounding fortifications and the building itself were empty. Only after it had been combed out was the hospital medical staff, numbering 200 people, found in the basement where they were hiding. Not one had been hurt.

A GENERATION'S DREAM
IS REALIZED

Scaling the Walls

At 9:00 came Motta's message that Augusta Victoria had been captured and everyone at Binyanei Ha'ooma was seized with its impact. The time had come. We were upon the walls.

"Shall we move?" I murmured impatiently.

We moved.

The forward H.Q. group – two half-tracks and two jeeps – were waiting and in we climbed, with Didi Menussi and Raffi Amir, a Kol-Israel man, whom Didi had graciously invited for "the experience of your life." We drove toward the Mandelbaum Gate, still blocked because of the mines, and therefore switched direction to the P.Ag.I. houses, taking the paratroops' assault axis to the police school. I wanted to get to the Rockefeller Museum to see Motta, since I'd had no contact with him after he announced the occupation of Augusta Victoria. We passed the East Jerusalem Y.M.C.A., whose smashed windows and besmirched walls gave bleak evidence of battle. The American Consulate on the right was also battle-scarred; a destroyed gas station stood next to the temporary memorial erected by the paratroopers to their fallen comrades. We sped by passing an undamaged mosque and the bullet-riddled buildings in an alley, called "the Alley of Death" by the paratroopers, for the fallen who had attempted to rescue their comrades.

Suddenly the wall rose before us, and the battlements of Nablus Gate. The Gate was not yet ours; Legionnaires guarded the parapet and we turned back to Salah e-Din Street, where broken windows, burned automobiles, and derelict electric wires spoke of war. Opposite the Rivoli Hotel was a damaged Egged bus and several paratroopers. I asked what they were doing.

"Wounded evacuation point," one replied.

"Are there wounded?"

"Two, not seriously."

"And what's ahead?"

"Don't know. Shooting."

Another group of paratroopers halted our advance, warning about shooting at the end of the road, where Salah e-Din Street meets Herod's Gate and the Old City walls. We could travel on it no farther and turned around, Haim Bar-Lev taking the wheel. Back on Nablus Road, we encountered all the terrible and pathetic remnants of war: death and destruction and chaos. Nothing stirred.

"I think they've all run away," I said to Bar-Lev.

The next day proved me wrong. The residents of East Jerusalem had simply hidden in their cellars, to emerge when the shooting stopped.

By 09.45 we were on Mt. Scopus, gazing at the town below, which seemed idle and empty. All at once I saw smoke rising inside the Old City, behind the walls, and contacted Arik: "Are the paratroopers shelling the Old City?" When he said that they were, I ordered him to stop immediately, and at the same moment, I heard the paratroop G. Branch officer commanding his mortar units to stop shooting. "We're going in," he cried.

"Where are you?" I called.

"At the Lion's Gate," and before the last word had been uttered we were back in our vehicles, racing down the mountain, our hearts as loud as the motors. We were going into the Old City!

Nineteen years earlier we had broken through the Zion Gate and entered the Jewish Quarter, only to leave it again in despair and bitter disappointment.

"Let us not go in if it's just to go out another time," I breathed.

"We shall never leave again," said Haim Bar-Lev.

Our convoy was on the slope of the hill below Rockefeller, where the road branches towards Gethsemane. From the corner position on the wall opposite, shots were still coming, and beneath, on the traffic island, was a silent Sherman tank and the sunshade of the policeman who was not on duty to use it.

The intermittent shots of the snipers could be heard from the walls. I threw a smoke-grenade, under cover of which we crossed to the abandoned tank, which had been hit the night before during the "Battle on the Bridge."

Snipers fired on a column of paratroopers, who marched on without changing pace, like men fatigued to the point of trance. One fell, and then another, but forward tramped the rest.

Next to the damaged tank, completely exposed, a paratrooper with a bazooka stood, legs apart, fighting a private duel with the snipers on the walls. He silenced the corner position.

We went back to the cars, abandoning the slow-moving half-tracks, and sped off in the jeeps. Ahead, on the road from the valley to the Lion's Gate, was a column of paratroopers, led by General Rabbi Shlomo Goren, Chief Army Chaplain, a *sefer torah* under his arm, a *shofar* in his left hand, his beard bristling like the point of a spear, and his face bathed in perspiration. He was panting.

"Rabbi," I called out, "come aboard. We're going to the same place."

"No," he replied, "to the Temple Mount one goes on foot."

"Then we'll meet there." The jeep sprang forward. On the move I contacted Motta to find out where he was.

"The Temple Mount is ours!"

I couldn't believe it.

"I repeat," said Motta. "The Temple Mount is ours. I'm standing near the Mosque el-Omar right now. The Wailing Wall is a minute away."

Now was the time for the jeep to sprout wings, but at the moment it lacked not just wings but one of its wheels. Bang, and the jeep veered so sharply that only with all my strength could I stop it before it tumbled off the road. The tire was in shreds. We had no time or inclination to change. We crowded into the second jeep, leaving Yoel Herzl with the radio, thus cutting ourselves off from contact and the possibility of finding out what was going on. But, more important, we drove up the narrow road toward the Lion's Gate. On the square in front of it an Arab bus was steadily burning. Electric cables were down. Legionnaires' bodies lay all around, a section of the gate had been torn from its hinges, the second section was flung open and the arch above the Gate had been hit, so that its loose masonry threatened the heads of passers-by. But the carved lions were undamaged.

We drove through, along the road to the Gate of the Tribes and the Temple Mount, and down the Via Dolorosa to the second arch. It was blocked by the lead tank of the paratroops. We climbed over it and continued on foot.

Yoel, behind us, picked off a sniper shooting at us from one of the houses. Except for that, the Via Dolorosa was cool and silent, the windows shuttered, the streets empty. Had our men been through

18. A tank stuck in the archway of the Via Dolorosa

19. An embrace from the Chief Rabbi Goren

here, I wondered. Beyond the second arch lay King Feisal Street, a brief, narrow, covered, tunnel-like lane, closed at the far end by a wide gate with a small wicket where pedestrians entered. This, too, was closed, but the bolt was not locked. We stepped through, and the breath caught in our throats.

We beheld the huge paved courtyard, crowned, against the blue sky of June 7th, 1967 (the 28th of the month of Iyar in the year 5727), by the golden cupola of the Dome of the Rock, gleaming, glistening, taking its gold from the sun.

A spectacle of legend.

We ran towards Motta Gur, standing on the Mount, where the flag of Israel flew. We were joined first by Moshe Stempel, Motta's deputy, and then by Rabbi Goren. We embraced and the Rabbi prostrated himself and genuflected towards the Holy of Holies. In a resonant voice he recited the ancient Prayer to Battle (Deuteronomy 20:3-4):

Hear, O Israel, ye approach this day unto battle against your enemies; let not your hearts faint, fear not, and do not tremble, neither be ye terrified because of them; for the Lord your God is he that goeth with you, to fight for you against your enemies, to save you!

Hastily, I visited the Mosque and was delighted to find no damage, except to a glass door from the brief battle in the courtyard. There had apparently been resistance from inside. As the cleaning up continued, I told Motta once again to make sure that no holy places or shrines were touched.

We made our excited way through the streets to the Mugrabis' Gate, along a dim alley, turned right down a flight of steps, impatiently faced another right turn – and there it was. The Wailing Wall. I quivered with memory. Tall and awesome and glorious, with the same ferns creeping between the great stones, some of them inscribed.

Silently I bowed my head. In the narrow space were paratroopers, begrimed, fatigued, overburdened with weapons. And they wept. They were not "wailing at the Western Wall," not lamenting in the fashion familiar during the Wall's millennia of being. These were tears of joy, of love, of passion, of an undreamed first reunion with their ancient monument to devotion and to prayer. They clung to its stones, kissed them, these rough, battle-weary paratroopers, their lips framing the *shema*. Returned, it seemed to the Temple ....

But more exalted, prouder than all of them, was Rabbi Goren. Wrapped in a *tallit* (prayer shawl), blowing the ram's horn, and

20. (From right to left) Rabin, Dayan and Narkiss entering the Lions' Gate

roaring like a lion: "Blessed be the Lord God, Comforter of Zion and Builder of Jerusalem, Amen!" Suddenly he saw me, embraced me, and planted a ringing kiss on my cheek, a signal to everyone to hug and kiss and join hands. The Rabbi, like one who had waited all his life for this moment, intoned the *Kaddish*, the *El Moleh Rahamim* (O, God, full of mercy . . .), in memory of those who had fallen in the name of the Lord to liberate the Temple, the Temple Mount and Jerusalem the City of the Lord: "May they find their peace in Heaven . . . and let us say Amen."

The restrained weeping became sobs, full-throated, an uncurbed emotional outburst. Sorrow, fervor, happiness and pain combined to produce this mass of grieving and joyous men, their cheeks wet, their voices unsteady. Again the *shofar* was blown: *tekiya* (a short, but unbroken sound), followed by the *shevarim* (a short but tremolo sound). And Rabbi Goren intoned, like a herald: "This year, at this hour, in Jerusalem!" (*le-shana hazot, be-sha'a hazot, be-Yerushalayim*).

Until that moment I thought I was immune to anything. Even the stones responded. "We shall stand at attention and salute! Attention!" I shouted. "And sing *hatikva*" [Israel's national anthem], came the choked voice of Haim Bar-Lev. We started to sing. To our voices were added those of the paratroopers, hoarse and indistinct. Sobbing and singing, it was as though through the *hatikva* we could unburden our hearts of their fulness and our spirits of their emotion.

We spent ten minutes in front of the Wailing Wall and at 10.55 were on our way back to the basement of Binyanei Ha'ooma. There was plenty of work to be done. The Old City had not yet been cleared of snipers and the West Bank had not yet been taken.

Meanwhile, we learned, the Jerusalem Brigade had at the last minute made an improvised entry into the Old City through the Dung Gate. Amos, the G-Branch officer, having heard the 55th Brigade's announcement that Augusta Victoria had been taken, realized that the paratroops would immediately break into the Old City and determined that Zahal's Jerusalem Brigade, which for 19 years had defended the divided city, must participate in that historic entry. Two companies of the battalion which took Abu-Tor were assembled at Mount Zion and moved along the Walls to the Silwan stream to enter through the Dung Gate. They reached the Temple Mount shortly after 10 a.m. and from there turned westwards.

While we were driving I suggested to Haim Bar-Lev that we begin demobilization of the Air Defense people at once. With the war over, there seemed little danger of bombardment, and things must return to normal, and the economy be revived as quickly as possible. Although he agreed, several days were to go by before the demobbing order was issued.

At Binyanei Ha'ooma an Order-of-the-Day was born:

We are standing on your threshold, Jerusalem. Today we entered your gates.
Jerusalem, city of David and Solomon, is in our hands.
This morning, in the shadow of the Wailing Wall, we sang Hatikvah, we mourned our dead, fallen in the battle for the city.
Troops of the Command, brave fighters, devoted warriors, this day and your valor shall be in our hearts forever.

Major-General Uzi Narkiss

Allenby at the Fortress

Indeed we are not a ceremony-minded people. When Jerusalem surrendered to the British forces on December 9th, 1917, the British Commander, General Allenby, waited outside the gates of the city for three full days, by order of his government, during which time complete and detailed plans were drawn up in London for the victorious entry of the Conqueror of Jerusalem. The British War Office composed the speech he was to deliver when he stood at the Jaffa Gate. The speech was confirmed by the Cabinet and cabled to Cairo. And only then, on December 11th, after the entire ceremony had been prepared and rehearsed to perfection, was the signal given for General Allenby's official conquest of Jerusalem.

It is amusing to read what the official British historian wrote about the event:

Sir Edmund Allenby drove in a car along Jaffa Road, between rows of troops standing on both sides of the road and near the Gate. He dismounted from his car and entered the city on foot like a pilgrim. In front of him marched two adjutants and behind him three staff officers, his personal secretary and the liaison officer of the British War Office. On the right and left marched the Commanders of the French and Italian garrisons, as well as Brigadier Clayton, Major Lawrence and Colonel Wyndham Deedes. With them walked the military (attachés) of Italy and France, Allenby's Chief-of-Staff and his Deputy, the Commander of the 20th Corps and his staff officers. Completing the procession were soldiers who marched in squads of four.

The Military Commander of Jerusalem met the Supreme British Commander and led him to the steps of the fortress of David's Tower, where he met the city notables. Soldiers stood on the steps on both sides of the entourage, and the speech marking the conquest of Jerusalem was read out to the assembled guests in English, French, Arabic, Hebrew, Greek, Russian and Italian.

The ceremony was simple and impressive, and it seemed clear to me that all those present enjoyed it. Nevertheless emotions did not run too high and flags were not flown to honor the event.

Jerusalem has been conquered or overrun thirty-seven times. In June, 1967, we liberated our city for what we hope will be the last time and for what we pray will be the first generation of its complete redemption.

And what of our ceremony? Grimy, sweating soldiers, the General, dry-mouthed and silent, the Deputy C.O.G.S. in a black beret, a driver, an adjutant, a civilian and the Chief Army Chaplain, who knew how to behave on such an occasion – not a reporter nor a cameraman, no polished and gleaming guards, not even a Victory Arch. "Jerusalem deserves better than this," said my heart.

I contacted G.H.Q. and reported officially: "Ancient Jerusalem is in our hands." I suggested that the Supreme Command should solemnize the day with an official announcement. It was too late for the 11 o'clock news broadcast, but I had no doubt that such news warranted a special bulletin.

A meeting in connection with the military administration was held in my chambers, where I announced that the Chief of the General Staff had appointed General Haim Herzog to be Military Governor of the West Bank, attached to Central Command. I handed him his assignments: to impose law and order throughout the conquered territories, safeguard religious institutions, prevent looting and plundering and establish a suitable government framework. The Green Line was to be closed in and Israeli citizens were to be prevented from crossing over. The paratroops, an infantry brigade and the border guards were to be at the disposal of the administration.

During the discussions, I bent one ear to the radio on my table, hushing everyone at 12 o'clock to listen to the news. Nothing. Not a single word.

Later I was informed that the Defense Minister and the C.O.G.S., General Rabin, were coming to Jerusalem at 1.30 p.m.

Uri telephoned to say that his unit had reached Hevera, just before Nablus, and to ask whether the other units of the Brigade should go to Jericho or Hebron. At 10 a.m. his Brigade was in observation-range of Jericho. He requested permission to attack. Arik put the question to the General Staff, but the Defense Minister, who was listening to the

21. December 1917. Allenby reads the Manifesto to the citizens of Jerusalem

conversation, shouted, "What's Uri doing near Jericho? Who authorized the action? Have him get back at once!"

The C.O.G.S. told me that Uri was to leave the Jericho area
immediately, since his presence there was unauthorized. When I
repeated the order to him, he argued fruitlessly, and in the end
returned with his troops to the Ramallah region.

The radio was on continuously – during my orders to the Gush
Lachish forces to take Id'na, and to the Jerusalem Brigade to advance
southwards, and during reports of what was going on from the Suez
Canal to the Golan Heights. But Jerusalem was never mentioned.
Finally, at close to 2 p.m., I contacted the Zahal spokesman to ask if
an official announcement had been released about the liberation of the
Old City, and was told that they had decided to wait.

The room was crowded with people, loud with their congratulations. Teddy Kollek arrived. We talked, tried to forecast the future.
Herzog said: "We ought to set up an autonomous state for the Arabs in
Judea and Samaria." To which Teddy replied, smiling, "On condition that they'll hold regional elections."

The defense minister walked in.

A Front Page Picture is Born

Whatever I said about our lack of ceremony does not apply to Moshe
Dayan. He has a flair for it, and a colossal feeling for historical events.
He came prepared. With him were the C.O.G.S., other General Staff
officers and many civilians, followed by a train of photographers,
newspaper reporters and radio broadcasters. The whole retinue was
orchestrated by "Moish" Perelman.

We drove to the Lions' Gate in a convoy, military policemen before
and behind, and two armored half-tracks for protection. At the Gate
the first to enter were the photographers. After them went the defense
minister, who stopped in mid-entry as though something were missing and signaled to Itzhak Rabin to stand beside him. A slight pause,
and he turned to me: "Uzi, come here." We marched along, the
photographers angling their cameras and clicking out the picture of
the official entry through the Lions' Gate that became the front page
cover for the Six Day War in Jerusalem.

We were at the Western Wall by 2 p.m., where the crowd was larger
than it had been in the morning. Soldiers cheered and made room for
Dayan and his contingent, so that all of us were standing at the Wall.
Dayan took from his pocket a bit of paper on which something had

22. The descent to the Wall. (From left to right) Dayan, Rabin and Narkiss

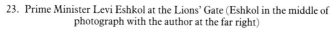

23. Prime Minister Levi Eshkol at the Lions' Gate (Eshkol in the middle of photograph with the author at the far right)

been written and pushed it between the old stones. "What did you write?" asked Koby Sharett.

"Let peace come to Israel," he replied.

He had prepared a statement and, in the presence of the batteries of cameras and microphones, delivered it:

"We have returned to the holiest of our holy places, never to be separated from it again. Israel extends the hand of friendship to its Arab neighbors, and to all those of other religions, with assurances that their complete freedom and right to observe and practice their religion shall be safeguarded. We have not come to conquer the shrines of others or to restrict their religious rights, but to insure the integrity of the city and to live in it in friendship and fraternity with others."

On the way back tension subsided somewhat and we talked about matters of military administration. Dayan ordered that the gates to the Old City be opened, but that unrestricted entry be forbidden. Soldiers were to guard the gates and check permits. But the gates would remain open. I suggested that we break open a passage to the Wailing Wall, but he preferred to wait and see what transpired.

We returned to Binyanei Ha'ooma at 2:30 and Dayan, Rabin, Chera, Gandi, Herzog, Moish Perelman and Moshe Kashti gathered in my chambers.

It was a small windowless room, lit by battery-fed lamps. There was a field table with telephones, a bench, a folding bed, and a radio transmitter in a corner. We were crushed together. Rabin asked: "How does one govern a million Arabs?"

"A million two hundred and fifty thousand," Gandi corrected.

"You'll have to open up supply axes in breadth," Rabin said to me. "And it would be best if Uri and Dado [the forces of Northern Command] were to contact us before dark. When are they going to Hebron?"

"The Jerusalem Brigade started towards Elias and Bethlehem about an hour ago," I replied.

A recording crew from *Kol Israel* (the Voice of Israel Broadcasting Service) arrived to record Dayan's statement about the capture of the Old City, and everyone was sent out of the room except Gandi, who shone a lamp on the paper from which Dayan was reading. Dayan settled in a corner with the recording crew. When he had finished, he invited Rabin to say a few words, after which his patience was exhausted. He smiled and shook hands and was off to Tel Aviv. Rabin

24. The morning after: destroyed military vehicle in front of the undamaged Church of Gethsemane

instructed me to inform the army spokesman that his statement and that of the defense minister were to be considered Zahal's official announcement of the liberation of the Old City.

Eshkol at the Wailing Wall

The Prime Minister, I was told by his office, was in Jerusalem and wanted to visit the Temple Mount. We prepared a convoy, but before I left I stopped to get a situation report from Arik Regev, who said that the Jerusalem Brigade was outside of Bethlehem and the 10th advancing on Jericho, whose capture had meanwhile been authorized.

"Let him try blowing up Allenby Bridge," I told Arik.

Entering Eshkol's chambers, I recalled the Tattoo on the eve of Independence Day, when we had met here to go to the auditorium. Who could then have conceived that three weeks later we would leave this place again, but for how different a purpose? In Eshkol's office were the Minister of Justice, J. S. Shapira, the Minister of Religion, Zerah Warhaftig and the Director-General of the P.M.'s Office, Jacob Herzog.

Before we left for the Wailing Wall I called Arik to find out about the 10th and learned that Uri was attacking Jericho, was going to blow up the Allenby Bridge, and that Eliezer was taking Bethlehem.

At 6:00 p.m., twenty minutes after we left the Prime Minister's office, we were at the Lion's Gate. For the third time that day I walked down the Via Dolorosa to the Wailing Wall, and for the third time found it packed with soldiers praying, crying or simply gazing at those old stones out of eyes reverent with love.

"Sanctity overflows," whispered the Prime Minister.

We went up to Mount Scopus. In the fading light, the sight was more magnificent than it had been at midday.

Jordan Bridges Falling Down

Permission to capture Jericho had been granted in the afternoon, so that Uri, who had worked hard all morning to send his Brigade back to Ramallah, now had to return to the valley. The Brigade used two movement axes, meeting only slight resistance, and finding that the narrow, twisting paths were the chief obstructions to their progress. Even so, by 6:30 p.m. they were deployed some three kilometers west of Jericho.

Uri planned to take Jericho by the so-called Ramallah Method: a tank strike and a powerful cannonade, a task that fell partly to the tank

25. With the Chief-of-Staff General Yitzhak Rabin at the Wall

26. Saluting the paratroopers on Temple Mount

battalion. The second battalion was ordered to capture the police fortress south of the city, and the reconnaissance and mortar companies dug in at Kfar Na'uma, about two kilometers north of the city. At 6:30 the mortars began their softening-up bombardment, the tanks fired, and the half-tracks followed.

Uri had ordered an assault by storm, but had not taken into account the tricky curves towards the bottom of the decline. The tanks had to maneuver back and forth to negotiate the hairpin turns, while other vehicles stood immobilized before the enemy. More than one tank commander shivered as his eyes swept the green Jordan plain and his mind dwelled upon the very real possibility that each banana plantation and every orchard concealed an anti-tank ambush. But the silence was total, and the commanders reminded the tankmen that the Brigade C.O. had said that the air-reconnaissance flights prior to the attack had glimpsed no sign of enemy tanks in the neighborhood. Air-reconnaissance proved, in fact, to be mistaken. No fewer than twelve Pattons, some with shells, were found the next day as well as two Long-Toms, of the type which had shelled Tel Aviv. Their crews had abandoned them.

After negotiating the final bend in the road, the vehicles stormed the town. The 10th Brigade burst into the police fortress, whose defenders, after sending several rounds of machine-gun fire into the first waves of attackers, had laid down their weapons and fled. The fortress was taken without casualties. At the same time, the tank battalion thrust into Jericho, still filled with army vehicles carrying Jordanian soldiers escaping to the east. The appearance of the tanks reduced the retreat to chaos. Jordanian soldiers leapt from the cars and jumped fences in their effort to get away, in some cases firing at the tanks and wounding some of the crew. But they could not stop the momentum of the force, which fired ceaselessly, set vehicles ablaze, and destroyed walls. When they drove out of Jericho, they left a shell-shocked and beaten town behind them.

As darkness fell, the Brigade commander ordered his forces to organize in night-laagers. But at midnight they were again on their feet, ordered to blow up the Jordan River bridges. Although organized resistance in the sector had dissipated, the enemy dispositions and strength on the other side of the river were unknown, forcing the Israelis to move as cautiously as if they were setting out for battle.

The Brigade had few high-explosives, certainly insufficient to blow up all four Jordan bridges, and therefore had to mobilize captured enemy landmines and even 120mm. shells to increase their explosive power.

The West Bank slept as the sappers drew near and laid their charges. Their commander, Lieutenant Mordechai Goldstein, had broken his leg when his vehicle overturned in the assault on the police fortress and was to be evacuated.But when he learned of his platoon's assignment, "the dream of every sapper," he refused evacuation and categorically demanded to participate. In spite of terrible pain, he supervised the laying of the explosives and heard the traditional roar of the sappers: "Blast!"

At six o'clock in the morning, the four bridges collapsed, and Palestine and the kingdom of Jordan were severed from each other. Columns of pitiful refugees plodded toward the river, reaching its banks after walking all night, their children and household goods on their backs. Their eyes pleaded for help. The men of the Brigade gave them water and helped them to carry their children across the submerged Abdullah Bridge.

Subduing the West Bank

The Jerusalem Brigade had started south, led by its commander, Colonel Eliezer Amitai. Before noon he deployed his forces opposite the Mar Elias Monastery, and upon order, signalled his men to attack, but they charged upon empty space. The Legionnaires' force had apparently withdrawn, and the thick-walled, fortress-like monastery, usually occupied by a company of Legionnaires, fell without resistance.

The Brigade advanced about a kilometer before it was stopped by the blown-up road. An anti-tank jeep, trying to bypass the demolition area, went off the road on to a mine. It took two hours to break a passage through the mines so that the column could continue. At 16.30 hours, it stood before Bethlehem, and the artillery began its softening-up procedure, which was stopped by Arik Regev when the first salvo landed near the Church of the Nativity, miraculously doing no damage. White flags began to appear on the roofs of Bethlehem's houses.

The sun was sinking when the force reached the ruins of Kfar Etzion.

At dawn they continued south in two forks; one, commanded by the G-Branch Officer, to Halchul, the other, with Zwicka Ofer at its head, on the main highway to Hebron.

At Binyanei Ha'ooma, the heads of the military administration – Haim Herzog, Chich, Raphael Levy, the district officer, the Chief of Police, Shaul Rosolio, and my staff officers – gathered for an 8 p.m. discussion. It was my third day without sleep, and I was impatient and tired, even though I recognized the importance of the meeting.

Herzog said: "I have settled in at the Ambassador and have set aside a floor for Chich. The border police have closed the communicating passages and thoroughfares. Colonel Raphael Vardi has been appointed my Chief-of-Staff, responsible for military coordination. Lt. Colonel Werbin will deal with the civilian side. I need a spokesman. I plan to invite the clerical heads and all other important *Goyim* for a meeting."

Now Chich took over: "They're still sniping in the Old City. Please broadcast an announcement that the public must not visit the Wailing Wall for the time being."

"There should also be warnings against mines," said Herzog. "There have already been casualties."

Summing up, I said, "We need a prison for soldiers found plundering. Gather all the captured vehicles in one place. Get fifty border police with arm-bands to patrol the Old City. Place guards on the Consulates to assure their diplomatic immunity, but for the moment consuls living in the eastern part of the city are not permitted to move about in both sectors."

At the staff meeting afterwards, Arik reported the capture of Jericho and Bethlehem, and of Kalkiliya and Tulkarm by Zunik's Brigade, which were now near Sabatiya. Yotvat's Brigade had begun to mop up from the mountain ridges to the Green Line.

"Tomorrow we shall finish subjugating the West Bank," I announced. "The 10th Brigade will occupy the Jordan plain, the Jerusalem Brigade, Hebron, and Yotvat's Brigade will complete mopping up. I expect everything to be finished by evening. The Command will concentrate on the two assignments of the Military Administration and collecting the spoils. The Command H.Q. must be moved up from Ramla."

Control from Ramla to the West Bank was impossible. The Command H.Q. had to be brought to the Jerusalem area. But much water was still to flow in the Jordan, and many problems were to crop up, before the foundation-stone for the new Command H.Q. could be laid in June, 1968.

I had to get some rest. Since the start of the battle, I had not closed my eyes. I went to the King David Hotel, hoping, no matter what, to sleep. The hotel was empty. The tourists had fled and the journalists appeared to have gone to Tel Aviv. Although the battles had ended, the blackout was still in force and the hotel was darkened. Behind the reception desk a clerk was barely discernible in the faint glow of the candles. I went up to my room, carrying two candles, thinking vaguely that I should call the command post to find out if Uri had blown up the bridges, but I was asleep before I could pick up the phone.

But its strident clang shattered my ears at 7 o'clock in the morning. My bones ached with tiredness and for a split second I didn't know where I was. I stretched out my hand. Colonel Arieh Raz, the President's A.D.C., was on the line.

"Uzi, my congratulations."

"To say that you had to wake me up?" I protested. "It's ancient history by now."

"Listen, Uzi, the President wants to go to the Wailing Wall."

"Under no circumstances," I replied, "there's still sniping there. They haven't finished mopping up."

But he refused to listen. "It's not a matter for a telephone conversation. I'm coming to see you," he persisted. And in fact he arrived before I finished dressing.

"The President insists, and I can't dissuade him. You have a try."

We drove to his house, and after we had shaken hands and he had congratulated me, he got down to business. "Everybody has been to the Wailing Wall. That the President should be the only one left out is inexcusable."

"But Mr. President, they are still shooting there. How can we expose the President of Israel to physical danger?"

"No problem: I'll wear a steel helmet."

"Your Excellency, no security measures yet invented can stop a bullet."

He stood straighter, seeming to become taller; he grew more serious; he fastened his eyes on mine. "Young man, listen well: The President of Israel is obliged to go to the Wailing Wall. We are not talking about someone called Zalman Shazar. He's an old man; whatever he was called upon to do during his lifetime, he has already done. If he lives or dies is of no consequence. But the President of Israel must get to the Wailing Wall. The matter is in your hands. I request that you make all security arrangements possible to protect the President of Israel, and afterwards that you assess the chances of danger. If they are great, then I shall not go, 'lest the daughters of the Philistines rejoice' [II Samuel 1:20]. But if the risk is not too serious, then the President shall go to the Wailing Wall."

"Your Excellency, Mr. President," I stammered, "when can you be ready?"

"I am ready now," he said.

Israel's Flag on Machpelah

While I was talking to the President, Eliezer Amitai was capturing Hebron. He in fact entered the town. We had expected strong opposition, not only because Hebron's residents were reputed to be vicious fighters, but because a sizable number of Arab Legionnaires was based there. The Brigade was therefore ordered to shell heavily before the assault and breakthrough.

But when Eliezer's column drew near, no Legionnaires were to be seen, having either crept eastward during the night, or having jettisoned weapons and uniforms and mingled with the civilians. The twenty Centurion tanks at Hebron were found abandoned in the wadis of the Judean Desert. No attempt had been made to destroy them. A white flag flew from every building. "How could I bring myself to bomb a town that wanted to surrender?" Amitai asked me later.

He took over the town and sent Zwicka Ofer's column south towards Beersheba. When Major Amos arrived at Hebron with his men, he said that Halchul, through which they had marched, had also been a ghost town, its streets empty, houses shuttered, white flags flying. Amos had just reached the Cave of Machpelah when a command-car shrieked to a stop, carrying Rabbi Goren, his *sefer Torah*, *shofar*, and whole entourage. The Rabbi, his eyes glistening, said a blessing. Catching sight of the Israeli flag on Amos' half-track, he said, "Bring your half-track close to the wall. I want to raise the flag of Israel above the Cave of Machpelah."

And the Israeli flag flew over the tombs of our forefathers, Abraham and Sarah, Isaac and Rebecca, Jacob and Leah.

It was reported that the 10th Brigade had dispatched reconnaissance units north and south to the Jordan plain to prevent infiltration eastwards of the remnants of the Jordanian armed forces; that about ten Egyptian commandos had attacked an Israeli fortified position and six of them had died; that the Jerusalem Brigade had joined the Gush Lachish force south of Hebron.

I transmitted all this to G.H.Q. and was told that Moshe Dayan was coming to Jerusalem immediately. He wanted to "cut the ribbon" in the south also.

Baron Edmond de Rothschild, at the head of a delegation that included Jean Rosenthal and Jean Friedman, came to Binyanei Ha'ooma directly from France.

Teddy Kollek telephoned to suggest that the liberation of the Old City be celebrated with a concert on Mt. Scopus.

We started for Beersheba. "We'll find a unit on the way and add it to our group for security," I told the Chief of Staff. "All Egyptian commandos in the area must be hunted down." And I added, "All Cabinet Ministers, Members of the Knesset and Directors-General are allowed to visit the Temple Mount."

In front of the building I saw David Ben-Gurion and his wife Paula approaching. A broad smile. A warm handshake. He wanted to know everything. But Moshe Dayan arrived, and I had to cut our conversation short so that we could drive south.

We picked our cautious way through the minefield near the Mar Elias Monastery and were in Bethlehem. White flags flew from every house, but nothing else to indicate that it was a captured town. The inhabitants strolled aimlessly or stood talking in groups, occasionally glancing at us or waving. The children clapped.

We stopped at the ruins of Kfar Etzion, which wakened memories of my days as commander of Gush Etzion during the precarious weeks of January 1948. The region had changed. The Russian Convent had been destroyed by the Arabs, although at Kfar Etzion the Secretariat building, which once doubled as headquarters, remained standing, as did the single tree, Gush Etzion's identification marker. A large mosque dominated the settlement, now a military camp.

At lunch, Dayan talked somewhat patronizingly to newspaper correspondents. "I promised that we would enter Sharm e-Sheikh on the evening of the 7th, but, in fact, we got there in the morning. Do you remember the mood a fortnight ago? And it is to Uzi's credit. The day before I was appointed defense minister, we went over his plans, and here we are; they were carried out unaltered."

Someone mentioned the eastward flight of the Arab residents of the West Bank, to which Dayan queried, "They fled?"

"Only about twenty-five percent of them."

"Because they knew it wasn't worth their while to run away. Their relatives from Israel told them the kind of life the Israeli Arab leads."

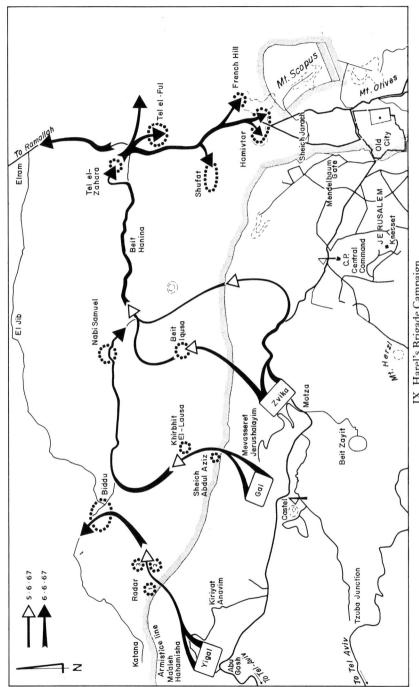

IX Harel's Brigade Campaign

The Commander of the Jerusalem Brigade was waiting at the junction of Beit-Zuriff to accompany us to Hebron. Because of the curfew, the streets, except for a few army people, were empty. We were impressed by the number of white flags on the rooftops and the complete lack of evidence of war. Gates intended as victory portals for Jordan's Army Day had been erected in the main road, but changed circumstances cancelled the ceremony.

At the Cave of Machpelah we visited the Tombs of the Fathers, to which for years Jews had been forbidden entry, allowed to mount only as far as the seventh step of the staircase outside the Cave. And that only by paying the watchman. "From now on we won't have to pay an entrance fee," somebody said.

The Arab watchman at the mosque asked Moshe Dayan for a chit that would protect him from being harmed by our soldiers. Dayan, in a good mood, pointed to me. "He'll give you a chit," he said, and from then on the watchman dogged my steps.

At three o'clock we left Hebron and drove south on a deserted road, in pastoral peace, through Daharya, the last large township before the Green Line, past Beduin camps, and at some point unceremoniously crossed the Green Line back into Israel. It was nearly 4 o'clock when we stopped at the Desert Inn Hotel in Beersheba, and flew from there to Tel Aviv. I returned to Jerusalem in the evening.

The entire staff gathered in my room, each with problems in immediate need of solution. The Chief-of-Staff had begun to organize Teddy Kollek's concert on Mt. Scopus, and Arik, the deployment of troops on the West Bank. G.H.Q. had ordered another force dispatched to Northern Command, and just afterwards ordered all armored units to the north. The war with Syria was about to begin. In town, disputes had arisen between the brigades and the military government. But outweighing all else was the knotty question of what was going to happen.

My staff hoped that I would at least drop a hint about future policy, especially since I had been with the Defense Minister for half the day. What were his views? I tried to marshall all his remarks, statements, slips-of-the-tongue and idle speculations, such as that Jordan, shattered, was no longer a factor and never would we leave Mt. Hebron or Jerusalem. But he had voiced no other opinions. We had, therefore, to plan as though nothing would change in the next three months.

Indeed, we did plan this. When the Brigade commanders gathered in my room at 9 o'clock that night, Arik informed them that from the

10*

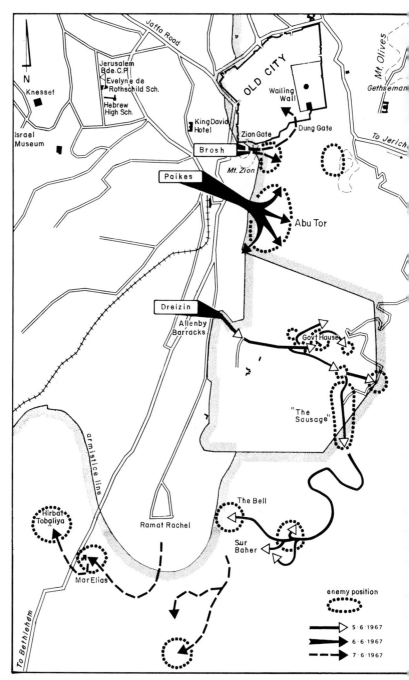

X Jerusalem Brigade Campaign

27. Ben-Gurion, Mrs Ben-Gurion and Shimon Peres visit the author at his command post

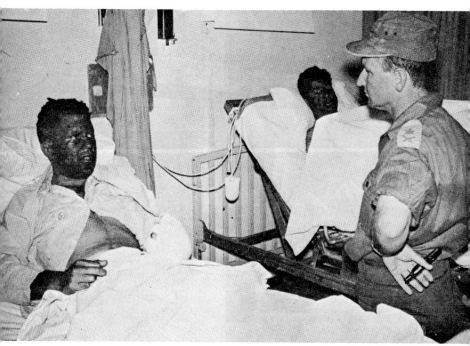

28. Visiting the wounded

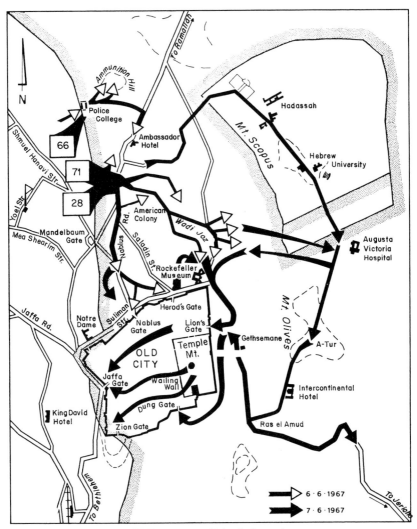

XI Paratroopers Brigade Campaign

next day on the entire West Bank would be within the area of Central Command. The Command forces were given their assignments.

Only One Jerusalem

But there was neither relaxation nor peace in the days and weeks that followed. New conditions demanded new treatment. Everything was in embryo, galvanizing. Plans made one day were discarded the next. Orders were issued and immediately inactivated. Only gradually did a policy emerge that could be carried out as formulated.

But not just day-to-day gloom darkened the days after the war.

I reviewed the parade of the paratroops on the Temple Mount and was filled with the sense of occasion and the solemnity of the times. When the standards of that Brigade, its blood still fresh on the Old City stones, were blessed and sanctified, my heart thundered. After that parade we were ordered to hold no others on the Temple Mount.

But the Old City gates were open for tens of thousands of Jews to swarm through. So that they could pray to their Maker in celebration of the Feast of Weeks, I authorized cleaning the square in front of the Wailing Wall.

Jerusalem became one city. The concrete partitions were demolished, the defense works destroyed, thousands of mines dismantled. Hordes of engineers and workers, at the Mayor's request, unified the two sections of the city and removed the barriers that separated it. After nineteen years of building and maintaining the partition called the municipal line, to protect the inhabitants of Jewish Jerusalem, the engineers eagerly destroyed it in a few days.

My visits to the families of the fallen all but cancelled my pride of victory.

Difficult days were to come. Fighting flared up in the Jordan Valley, cannons roared, men died. The battle of Karameh took Arik Regev and Gadi Manella, Zwicka Ofer and Siemnel, and countless others who had survived the war but not the sorties and terrorist hunts that followed it. Slowly the exaltation of spirit that accompanies victory diminished as the war to end war became a mockery and the growing question, "How long?" eroded our collapsing belief.

On the 6th day of Iyar, 5728, May 4th, 1968, Israel celebrated its twentieth year of independence. And the Eternal City celebrated its first united birthday. Again Jerusalem was host to the Zahal parade, no longer miniature, but a great and impressive display. Once again, as I had done the year before, I stood with the President, the Prime

29. There is only one Jerusalem

Minister, the Defense Minister and the Chief of the General Staff and saluted the units as they marched by. Air Force planes streaked overhead, tanks ploughed up roads and highways, and the uproar of the cannons drowned out the tumultuous applause. There was no Mixed Armistice Commission, no discussion about what could or could not be done; perhaps never again would there be.

All Jerusalem, its babies and its old men, its laughing couples and its staid professors, burst out of their homes and lost their senses at the sight of the marching columns. All Jerusalem, as though it had known naught but celebration and holiday, was a stranger to barbed-wire and concrete walls and hidden sniping.

The buildings on Mt. Scopus were gay with holiday flags, and the two cupolas, one silver and one gold, on the Temple Mount shone as though God Himself had polished them for the occasion.

And Jerusalem seemed to have returned to tranquility, to have inherited its biblical legacy.

I knew: this time, unlike in 1948, the job had been thorough.

EPILOGUE

But it had not been.

For on Yom Kippur in the year 5733 – October 6th, 1973 – the day when Jews, in their prayer shawls, commune with their Creator, air raid sirens wailed in the air.

Israel was being attacked.

The armies of Egypt and Syria surprised us with an assault in enormous strength. The Golan was blitzed and inundated, and the defense of the Suez Canal collapsed.

Zahal had been caught napping.

Israel could not believe it.

But early bungling and panic notwithstanding, Zahal recovered, and the military machine began to function. Thanks to the regular army units, whose men died defending the Golan and the Suez Canal, and to massive air force coverage, the reserves were quickly organized to rush into the breach. Slowly, in Israeli terms, but with unbelievable speed, in classic military ones, the Israeli Defense Force counterattacked.

Within days they were within gunshot of Damascus, having beaten the Syrian, Jordanian and Moroccan armies. And a little later they crossed the Suez Canal and lacked only a few kilometers of reaching Cairo.

That time, too, Zahal was victorious...but...

- The tactical defeats in the initial stages of battle affected the war as a whole.
- The shock of being taken by surprise undermined the nation's confidence in the intelligence services and their exalted reputation.
- The poor start multiplied the confusion inherent in wartime, casting doubt upon Zahal's reputed invincibility.
- The thousands of dead and wounded corroded and deflated victory until it was indistinct from defeat.

On the other hand...

- The Arab soldier was recognized as one who fought well in the beginning.
- The Russian armaments proved effective even when used by Arab soldiers.
- Manpower was properly utilized in the initial schematic stages of battle.
- The Arab Command planned the war with admirable strategy, both tactically and logistically, and especially from the point of view of camouflage.
- The Pan–Arab political leadership planned daringly and exploited the oil weapon effectively.

Israel was frightened and its self-confidence shaken.

The fundamental question of its existence surfaced once again. What would happen to a comparatively small Jewish entity among a disproportionately large number of Arabs, consumed with congenital hatred, who act upon the Muslim precept: "The religion of Mohammed will prevail in the end." Israel's other victories seemed fruitless, and the pre-State doubts threatened to devour the Jewish State.

The end of the Six Day War had brought with it a sense of finality, of no more war. It was truly one of those "finest hours," a time of prophetic and spiritual ascendancy, fulfillment of decades, generations of dreams.

It benefited the Jewish communities in the diaspora, helped them to identify with their Jewishness with a pride and openness not manifest even when the State was born.

A mechanic newly emigrated from Odessa said, "The brilliant victory gave us courage to stand up to the Soviet authorities and demand to go to Israel."

The rabbi from Gruzia said, "We began to pack. We wanted to set out at once for a redeemed Jerusalem."

A young girl from Warsaw said that it was the high point of her life, that "even the Poles were pleased at the Israeli victory."

But the hour ended without our noticing, without our willing it. We rejoiced in our crown of victory, were comfortable resting on our laurels, not realizing that Nasser's "telephone call" never came because we were not connected. We fell in love with the cease-fire lines and the pleasant maps they made, outlining an Israel large and respectable and identifiable even on a map of international scale.

The Jordan River seemed to us impassable, the Golan Heights impenetrable, the Suez Canal an insurmountable obstacle. We copied the French with their Maginot Line. We committed ourselves, in other words, to a concept of an insuperable line of defense, which permitted us to take a little nap, to shut our eyes to reality and its inexorable demands. We paid no attention to consequences, to the possibility that others might not be as happy as we were with the new status quo.

We also under-estimated our enemies. We never inquired into the new social processes the Arab armies had been exposed to, nor did we properly comprehend the implications of the new weapons in their possession. The significance of the massive Russian effort and investment to improve Arab muscles and brains was lost on us.

The Soviets succeeded. The Egyptian and Syrian army corps learned the strategy of a break-through battle, the importance of cooperation between infantry and armor, artillery and engineers. And with the Yom Kippur War they staggered the world with an achievement that roused all Israel from its seven-year nap.

We seemed to have forgotten that "With wiles and cunning shall ye make war," although it underlies our military studies.

The Six Day War was won by an army spoiled and pampered by a nation yearning for peace and deceiving itself into believing that its achievement might be synonymous with peace.

But fundamentally, nothing has changed. Anti-semitism, to a degree dormant for twenty-five years, once again prowled the world, exploiting the connection between Jews and Israel to justify its venom. Israel, the Jewish State, became the target of a modern anti-semitism envious of its growth and achievement. The Arab States abetted the world's attitude. Russian international interests generally and Middle Eastern concerns particularly are furthered by the condition of "No Peace and No War," which it continues to exploit advantageously. The Arab States are growing stronger, raising their standards, increasing their wealth and extending their political power.

The attitude of the United States, always well-disposed, always generous, encouraging, helpful, cannot in the final analysis be guaranteed.

What, then, of us?

Because we believe that the Jewish people can survive only in the State of Israel, we must live by strength. We cannot sheathe our swords or escape their shadow. We cannot trust to appearances or yield to weariness and carelessness. Because we have no option, we must be prepared and on guard, as though we ourselves had come out of Egypt.

EPILOGUE FOR 1983

Neither joyously nor of its own volition did the Israeli government go to war on the morning of June 5, 1967. Even if technically it was the Israeli airforce which launched the initial attack against the Egyptian airforce, destroying it within several hours, and the Israeli armored force which penetrated into the expanses of the Sinai peninsula, overpowering the Egyptian army within six days – the Six Day War was not launched on Israel's initiative.

Only after the government had exhausted all the political and diplomatic possibilities during the "waiting period" which preceded the war, was the decision made. The Israeli Defense Forces embarked on a defensive war against Egypt which threatened to attack and to destroy the Jewish state. Israel had made every effort to communicate with Egypt so as to reach an agreement on free navigation in the Red Sea and the evacuation of the Egyptian troops from the Sinai peninsula, after the Egyptians had violated the demilitarization pact there.

This reluctance to initiate hostilities was even more pronounced with regard to Jerusalem.

The government of Israel, which found itself forced to go to war, wished to restrict the war to a single front. At the outset of the campaign against Egypt, Prime Minister Levi Eshkol sent a telegram to King Hussein, through the good offices of the U.N., asking the king not to join Egypt and not to attack Israel. No harm would then come to him, the telegram stated.

King Hussein did not heed Levi Eshkol's warning. The Jordanian army was sure of Nasser's victory and, wishing to share the fruits of that victory, it opened fire along the armistice line in Jerusalem, which had divided the city between Israel and Jordan for nineteen years.

The U.N. requested a ceasefire repeatedly on the first day of fighting in Jerusalem. In response the IDF General Staff imposed a ceasefire on the unwilling troops of the Central Command. They held their fire reluctantly but to no avail, for the Jordanians did not respond and continued their attack.

The armored brigade of the Central Command which had conquered Ramallah on the second day of fighting began to descend along the eastern slopes of the hills of Benjamin towards Jericho. When Defense Minister Moshe Dayan learned of this movement, he ordered a halt and commanded me to return the force to Ramallah, on the grounds that the government had not decided to advance as far as the Jordan River. The brigade withdrew. Perhaps Dayan wished to indicate to the Jordanians that the IDF would not advance to the Jordan in order not to preclude the possibility of some arrangement which would satisfy the security needs of Israel while preserving the pride of the Kingdom of Jordan. And perhaps this was the beginning of the conception of territorial compromise with Jordan. But the rapid flow of events overran Dayan's restraint and the IDF swooped down to the Jordan River.

As commander of the campaign it was clear to me that once the lines of the Jordanian army in Jerusalem had been breached the time had come for the Old City to be liberated from the yoke of the enemy. But it was only after many hours of hesitation that the government finally decided to allow me to enter the Old City and reach the Western Wall – the jewel in the crown of the Jews.

As with a decisive wave of the hand, Judea and Samaria were conquered and Jerusalem was reunited. For the first nineteen years of its existence the State of Israel had in effect been based on the land of the Philistines and the Nabateans. Now it suddenly gained control of the land of the Bible. Nablus and Shiloh, Bethlehem and Hebron, were joined to the Jewish state. Thus, the crown of the ancient kingdoms of Judah and Israel was restored.

The force of emotion swept aside sober logic. That impatience lacked logic's ability to pierce mists of the future. Somewhat later a creeping annexation of the West Bank began. Should it be allowed to run its course the Arab population of the land of Israel will triple. The original idea of the Jewish state – a state with a clear Jewish majority, in which the Jews will be able to live in safety forever – would be eroded by such a development.

True, annexation of the West Bank also presents a clear strategic advantage, namely: enhancement of Israel's physical security. But this advantage is nullified by the drawback which threatens Israel's very existence by the addition of over a million Arabs to the population of Israel. Lebanon, where ethnic and communal strife exceed factors which unite the country, serves as an example. In such a